If The Keystone Is Removed

If The Keystone *Is* Removed
An Evangelical Review of the Church of Jesus Christ of Latter-Day Saints

Samuel Hesman

RESOURCE *Publications* · Eugene, Oregon

IF THE KEYSTONE IS REMOVED
An Evangelical Review of the Church of Jesus Christ of Latter-Day Saints

Copyright © 2025 Samuel Hesman. All rights reserved. Except for brief quotations in critical publications or reviews, no part of this book may be reproduced in any manner without prior written permission from the publisher. Write: Permissions, Wipf and Stock Publishers, 199 W. 8th Ave., Suite 3, Eugene, OR 97401.

Resource Publications
An Imprint of Wipf and Stock Publishers
199 W. 8th Ave., Suite 3
Eugene, OR 97401

www.wipfandstock.com

PAPERBACK ISBN: 979-8-3852-3798-2
HARDCOVER ISBN: 979-8-3852-3799-9
EBOOK ISBN: 979-8-3852-3800-2

VERSION NUMBER 02/04/25

This was the Prophet Joseph Smith's statement. He testified that "the Book of Mormon was the most correct of any book on earth, and the keystone of our religion" [. . .] Just as the arch crumbles if the keystone is removed, so does all of the Church stand or fall with the truthfulness of the Book of Mormon.

—Ezra Taft Benson

Contents

Introduction | ix

Part 1: **Epistemology**
Chapter 1: How do we find truth? | 3
Chapter 2: A Critique of the Religious Epistemology
       of the LDS Church | 11
Chapter 3: "Come let us reason together" | 19
Chapter 4: Objections to the Rational Pursuit of Truth | 31

Part 2: **Theology**
Chapter 5: Are Latter-Day Saints Christians? | 41
Chapter 6: Who is Jesus? | 50
Chapter 7: Comparing LDS and Evangelical Soteriology | 67
Chapter 8: A Response to LDS Soteriology | 81
Chapter 9: A Call to Sola Fide | 89

Part 3: **Interior**
Chapter 10: Flaws Within the Book of Mormon | 101
Chapter 11: Anachronisms | 104
Chapter 12: Theological Anachronisms | 117
Chapter 13: Inaccuracies and Missing Evidence | 126
Chapter 14: Thomas Stuart Ferguson | 138
Chapter 15: DNA Evidence | 142
Chapter 16: Changes to the Book of Mormon | 148

Part 4: **Exterior**

Chapter 17: Joseph as Translator | 161
Chapter 18: The Book of Abraham | 171
Chapter 19: The Kinderhook Plates | 185
Chapter 20: Joseph's Missing Works Cited Page | 190
Chapter 21: Joseph's Abilities | 192
Chapter 22: 10 Sources | 199
Chapter 23: 2. The View of the Hebrews | 209
Chapter 24: 3. The Lost 116 Pages | 215
Chapter 25: 4. Denominational Debates | 219
Chapter 26: 5. Joseph's Literary Style | 222
Chapter 27: 6. The Late War of 1812 | 225
Chapter 28: 7. Methodism | 230
Chapter 29: 8. Names and Geography | 237
Chapter 30: 9. Captain Kidd | 240
Chapter 31: 10. Joseph's Family | 243
Chapter 32: Polygamy and Polyandry | 252
Chapter 33: The Eleven Witnesses | 265

Chapter 34: Conclusion | 277

Exhortation | 279

Appendix A: King Follett Discourse | 281
Appendix B: Joseph Sr.'s Dream | 289
Bibliography | 295

Introduction

This was the Prophet Joseph Smith's statement. He testified that "the Book of Mormon was the most correct of any book on earth, and the keystone of our religion" [. . .] Just as the arch crumbles if the keystone is removed, so does all of the Church stand or fall with the truthfulness of the Book of Mormon.

—Ezra Taft Benson

IN THIS BOOK I hope to make a case that successfully "removes the keystone." This book is an evaluation of the doctrines of the Church of Jesus Christ of Latter-Day Saints. The truthfulness of the Book of Mormon is the key piece of evidence that confirms that Joseph Smith was truly a prophet of God. If Joseph was a prophet, the Church of Jesus Christ of Latter-Day Saints reasons, (hereafter LDS Church) "then the Church is true, the Book of Mormon is scripture, the doctrines of the Church are true, and the church is still led by prophets today."[1] On the other hand, if the Book of Mormon is not true, then Joseph was not a prophet, and his church is not true. Yes, as President Benson puts it, "so does all of the Church stand or fall with the truthfulness of the Book of Mormon." In the pages to follow I present a case for readers to evaluate the truthfulness of the Book of Mormon and Joseph's status as a prophet.

In my study of the LDS Church, I found that most books considered either the theological teachings of the Church, like the atonement, the attributes of God, or the practical teachings such as history, translation, and polygamy. I thought it was important to have a book that combined these two important aspects of the LDS Church and reviewed them in a

1. Joshua J. Perkey Church Magazines, "Why Do I Need to Know Joseph Smith Is a Prophet?,".

single volume. This is because the practical conclusions about the Book of Mormon create important theological conclusions as well.

The second goal that I had in writing this book was modeling an effective truth-finding strategy and applying it to the LDS Church. The belief of many Saints is built from feeling or identity. As we will get into, the Saints believe that strong emotional experiences testify of truth. Many adherents of this Church have been drawn by passionate feeling. The other factor is identity. The LDS community has an incredibly strong sense of identity. As a result, if born into an LDS home one may continue in the Church as a matter of identity more than belief.

These belief-forming approaches are unsuccessful if truth is the ultimate goal. One of the results of these methods is that when Saints are confronted with evidence that leads them to leave the Church they often give up on organized religion as a whole. Upon finding that many of the teachings of the LDS Church are untrue they feel that they have been misled their entire lives. They project this negative feeling upon all religion and find themselves as skeptics who don't know what to believe and don't want to be fooled again. I am not saying that it is the intent of the LDS Church to deceive, I am just trying to explain the perspective of those who have been victimized by poor truth-finding strategies.

Rather than merely critiquing the LDS structure of belief, and leaving readers to find their own way, I want to show how beliefs should be evaluated. After we review the LDS Church, I want to encourage readers to evaluate Christianity using the same strategy. The same tool that demonstrates the weakness of the LDS view can be used to find the robustness of the Christian view. In short, I'm writing this book to help readers evaluate and form beliefs that more align with the truth. This book is intended for two main groups of people. The first group is LDS investigators, those within the LDS Church who are curious or have doubts and are interested in understanding their church from a Christian perspective. Second this book is for Christians who are interested in better understanding the LDS Church; especially those with the intent to be more effective witnesses to the LDS community.

I have given my practical reasons for writing this book and they are why I believe it will be a valuable contribution to the literature. More importantly, however, I wrote this book because I love the LDS community. I have found the Latter-Day Saints to be some of the kindest, most hospitable, friendliest, and most devoted people I have ever met. I respect their virtue, selflessness, the strength of their families, and so many other things about them. Over the years that I have spent researching and writing this book I have met with many missionaries, spoken with Church leadership, met in the homes of Church members, been to LDS Church meetings, and more. In all my encounters with these people I have found them to be unbelievably kind.

I have the deepest respect for LDS missionaries. These are young adults who sacrifice two years (or eighteen months) of their young lives to devote themselves to sharing their beliefs with the world. I wish that more of the young evangelicals I know possessed even a fraction of the devotion exhibited by these young Saints. If we possessed, in the evangelical church, just half of their passion and devotion the world would be changed overnight. Held to a rigorous schedule, frequently encountering rude people slamming doors in their faces these young adults remain unbelievably warm and friendly. I am convinced that it is not the strength of their doctrine that makes the LDS church grow, but rather the kindness of their community.

I *love* the LDS people and that is why I am writing this book. I am not an "anti-Mormon." My goal here is not to attack the LDS people. On the contrary, it is my love for these people that has motivated me to perform this study. I have often shed tears in prayer over my friends in the LDS Church. This study is necessary because, contrary to what it teaches, I do not believe that the LDS Church contains the "fullness of the gospel." Rather, Joseph's teaching egregiously distorts the gospel in a number of ways. It is because I love these people that I feel compelled to point out the errors in this Church and point the Saints towards the true gospel of Christ. If you are LDS and are reading this, please hear my heart. I do not want to attack or condemn you. I offer this book hoping to help you know how deeply our Heavenly Father loves you, and to help you see Him more clearly.

Before we dive into epistemology, I have a few final notes regarding choices I made when writing this book.

First, I have deliberately excluded my use of the word "Mormon" from this book wherever possible. The public is, no doubt, most familiar calling the Latter-Day Saints "Mormons" and their Church the "Mormon" Church. Out of respect and courtesy for my LDS friends I have chosen not to use this title. In 2018 President Russell M. Nelson emphasized the importance of using the full name of the Church. He stated: "To remove the Lord's name from the Lord's Church is a major victory for Satan."[2] In an attempt to address them by their chosen name and to demonstrate my respect for them, I use "LDS Church" throughout this book.

Second, many of the sources in this book are not academic. Rather than referencing scholarly works or the essays of BYU professors I made much greater use of essays from the LDS Church website or quotations from past Church presidents. This is because the academics have no authority in the LDS Church. They may contribute to the discussion or provide elaboration on doctrinal points, however, it is the Church *only* who has the authority to define doctrine. In the LDS Church the President is considered a living prophet. He is, in a very real sense, believed to be a mouthpiece of God. His authority is supreme. For this reason, rather than engage in academic tedium, I have used authoritative church sources. If it has been published by the LDS Church, for the most part, it is their doctrinal stance. For this reason, I utilize church sources rather than academic ones.

Third, I want to make a brief note about translation and quotation. Where I quote the Bible throughout this book, I use either the ESV translation or the KJV translation. While the KJV is the favored translation of the LDS Church[3], I prefer the ESV and find it to be a more accurate translation.

I quote a number of Bible verses at length in this book. I did this because I believe that it is important for readers to read the Scriptures in this book rather than just skimming over references and moving on. As I attempt to make a biblical case for my views, the Scriptures themselves are essential pieces of my arguments. I reproduce the verses here for reader convenience. I must also note that where I selectively exclude parts of verses or passages it is not my attempt to twist the text or provide only the parts of verses that support my view. I have limited space and frequently considered how much of a verse or passage to include. I am not trying to obscure the text and would love nothing more than for the reader to review every verse I quote in its full context. For that matter, read every verse that I don't quote in its full context as well.

I also quote somewhat extensively from the Book of Mormon. As I previously mentioned, my intended audience is both Christians and Saints. While every Saint, no doubt, has a Bible in their home it is likely

2. President Russell M. Nelson President of the Church ImagePresident Russell M. Nelson, "The Correct Name of the Church,".

3. They predominantly use the KJV over the JST (Joseph Smith Translation.)

that few Christians have a Book of Mormon in their home. Again, for reader convenience, I quote verses from the LDS scriptures at length. I made this choice also because it is important to critique opposing views in the words of their adherents. I quote LDS sources in an attempt to avoid caricaturing the teachings of the LDS Church.

I will reiterate what I said previously. I have limited space and I encourage the reader to review the LDS scriptures in their context. I have read the Book of Mormon cover to cover numerous times. I have read Doctrine and Covenants and Pearl of Great Price in their entirety as well. This is, of course, is excluding my frequent personal study that did not take the form of cover-to-cover reading and my reading of hundreds of LDS church essays.

Finally, I want to thank you for picking up this book. I hope that it is useful to you and that it encourages you to think deeply about what you believe. We now proceed to removing the keystone.

Part 1: Epistemology

Chapter 1: **How do we find truth?**

THE LDS CHURCH WAS founded by Joseph Smith, a man born in 1805, and they believe his claims of being a Prophet. They believe in the Book of Mormon (hereafter BOM) which is "an abridgement of the record of the people of Nephi," a community ancient Jews who left Jerusalem and sailed to North America around 600 B.C. They believe that this record was engraved upon golden plates which were discovered and translated by Joseph Smith. The BOM contains a host of historical and theological assertions which members of the LDS Church are bound to believe. Many of these claims will be evaluated in this book.

The fundamental question of this study is—*is it true*? Is the Book of Mormon true? Was Joseph Smith a prophet? Does the LDS Church today contain the fullness of the gospel and the governing, guiding voice of a living prophet? When we ask if Joseph Smith can be believed and whether what he teaches is true, we are trying to ascertain whether his claims correspond to reality. Are the teachings of the LDS church *true* or merely a useful, fictional narrative?

Essential to answering this question is a responsible and effective method of evaluation. One cannot reliably tell the weight of any given object by looking at it, but must place it on a scale. In a similar way, one cannot reliably determine the truthfulness of Historical/Theological claims by feeling them. Rather, the claims must be weighed by methods appropriate to evaluating these kinds of claims.

In these next few pages I am going to make the case that reason and study are the best ways to uncover this kind of truth. This approach deviates from the typical LDS perspective which focuses on personal revelation (typically conveyed as a feeling) to discover spiritual truths. In this study, we will consider a number of LDS sources which teach how one comes to know the truth. After the LDS view is supported, I will respond by describing why I believe this method is unreliable and what methods I believe ought to be preferred.

In the field of philosophy, this category of study is known as epistemology. "Epistemology is the study of knowledge" and those who commit themselves to this field of study possess two central focuses; "the nature of knowledge [. . .] and the extent of human knowledge[.]"[1] This chapter is concerned with religious epistemology, questioning how we can reliably discern spiritual religious truths.

The most prominent approach used by the LDS church to validate their beliefs is personal revelation from the Holy Ghost. For them, the most important evidence to support the truth of their beliefs is found in the witness of the Holy Spirit to the heart of an individual. What does this look like in practice? This epistemological strategy is described in many LDS sources and is firmly instantiated within their church tradition. Perhaps the primary passage used to teach this method of truth-finding is Moroni 10:4–5 which reads:

> **Moroni 10:4–5**
>
> ⁴And when ye shall receive these things, I would exhort you that ye would ask God, the Eternal Father, in the name of Christ, if these things are not true; and if ye shall ask with a sincere heart, with real intent, having faith in Christ, he will manifest the truth of it unto you, by the power of the Holy Ghost. ⁵And by the power of the Holy Ghost ye may know the truth of all things.

These verses give an important insight into the way that the LDS Church endeavors to validate its truth claims. The first step is to ask God if "these things are not true." After stating the necessity of an active request, a stipulation is given on how we are supposed to ask. When you ask God if these things are true, it must be done with a "sincere heart" and with faith. If the seeker meets these qualifications, Christ will "manifest the truth of it [. . .] by the power of the Holy Ghost." This theme of asking with sincere interest and the truth being revealed spiritually is the dominant model for LDS epistemology. I will provide here three other passages that the Saints frequently appeal to for this teaching.

---

1. "Epistemology | Internet Encyclopedia of Philosophy." Accessed December 20, 2022.

CHAPTER 1: HOW DO WE FIND TRUTH?

James 1:5–6

⁵If any of you lack wisdom, let him ask of God, that giveth to all *men* liberally, and upbraideth not; and it shall be given him.

⁶But let him ask in faith, nothing wavering. For he that wavereth is like a wave of the sea driven with the wind and tossed.

Alma 5:46

Behold, I say unto you they are made known unto me by the Holy Spirit of God. Behold, I have fasted and prayed many days that I might know these things of myself. And now I do know of myself that they are true; for the Lord God hath made them manifest unto me by his Holy Spirit; and this is the spirit of revelation which is in me.

DC 8:1–2

Oliver Cowdery, verily, verily, I say unto you, that assuredly as the Lord liveth, who is your God and your Redeemer, even so surely shall you receive a knowledge of whatsoever things you shall ask in faith, with an honest heart, believing that you shall receive a knowledge concerning the engravings of old records, which are ancient, which contain those parts of my scripture of which has been spoken by the manifestation of my Spirit. ²Yea, behold, I will tell you in your mind and in your heart, by the Holy Ghost, which shall come upon you and which shall dwell in your heart.

DC 42:61

If thou shalt ask, thou shalt receive revelation upon revelation, knowledge upon knowledge, that thou mayest know the mysteries and peaceable things—that which bringeth joy, that which bringeth life eternal.

These scriptures lay out the process that believers or investigators should follow to acquire a testimony of the truthfulness of the church's teachings. One of the most common requests that an LDS missionary will pose to an investigator is that they read the BOM and pray about whether it is true. For the Saints, the process for discovering whether or not a teaching is true is by asking God with faith and a sincere heart. If we ask with a proper heart posture the scriptures claim we will be given a revelation verifying their truth. This process appears simple enough, but how can we know that what we feel is the Spirit testifying of truth rather than a mere emotional impression? This question is answered in D&C 9:8–9.

> **D&C 9:8–9**
>
> But, behold, I say unto you, that you must study it out in your mind; then you must ask me if it be right, and if it is right I will cause that your bosom shall burn within you; therefore, you shall feel that it is right. ⁹But if it be not right you shall have no such feelings, but you shall have a stupor of thought that shall cause you to forget the thing which is wrong; therefore, you cannot write that which is sacred save it be given you from me.

Here is maybe the most striking element of the LDS epistemological strategy. Once the request for knowledge is extended with the proper heart, the Holy Ghost will cause "that your bosom shall burn" and that is supposed to be taken as a reliable sign that to "feel that it is right." It is assumed by LDS scripture that the method for discovering what is true in spiritual matters is by praying and experiencing a feeling. In her book *Leaving Mormonism*, Latanye K Scott explains the way that this approach is commonly understood. "A physical sensation called a "burning in the bosom" is the spiritual confirmation from the Holy Ghost often said to accompany the conviction that a given thing is "true."[2] Scott describes the LDS confirmation of belief as a phenomenological religious experience. This process for truth finding is more explicitly articulated in an influential speech made by the First Counselor in the First Presidency, Dallin H Oaks.[3] Below are a couple excerpts from his notable speech entitled *Testimony*.

> A testimony of the gospel is a personal witness borne to our souls by the Holy Ghost that certain facts of eternal significance are true and that we know them to be true [. . .] While there are some "evidences" for gospel truths (for example, see Psalm 19:1; Helaman 8:24), scientific methods will not yield spiritual knowledge.[4]

Oaks begins by defining what a testimony is. Corey Miller, a contributor to the book *Leaving Mormonism*, elaborates that Christians and members of the LDS church have different meanings when they use the

---

2. Leaving Mormonism Why Four Scholars Changed Their Minds, 105.
3. Dallin H. Oaks
4. Testimony Dallin H. Oaks

word "testimony." For typical Christians, a testimony is the story of how they came to know God or a description of some way that God has worked in their life. In contrast, Oaks' definition states that a testimony is a witness of certain facts. He continues to say that scientific methods do not yield spiritual knowledge. He advises that the way spiritual knowledge is acquired is through the witness of the Spirit to our souls. He relates:

> One of the greatest things about our Heavenly Father's plan for His children is that each of us can know the truth of that plan for ourselves. That revealed knowledge does not come from books, from scientific proof, or from intellectual pondering. As with the Apostle Peter, we can receive that knowledge directly from our Heavenly Father through the witness of the Holy Ghost. When we know spiritual truths by spiritual means, we can be just as sure of that knowledge as scholars and scientists are of the different kinds of knowledge they have acquired by different methods.

The view presented above, to some, may appear questionable. This is the orthodox LDS view. An especially notable element of this perspective is the level of confidence with which they hold their beliefs acquired by testimony. Oaks not only excludes the necessity of reason and study, but goes a step further and rejects them claiming that the justifying evidence does not come from "books, from scientific proof, or from intellectual pondering." Rejecting these traditionally trusted methods for the evaluation of evidence, he shares the opinion that Saints may be equally confident in their revealed knowledge as a scholar or scientist might be with their conclusions from traditional forms of study.

This level of confidence is echoed by other LDS sources. Respected LDS Apologist and member of the First Council of the Seventy, Elder B.H Roberts[5], claimed that the witness of the Holy Ghost "must ever be the chief source of evidence for the truth of the Book of Mormon. All other evidence is secondary to this."[6] President Boyd K Packer claimed that "each of us must accommodate the mixture of reason and revelation in our lives. The gospel not only permits but requires it." There are many other quotations by influential members of the Church that are consistent with this theme of the confidence that can be achieved by bearing testimony. LDS apologist Tad R. Callister touches on this

---

5. B.H. Roberts Seeker After Truth

6. Tad R. Callister, *The Case for the Book of Mormon* (Salt Lake City: Deseret Book, 2019), 66–67.

subject in his book of LDS apologetics entitled *The Case for the Book of Mormon*, saying:

> When all is said and done, the Spirit is the ultimate evidence. It is the decisive, determining factor—not archaeology, not linguistics, and certainly not theories of man.[. . .] In essence, the Spirit is that one indisputable piece of evidence in the courtroom of truth that cannot be discredited, diluted, or denied. It speaks for itself without the need of any external confirmation or corroboration.

Ex-LDS scholar Corey Miller articulates this perspective saying: "Testimony will trump any and all arguments that can ever be forged against it. It's that powerful." The essential importance of a testimony is understood, but how is a testimony of the truthfulness of the gospel acquired? To answer this question, we return to Oaks' speech where he teaches that a testimony is found in the bearing of it.

> Another way to seek a testimony seems astonishing when compared with the methods of obtaining other knowledge. We gain or strengthen a testimony by bearing it. Someone even suggested that some testimonies are better gained on the feet bearing them than on the knees praying for them.

In full recognition of how unlikely it sounds, Oaks teaches that the power of a testimony is found in repeating it. He teaches that if you do not feel that your testimony is very strong or if you have difficulty believing what you say, you ought to proclaim it more fervently and frequently. Oaks, Packer, and others hold firmly to this notion and teach it as official church doctrine.

The way that members of the LDS Church construct their beliefs and strengthen them is by receiving and bearing a testimony. This testimony, they believe, is actual evidence of the truth of their beliefs. In addition, they believe that the knowledge of their beliefs is given by the Spirit. If you ask with faith and a sincere heart, then God will bless you to know his truth. The ultimate evidence that a person can receive is a witness of the truth from the Holy Ghost confirmed by a "burning the bosom" feeling. This feeling causes people to understand that whatever they are pondering (typically the truth of the restored gospel through the prophet Joseph Smith) is true. This approach is unapologetically exclusive of reason.

When religious beliefs are justified by spiritual feelings alone, it creates a culture in which reason itself is questioned. Doubts may be seen as evil and critical questioning of one's beliefs becomes very difficult. This is clearly the case in strict fideist circles such as have been cultivated in the LDS community. One powerful illustration of this condemning view of doubt is found in an article by Elder Hugo Montoya of the Seventy. Even the title of his work gives a clear picture of what church's view of doubt. In *Overcoming the Danger of Doubt*, Montoya says "Like the fungus that enters these trees, doubts can invade our thoughts. If we let them grow, over time they can affect our roots and rot our foundation of faith until we too may be cut down."

First, he claims that doubt is a danger and, if left unchecked, may kill one's faith. Montoya goes on to assert how we are to deal with doubts if/when they arise, and the answer is in accord with everything that has been presented above. He states "Whenever we are tried with doubts, let us ponder our spiritual experiences. Doing so will help us to erase the doubts."[7]

It appears to me that the danger is not, as is described by Montoya, engaging doubts. Rather, the true peril lies failing to engage our doubts with open, truth-seeking minds. It is often the case that both LDS and Christian individuals utilize religious experience as an excuse to brush off legitimate questions regarding their faith. Though religious experience is certainly valuable, it should not form an unassailable foundation for one's belief.

I find this strategy to be an incredible danger for multiple reasons. Firstly, open-mindedness is essential to finding truth. I am painfully aware of the possibility that I could be wrong about any number of my personal beliefs. I am not the smartest or most well-researched person in the world on any given topic. This realization prompts me to hold my beliefs with a little more humility. Of course, I believe that I have good reasons for holding the beliefs that I do. However, I am aware that I cannot know everything with 100% certainty. Because of this, I am open to plausible arguments from others. Even now I do my best to approach conversations with LDS missionaries with an open mind to what they have to say. I am incapable of doing this if I am ensnared in the trap of close-mindedness.

---

7. Overcoming the Danger of Doubt

How is one to grapple with religious experience as an epistemological strategy? If we appeal to the words of Callister quoted previously, it appears that we cannot. He claims that the Spirit is "the one indisputable piece of evidence" in the conversation of truth. It appears to me that the LDS approach to discovering and testing religious beliefs is ineffective, problematic, and prone to the threat of close-mindedness. As we continue, I will elaborate on the inherent problems with this strategy. Following this, I will build the case that we ought to appeal to reason and study in our collaborative effort to find the truth.

Chapter 2: **A Critique of the Religious Epistemology of the LDS Church**

THE LDS APPROACH TO finding spiritual knowledge is deeply unreliable. I will note, unfortunately, that many Christians exercise a very similar strategy. Though it is claimed that its basis is the Spirit, it is challenging to determine whether this is the case. I cannot bring myself to agree with the notion that something as important as one's religious beliefs ought to be justified primarily by what is often indistinguishable from a mere emotional experience.

Before I address spiritual experience as an epistemological strategy, I want to clarify that I am not a fervent skeptic of all religious experience. I believe religious experiences to be very real and know they can be incredibly compelling to those who receive them. When I ask both Christian and LDS friends why they believe as they do, one of the most common answers I receive is an appeal to a religious experience. These experiences are often profoundly moving and frequently used as confirmation. Ultimately, I have no objections with using a religious experience to *confirm* one's faith. Religious experience is valuable and can be deeply compelling.

In his book, *Is there a God?* Christian apologist and philosopher Richard Swineburne makes the case that if there was a God, then we would reasonably expect to see powerful religious experiences.[1] I completely agree. We have phenomenal experiences that make us feel as though we are connected to God. What I intend to point out here is that I believe religious experience is real. I do not want to appear as

1. Richard Swinburne, *Is There a God?* (New York: Oxford University Press, 1996).

though I am relegating every spiritual experience to the realm of mere emotionalism. What I am saying is that though these experiences have great value, it is problematic when they are used as a primary grounding for our propositional beliefs.

It is useful to draw a distinction between *justification* and *confirmation* for one's beliefs. It appears to me that there are many situations in which evidence may be confirming to a particular belief without actually entailing that specific conclusion. *Confirmation*, as I am using it here, is when a feeling, experience, or evidence encourages confidence in a previously held belief. *Justification* is when a feeling, experience, or evidence reliably leads to a specific conclusion.

I believe that the LDS approach of receiving a numinous feeling when reading the Book of Mormon, and concluding its truth based upon that feeling falls into that first category. The teaching of the Church encourages seekers to assume that the feelings they receive justify the very truth claims they are investigating. One of the reasons that people are so easily tricked by this is that they are blinded by their situational context.

Consider the following example. When a person goes to a church event, often those involving music, and gets the chills they may believe that the sensation is caused by the Holy Spirit moving. However, when a person is watching a movie and gets the chills, they are significantly less likely to attribute their experience to the presence of the Holy Spirit. Physiological responses such as these occur in a variety of situational contexts. Because the physical response does not self-identify whether it is from music or the Spirit, it is equally possible that the chills during the movie are from the Holy Spirit and the chills during the worship event are from the music.

We tend to interpret our experiences by their context even when there is no certain link between them. While the feeling of a "burning in the bosom," as Joseph Smith describes in D&C 9:8, is presented as meaningful proof testifying to the truth of the Book of Mormon, there is no reason to believe that the feeling is actually tied to the access of some great spiritual truth. Just as the taste of a food has little bearing on its nutritional value, the emotions conjured when reading the BOM are no certain attestation of its accuracy. These kinds of experiences would constitute confirmation rather than justification. While they may encourage confidence in a belief, they have no ability to demonstrate the truth of something when separated from situational context.

Archaeological evidence, the writings of ancient historians, or chains of logical reasoning, on the other hand, provide direct conclusions. When we dig up the ruins of old cities with inscriptions of the names of the people who lived there, there is a direct connection between the evidence and the belief attained from that evidence. Syllogistic reasoning acts similarly. With a great deal of precision, logic processes a claim and directs itself towards a specific conclusion. For numerous reasons, it is my opinion that when forming religious beliefs justification-type evidence is superior to confirmational. I will address this more thoroughly further on.

With this important clarification on the nature of religious experience as evidence and to what degree it ought to be relied upon, I will level five main arguments against the approach to seeking religious truth from Moroni 10:4–5.

First, Scripture warns us not to put too much trust in ourselves or our feelings when deciding if something is true. Here are a couple of verses that support this perspective.

Jeremiah 17:9

The heart is deceitful above all things, and desperately sick; who can understand it?

Hebrews 3:10

Therefore I was provoked with that generation, and said, 'They always go astray in their heart; they have not known my ways.'

Proverbs 16:2

All the ways of a man are pure in his own eyes, but the LORD weighs the spirit.

Matthew 15:19

For out of the heart proceed evil thoughts, murders, adulteries, fornications, thefts, false witness, blasphemies:

These verses caution us about the condition of our hearts. If the Bible tells us that our hearts are "deceitful above all things," it would be foolish to assume that we may have complete confidence in any conclusion we receive from them. Further, Scripture makes clear that the corruption of our hearts keeps us from God. If we were left to our own devices our hearts would inevitably lead us astray. We must ask ourselves what we want to follow. What is our proper basis for grounding beliefs? If the Bible tells us that our hearts produce "false witness, [and] blasphemies" and that they "always go astray" it would be an understatement to say that they are unreliable for justifying religious beliefs. There are better methods for determining what is true than a warm feeling. I praise the Lord for His grace in giving us alternative methods. If the heart were the only tool at our disposal, we would be desperately and hopelessly lost.

The second main argument is that personal spiritual revelation, particularly that which the LDS church teaches, does not provide specific facts or doctrines. I can demonstrate this with a couple of examples. In my meetings with missionaries, one of the most common passages used to present the idea of spiritual truths and doctrines being confirmed for an investigator was from James 1.

James 1:5–6

⁵If any of you lacks wisdom, let him ask God, who gives generously to all without reproach and it will be given him. ⁶But let him ask in faith, with no doubting, for the one who doubts is like a wave of the sea that is driven and tossed by the wind.

They present this verse to indicate the idea that if there is anything that we do not know we may ask God in faith and receive the answer. This does not appear to be a proper interpretation of these verses. For instance, if I was sitting in a math course and had completely forgotten to prepare for the exam, could I simply request by faith and be given the answers to all of the problems on my test in front of me? Does the witness of the Spirit give the kind of propositional knowledge that I would need in order to mark down the correct answers and not fail my exam?

If you are of the opinion that this passage means that we are given specific facts, through the witness of the spirit, I encourage you to try this approach on your next exam rather than studying. This is not typically the way that the Spirit operates. I will grant, that this does not sound exactly like what the LDS church teaches. After all, each church member is not receiving facts in their minds, but an intimation of the truth of the BOM. Far from being the answers to many questions on an exam, the seeker has only one question and it is yes or no. Is the BOM true? While I do notice the ways in which this is dissimilar to the example I provided, we must also recognize what the BOM contains. It contains hundreds of years of history and an immense number of religious discourses. Thus, while an

CHAPTER 2: THE RELIGIOUS EPISTEMOLOGY OF THE LDS CHURCH

investigator is only technically seeking the answer to one question, they are, at the same time, trying to reach conclusions to thousands.

There are some exceptions to this rule about religious experience imparting propositional knowledge. Two notable examples include Paul who was spoken to directly by God and, Joseph Smith who, as we will evaluate further on, claimed to have received many special revelations from God. It is easy to notice, however, that the revelations of Joseph Smith or Paul are quite different from what most of us are blessed to receive. For the majority of the Church, it appears as though the "burning in the bosom" is the extent of our religious experience. This feeling may be confirmational but does not produce new propositional beliefs akin to God's revelations to the prophets. For these reasons, I am of the belief that religious experience can very rarely be used to justify truth claims in the way that the LDS interpretation of James would have us believe.

Third, the promise of the LDS church is that if I read the Book of Mormon and ask God if it is true, I will receive a revelation confirming its veracity. In my own life I have put this to the test. Virtually every LDS missionary who I have crossed paths with has encouraged me to read and pray about the truthfulness of the BOM. I took this suggestion very seriously. As I said earlier, I am acutely aware of the possibility that I could be wrong. True, I have examined compelling research that leads me to disbelieve the doctrines of Joseph's religion, but I may have missed something and am willing to test the scriptures as the missionaries suggest.

I have read the Book of Mormon cover to cover multiple times, have prayed earnestly asking God if it is true, and have received no confirmation. I readily admit that my lack of experience confirming the BOM is no more an argument against its veracity than another person's experience is for it. Religious experience, or lack thereof, is unreliable. Despite this, if the Saints promise a confirming experience, what are we to do with people like myself who read the Book of Mormon and pray about it but receive no testimony of its truth? Indeed, not only did I fail to receive spiritual confirmation of the truthfulness of the BOM, but my religious experiences typically occur when engaging with the Evangelical community and teaching. I have a personal testimony of God from the Evangelical tradition despite my having requested one from God confirming the truth of the BOM.

My fourth objection to the LDS epistemological strategy has to do with the idea that a testimony is found and strengthened in the bearing of it. This concept is especially concerning to me. If any approach is indicative of blind faith it is this one. It demonstrates a complete disregard for attempting a responsible approach in forming personal beliefs. According to this view, one should willfully accept something that they do not necessarily believe and continue to repeat it until they feel with confidence that it is true. There is a psychological theory called the illusory truth effect which explains this process. The illusory truth effect shows that "repeated statements are easier to process, and subsequently perceived to be more truthful, than new statements." This theory plays with mental retrieval of information and demonstrates that a powerful element in this process is fluency on the subject of a belief. When a person has a memory that is more recent or more frequent than others, they are more likely to retrieve that information and assume its truth. The essay *Knowledge Does Not Protect Against Illusory Truth* analyzes how these fluency factors are, in many cases, more relied upon than a prior knowledge base.

> Contrary to prior suspicions, illusory truth effects occurred even when participants knew better.[. . .] Participants sometimes rely on fluency even if knowledge is also available to them (Experiment 2). Thus, participants demonstrated knowledge neglect, or the failure to rely on stored knowledge in the face of fluent processing experiences.[2]

This is a problematic strategy. I do not think the recommendation of Oaks and Packer to gain confidence in a testimony by bearing it is a deliberate attempt to mislead the faithful, but it is an unfortunately irresponsible method to find what is true. Investigators should be cautious of this approach and note that fluency can be biasing. For this reason, it is essential to engage in deep reflection and try to cue our minds towards understanding and finding our own reasons for belief. Blind faith and building confidence by increasing fluency through repetition is a problematic, misleading, and irresponsible way to find the truth.

---

2. Lisa K. Fazio et al., "Knowledge Does Not Protect against Illusory Truth," *Journal of Experimental Psychology: General* 144, no. 5 (October 2015): 993–1002.we frequently encounter false claims in the form of consumer advertisements, political propaganda, and rumors. Repetition may be one way that insidious misconceptions, such as the belief that vitamin C prevents the common cold, enter our knowledge base. Research on the illusory truth effect demonstrates that repeated statements are easier to process, and subsequently perceived to be more truthful, than new statements. The prevailing assumption in the literature has been that knowledge constrains this effect (i.e., repeating the statement "The Atlantic Ocean is the largest ocean on Earth" will not make you believe it

CHAPTER 2: THE RELIGIOUS EPISTEMOLOGY OF THE LDS CHURCH

My fifth point is demonstrating that there may be many false confirmations from what only appears to be the Holy Spirit. In my meetings with LDS missionaries, I frequently hear them bear their testimonies and tell me with full confidence that they *know* that Joseph Smith is a prophet because of the feeling that God has given them. After they claim to know the truth, a claim often based solely on their religious feelings, I ask "What about other religions?" What about them? There are an incredible number of other religions that claim to impart the same religious feelings and experiences that the LDS Church exalts. Muslims[3], Buddhists, Evangelical Christians,[4] Jehovah's Witnesses, and many others also report phenomenological religious experiences.

University of Dundee philosopher David Bastow confirms this saying the following. "All religions involve and rest on experience of the numinous, which affords a positive knowledge of the central object of religion - God."[5] If all the other religions have religious experiences that they use to support their diverse beliefs why does the LDS experience deserve to be treated differently? You might say that all of the other religions are wrong when they claim that their religious experience is real. Because they do not have true contact with the divine, their experiences do not justify their unique religious beliefs. However, just as we might say that all other religions are not truly experiencing God, but rather, some emotional or psychological deception, we could say the same about the LDS situation. If every religious community claims these experiences as evidence for their teachings, how are we to distinguish which truly experience God and receive the spiritual witness of His truth?

Alternatively, it is frequently granted that all of the religions which claim religious experience are having genuine encounters with the divine. This was a response that I received from two missionaries as we were engaged in discussing this topic. I asked them the same question—why do all religions claim that they have confirming spiritual experiences? Who is right? Are they all wrong and the LDS Church is right? To this they replied that all the experiences may be real. They told me that all religions

---

3. Brannon M. Wheeler, "Deciphering the Signs of God: A Phenomenological Approach to Islam. Annemarie Schimmel," *History of Religions* 36, no. 3 (February 1997): 283–85.

4. Julia L. Cassaniti and Tanya Marie Luhrmann, "The Cultural Kindling of Spiritual Experiences," *Current Anthropology* 55, no. S10 (December 2014): S333–43,1.

5. David Bastow, "Otto and Numinous Experience," *Religious Studies* 12, no. 2 (1976): 159–76.

contain pieces of the truth and that the confirmation their adherents experience is just God, in his love, allowing his children to find the pieces of His truth. At first glance, this seems to solve the problem. Why do all religions experience a similar numinous feeling that they so often cite to justify their claims? It is because all religions *do* have spiritual experience which confirms the pieces of the truth that they hold.

This response does little to resolve the tension. In my response I asked them if they believed that the LDS tradition contained more truth than the other religions. They firmly agreed. This prompted me to ask why they believe that their church contains the fullness of the gospel while all the other religions have merely bits and pieces of the truth. Is it not possible that Islam contains the fullness of the truth and that the "burning in the bosom" that the LDS community experiences is just confirmation that they have a few of the pieces right? The same question remains. Based on religious experience alone, how can we know who is right?

To this line of questioning, my missionary friends had no further responses. If the only tool at our disposal for discerning spiritual truth is a numinous, religious feeling we are lost. I do, however, believe that there is another way that we can use to know who has the truth. The answers can be found through reason and evidence. As I will lay out in the next chapter, God wants us to think deeply and come to a knowledge of him. Further, the approach I propose of evaluating arguments and evidence is far more capable of leading us to what is true than is vague spiritual revelation.

The LDS church relies heavily upon the witness and testimony of the Holy Spirit in supporting their truth claims. While I do believe in religious experience and believe that it may be very confirming for those who have it, I see a limitation on what it provides in the vast majority of situations. A "burning in the bosom" does not necessitate that what one is inquiring after is the truth. It is incapable of providing propositional knowledge for the foundations of religious belief. As I previously elaborated, experience is great for confirmation but fails to provide justification for beliefs. Thankfully, there are far more effective ways to evaluate what is true as I will go on to describe in the pages that follow.

Chapter 3: "Come let us reason together"

> Teach me how to seek you, and show yourself to me when I seek. For I cannot see you unless you teach me how, and I cannot find you unless you show yourself to me. Let me see you in desiring you; let me desire you in seeking you. Let me find you in loving you; Let me love you in finding you.[1]
>
> —St. Anselm of Canterbury

IN THE LAST CHAPTER we addressed the fact that religious experience alone is not enough to bring us to a clear, justified understanding of God. Here I want to champion reason and study as the most effective tools for Christian and LDS investigators to find the truth. To be clear, when I use the word "reason" here I am speaking of a person's intellectual faculty. We use reason to consider things critically, that is, to create and critique arguments. For my following points I will draw upon Scripture, great thinkers of the past, and some current theological literature. Following this, I will list a couple objections that many have to this reasonable faith model and provide responses to them.

Initially, it is important to ask ourselves, why should we use reason to find the truth? I believe that there are two main reasons for this. First, the intellectual faculty is a tool that directs itself towards finding the truth. Secondarily, reason, in and of itself, is objective and unbiased. The problems with reason arise not in its use, by critical analysis and application of the laws of logic, but rather in the minds of the reasoners. Unlike our feelings, reason necessarily directs itself towards finding what corresponds with reality and is a reliable process for doing so.

---

1. Anselm et al., *Monologion and Proslogion: With the Replies of Gaunilo and Anselm* (Indianapolis, Ind: Hackett, 1996),99.

The great problem of faulty conclusions emerges from our inability to reason perfectly. How can we get around this glaring issue? We must reason together. This, in part, is why open-mindedness is so important to the pursuit of truth.

I may be unable to reason perfectly on my own due to any number of reasons. This realization encourages me to join a community of thinkers who will assist me in my quest to discern what is true. I may accomplish this through conversations with other investigators or by reading the works of the greats. Another important way that we may evade the issue of our flawed intellect is by the guidance and revelation of God in His Word.

There are two extremes that must be avoided as we engage the question of how spiritual knowledge is discerned. The first is that of the strict rationalist. There are those who believe that the only way we can know anything is by reason and reason alone. While reason is reliable, it is incapable of proving *everything*. For instance, the belief that there is truly an external world and that it is not a mere creation of one's imagination is difficult to demonstrate rationally. While it may be challenging to prove the reality of an external world, I still accept this belief and hold it as true. There are some beliefs, referred to as "foundational beliefs," which must be assumed in order to make sense of the world around us. They form the foundation that reason helps us to build upon.

On the opposite end of the spectrum, sits the strict fideist. Those who subscribe to this perspective suppose that reason and faith are separate and potentially opposed.[2] As is expressed in the famed quote of Tertullian, "What has Athens to do with Jerusaelm?"[3] This view asserts that reason has nothing to do with theological truths. This position falls short in numerous areas and is similar to what is practiced within the LDS Church.

---

2. Richard Amesbury, "Fideism," in *The Stanford Encyclopedia of Philosophy*, ed. Edward N. Zalta, Summer 2022 (Metaphysics Research Lab, Stanford University, 2022). and it remains acentral preoccupation among contemporary philosophers of religion., "Fideism" is the name given to that school ofthought —to which Tertullian himself is frequently said to havesubscribed —which answers that faith is in some sense independentof, if not outright adversarial toward, reason. In contrast to themore rationalistic tradition of natural theology, with its argumentsfor the existence of God, fideism holds —or at any rateappears to hold (more on this caveat shortly

3. "'What Has Athens to Do with Jerusalem?': Apostasy and Restoration in the Big Picture," *FAIR* (blog).

My approach lies between these two extremes and is a model known as 'reasonable faith.' I place my faith in Scripture and hold great confidence in tradition. While holding these, I try to come to an understanding of the truth by way of reason. Whenever a belief of mine is in contradiction with Scripture, I assume that the problem is found in my failure to interpret accurately. 11th century Christian philosopher, Anselm, provided some of the foundational thinking that has helped to form this rational faith view. His desire to walk from mere belief into knowledge of God is beautiful, inspiring, and should be the model for all who truly want to know God. In a powerful expression of his process, he says: "for what I once believed through your grace, I now understand through your illumination."[4]

This "faith seeking understanding" approach is moving. Unfortunately, and all too frequently, it seems that people forget the "seeking understanding" part. It is necessary to embark on the rational questioning of our faith to develop and support our beliefs with a solid intellectual grounding. To apply this system of thought we must have our reason mediated by faith and the guidance of God. What does this process look like? How does God guide our minds towards him? Powerful tools that assist the Christian mind in this journey are study of Scripture, teachings of great thinkers, and the working of the Holy Spirit.

The doctrine of the Holy Spirit guiding our minds has an occasional tendency to create confusion. Rather than assume that the Spirit imparts knowledge, I believe that the Spirit's function is more typically involved in the movement of the heart.

Christian philosopher J.P. Moreland provides his thoughts on this subject in his book *Love Your God With All Your Mind*. He says "In my view, the Spirit does not help the believer understand the meaning of scripture. Rather, He speaks to the believer's soul, convicting, comforting, opening up applications of His truth through His promptings."[5]

If this is the work of the Holy Spirit, then we have yet to be liberated from the necessity to engage with critical study of Scripture and theology. Reason plays an invaluable role in the process of Christian spiritual formation.

---

4. Anselm et al., *Monologion and Proslogion: With the Replies of Gaunilo and Anselm* (Indianapolis, Ind: Hackett, 1996).101.

5. James Porter Moreland, *Love Your God with All Your Mind: The Role of Reason in the Life of the Soul*, 2nd ed (Colorad Springs, CO: NavPress, 2012).47–48.

The practice of using reason and Scripture to strengthen, test, and share our faith is taught all throughout the Bible. Below I will provide scriptural references that present the case that reason and study are necessary and valuable for the foundation of belief.

Isaiah 1:18

"Come now, let us reason together," says the LORD: though your sins are like scarlet, they shall be as white as snow; Though they are red like Crimson, they shall become like wool.

Hosea 4:6

My people are destroyed for lack of knowledge; because you have rejected knowledge, I reject you from being a priest to me. And since you have forgotten the law of your God, I will also forget your children.

Proverbs 28:26

Whoever trusts in his own mind is a fool, but he who walks in wisdom will be delivered.

1 Thessalonians 5:21

but test everything; hold fast what is good.

1 Peter 3:15

but in your hearts honor Christ the Lord as holy, always being prepared to make a defense to anyone who asks you for a reason for the hope that is in you; yet do it with gentleness and respect,

Colossians 2:2–3

that their hearts may be encouraged, being knit together in love, to reach all the riches of full assurance of understanding and the knowledge of God's mystery, which is Christ, ³in whom all things are hidden all the treasures of wisdom and knowledge.

Romans 12:2

Do not be conformed to this world, but be transformed by the renewal of your mind, that by testing you may discern what is the will of God, what is good and acceptable and perfect.

CHAPTER 3: "COME LET US REASON TOGETHER" 23

Romans 15:14

I myself am satisfied about you my brothers, that you yourselves are full of goodness, filled with all knowledge and able to instruct one another.

Acts 17:11

Now these Jews were more noble than those in Thessalonica; they received the word with all eagerness, examining the Scriptures daily to see if these things were so.

2 Corinthians 10:5

We destroy arguments and every lofty opinion raised against the knowledge of God, and take every thought captive to obey Christ.

These are just a handful of the verses that may be used to support the idea that reason is important and useful for spiritual formation. When you read over these verses it is nearly impossible to leave with any other conclusion than that we ought to value knowledge and the ability to think critically. God is a God of knowledge. This concept is embedded throughout the entirety of the Bible. In Hosea 4:6 God declares that His people are *destroyed* from a *lack of knowledge*. In Isaiah 1:18 God invites, "Come let us reason together." God encourages us to reason with Him. If God asks us to join Him in this process, we can be confident that it is good and beneficial for us.

In the New Testament, Paul tells the Thessalonians to "test everything" and to hold to what is good. In 2 Corinthians he tells us to "take every thought captive." He explicitly calls for reason and argumentation to support our beliefs. This exhortation comes from Paul, one of (if not) the best evangelists of all time. The apostle Peter tells us of the importance of being prepared to offer a defense for our beliefs.

Another consistent theme in the verses listed is the value of knowledge and coming to a "full assurance" and understanding of our beliefs. We do not have to hide the confidence which we have in our beliefs about God. He has blessed us with a wealth of Scripture and evidence that we may use to know Him and proclaim Him confidently!

We can see that Scripture repeatedly commits itself to the necessity that we come to an understanding of God. We are called to pursue knowledge. This process leads us closer to God and helps us to distinguish what is true from what is not. Matthew 7:15 warns us to "Beware of false prophets." Colossians 2:8 tells us not to let anyone take us "captive by philosophy and empty deceit." Another translation of that verse commands us not to be taken captive by "hollow and deceptive philosophy." What is the best approach to prevent ourselves from being swayed by hollow philosophy and deceit? The answer is found in 1 Thessalonians 5:21. We are to test everything. Whatever does not hold up to examination must be thrown out. The Bible consistently commits itself to the importance of reason and study.

In addition to the many biblical sources that may be used to support this line of thought, Christian tradition asserts the same. Below I will provide perspectives from just six (although I could add many more) of the great thinkers from church tradition affirming this position.

The Church has been blessed with a powerful intellectual tradition. Some of the world's greatest thinkers- philosophers, scientists, inventors, and others were a part of the Christian community. The Christian faith is deeply committed to the use of our rational faculty to glorify God.

We will examine six views on religious epistemology. These will be three classical thinkers (Augustine, Aquinas, and Galileo) and three contemporary thinkers (Wesley, Moreland, and Plantinga).

These views will be presented in the order that they appear in history. We will begin by examining the statement of St. Augustine. Augustine was a fourth century theologian and philosopher in North Africa.[6] He is widely thought of as one of the most influential Christian thinkers of all time. His writings have been heavily relied upon by nearly every western denomination as well as virtually all of the influential theologians who have followed him. He was one of the strongest proponents of a faith first standard. He rejects the kind of evidentialism that many have argued in support of. Although he denies the idea that everything may be known by reason and evidence, he fails to fall in line with the fideist. Under Augustine's epistemological process, faith comes before understanding in terms of time but not necessarily in value or importance.

For Augustine, to claim that one has true religious knowledge, a person must embark on a personal intellectual journey to find what is true. For this knowledge to be integrated it may not merely be given by a teacher but is evaluated based off of standards that are purely within oneself. The type of introspective criterion that Augustine wants each investigator

---

6. "Saint Augustine | Biography, Philosophy, Major Works, & Facts | Britannica,".

to appeal to are similar to logical trains, proofs of mathematics, or some deeply held moral value. While these may be taught by others, for them to be held strongly within oneself, they must be acquired as a conclusion of one's own. Augustine wants us to first, put our faith in Scripture and then strengthen that faith by means of reason and study; an exercise which must be achieved through personal, intellectual effort.[7]

We now consider the viewpoint of St. Thomas Aquinas. Aquinas was a 13th century Dominican friar, theologian, philosopher, and Catholic priest. He is esteemed by many to be one of the greatest philosophers of all time. He is widely respected for his great contributions to rational Christianity. He appeals more to reason than many before him and takes influence from the works of Aristotle. Many of his thoughts are recorded in his seminal work the *Summa Theologica*. The size of this work alone is a testament to Aquinas' commitment to reason and the critical and intellectual understanding the faith. The Summa is arranged in a question and response format. It has over 500 questions which are answered in over 2,500 articles. In total, it contains nearly 10,000 objections and replies.[8] In question 12 Aquinas shares his wisdom on "How God is Known by Us."

> Since everything is knowable according as it is actual, God, Who is pure act without any admixture of potentiality, is in Himself supremely knowable.
>
> [. . . F]or example, the sun, which is supremely visible, cannot be seen by the bat by reason of its excess of light. Therefore some who considered this, held that no created intellect can see the essence of God. This opinion, however, is not tenable. For as the ultimate beatitude of man consists in the use of his highest function, which is the operation of his intellect; if we suppose that the created intellect could never see God, it would either never attain to beatitude, or its beatitude would consist in something else beside God; which is opposed to faith. For the ultimate perfection of the rational creature is to be found in that which is the principle of its being; since a thing is perfect so far as it attains to its principle. [. . .] Hence it must be absolutely granted that the blessed see the essence of God.[9]

---

7. Christian Tornau, "Saint Augustine," in *The Stanford Encyclopedia of Philosophy*, ed. Edward N. Zalta, Summer 2020 (Metaphysics Research Lab, Stanford University, 2020),

8. https://www.sas.upenn.edu/~jross/summatheologie.htm

9. Thomas Aquinas, *Summa Theologiae*, I–II, q. 12, a. 4, accessed March 5, 2024.

As is demonstrated by his statements above, Aquinas is a firm believer in the idea that God is knowable to humans by use of the intellect. He readily acknowledges that we may not see all of God because He is infinitely too great for us to understand. He compares our ability to see God to that of a bat trying to see the sun. The sun is infinitely too bright for a nocturnal bat to be able to access. He further argues that man has a natural desire to know and that this intellectual desire is the fulfillment of man's highest function. This faculty is either purposed towards understanding God or something else. If our intellects were directed toward something else or were incapable of finding God, they would remain unfulfilled because they do not access that for which they were intended.

Human desires tend to have objects which fulfill them. Hunger is filled by food, and fatigue with sleep. Aquinas makes the case that the object of the desire for understanding is fulfilled in God. Galileo makes a similar argument for reason as an essential element of human nature in his letter to the Grand Duchess Christina.

Galileo was a 17th century philosopher, astronomer, and mathematician. He is best known for his defense of the Copernican model of the solar system despite persecution from the Church. He began his life desiring to be a priest before moving on to academic specialties. The Catholic Church, at the time, taught a different view of the celestial bodies.[10] They believed that the earth was the center of the solar system and thought that they had Scripture to support that view. Galileo pursued a different methodology for discovering what was true. Rather than relying upon a fideist faith alone model, he used reason and experimentation to find what was true. In his famous letter to the Grand Duchess Christina, He says:

> But I do not feel obligated to believe that the same God who has endowed us with senses, reason, and intellect has intended us to forego their use and by some other means give us knowledge which we can attain by them. He would not require us to deny sense and reason in physical matters which are set before our eyes and minds by direct experience or necessary demonstrations.[11]

10. Peter Machamer and David Marshall Miller, "Galileo Galilei," in *The Stanford Encyclopedia of Philosophy*, ed. Edward N. Zalta, Summer 2021 (Metaphysics Research Lab, Stanford University, 2021). \\uco\\u8220{}Galileo Galilei,\\uco\\u8221{} in {\\i{} The Stanford Encyclopedia of Philosophy}, ed. Edward N. Zalta, Summer 2021 (Metaphysics Research Lab, Stanford University, 2021

11. "Letter from Galileo to Grand Duchess Cristina (1615),".

I find this argument especially compelling. Galileo notes that God created human beings with minds. He was the one who endowed us with our intellectual faculty. After gifting this to us why would He expect us to take some other route to find knowledge? Worse even, why would He expect us to believe something that might contradict what reason leads us to believe? A God who would require this from us would be cruel and deceptive. If the only way to come to an understanding of spiritual truth was through the witness of the Holy Spirit, why would God have given us reason?

Galileo expresses this brilliantly saying, "But I do not feel obligated to believe that the same God who has endowed us with senses, reason, and intellect has intended us to forego their use."

These three classical Christian thinkers all champion reason and study as important elements in knowing God. Of course, these proofs must be mediated with faith and reliance on God and his Spirit. However, we are obligated to make a personal action to use our intellectual faculties to come to a more complete understanding of the principles that have been revealed to us. God gave us our rational capacity and, as with every other part of our lives, we ought to use it to His glory. One of the most basic methods for doing this is by using our minds to contemplate Him and His Word. This was certainly the opinion of the classical thinkers and is currently echoed by many of today's great intellectuals. We next turn to the thoughts of three contemporary Christian thinkers.

John Wesley was an 18th century Anglican clergyman, evangelist, and is the primary founder of the Methodist movement[12](which was Joseph Smith's favorite denomination prior to his revelations as we soon will address.) Wesley also had a deep commitment to developing the rational faculties of the Christian faithful. He, however, targets clergy specifically in his call to action. He finds it to be of vital importance that those who share the gospel be well equipped to do so. In one of his famous addresses, he elaborates on what it means to be well equipped for sharing the gospel.

> Ought not a Minister to have, First, a good understanding, a clear apprehension, a sound judgment, and a capacity of reasoning with some closeness?" [. . .] "Some knowledge of the sciences also, is, to say the least, equally expedient. [. . .] I mean logic. For what is this, if rightly understood, but the art of good sense of apprehending, things clearly, judging truly,

12. "John Wesley | Biography, Methodism, Beliefs, & Facts | Britannica,".

> and reasoning conclusively What is it, viewed in another light, but the art of learning and teaching; whether by convincing or persuading What is there, then, in the whole compass of science, to be desired in comparison of it [. . .] Should not a Minister be acquainted too with at least the general grounds of natural philosophy Is not this a great help to the accurate understanding several passages of Scripture Assisted by this, he may himself comprehend, and on proper occasions explain to others, how the invisible things of God are seen from the creation of the world; how "the heavens declare the glory of God, and the firmament showeth his handiwork;" till they cry out, "O Lord, how manifold are thy works! In wisdom hast thou made them all."[13]

Wesley was of the opinion that in order to be well equipped for sharing the gospel, ministers ought to have training in logic and even natural philosophy. He claims that these skills will make them better capable of understanding the doctrines for themselves and of presenting those ideas to other people. In addition, this kind of training better prepares ministers to defend their beliefs. Wesley is a powerful representative for intellectualism within the Christian community and his contributions have inspired many.

J.P. Moreland is the Distinguished Professor of Philosophy at Talbot School of Theology at Biola University. He holds three Graduate level degrees in Philosophy and Theology and has a reputation for being a brilliant Christian mind. In his book *Love Your God With All Your Mind*, he shares his views on the role of the mind in the Christian life.

> I was saddened to be reminded of how unusual it is for Christian people to be taught how to think carefully and deeply about what they believe and why they believe it. [. . .] the church must overcome the neglect of this critical area of development of the Christian mind, perhaps the most integral component of the believers' sanctification. The role of intellectual development is primary in evangelical Christianity, but you might not know that from a cursory look at the church today. [. . .] As our Savior has said, "Love the Lord your God with all your heart and with all your soul and with all your mind" (Matthew 22:37). To do this, we cannot neglect the soulful development of a Christian mind.

---

13. John Wesley, *An address to the clergy. By John Wesley*, . . . *1756*, 1756.

CHAPTER 3: "COME LET US REASON TOGETHER"

I highly encourage readers to read Moreland's book in its entirety for themselves. It is very compelling regarding the importance of the mind to faith. Moreland rightly points out that, in the Bible God commands us to love Him with our minds. If this were not enough to convince us to apply our minds to our religion, Moreland lists numerous additional benefits and his opinion that the mind is an incredibly important element for sanctification.

As Moreland exhorts us, we should consider being more active in faith through our minds. One of the processes for doing this is through the study of theology and philosophy. The final thinker to be presented is one of the most well-respected philosophers of the last hundred years, Alvin Plantinga.

Alvin Plantinga is most well-known for his great contributions to philosophy including, rationality of belief in God and the free-will defense. In 2017 he received the Templeton Prize Laureate for his contributions to "affirming life's spiritual dimensions."[14] He says:

> This capacity for knowledge of God is part of our original cognitive equipment, part of the fundamental epistemic establishment with which we have been created by God. [. . .] Another part of God's response to our condition, however, is Scripture and the testimony of the Holy Spirit. God speaks to us in Scripture, teaching us his response to our fallen condition and the way in which this response is to be appropriated by us. By virtue of the inward instigation of the Holy Spirit, we see that the teachings of Scripture are true. This work of the Holy Spirit, therefore, is a very special kind of cognitive instrument or agency; it is a belief-producing process, all right, but one that is very much out of the ordinary. It is not part of our original noetic equipment (not part of our constitution as we came from the hand of the Maker), but instead part of a special divine response to our (unnatural) sinful condition.[15]

Of these last couple of thinkers listed, Plantinga certainly leans the least towards the side of evidentialism. The second half of that paragraph reads similarly to how one would expect an LDS epistemologist to teach. However, it is important to recognize that he addresses this after two essential elements.

14. Marketing Communications: Web | University of Notre Dame, "Alvin Plantinga | Features | University of Notre Dame," Alvin Plantinga, accessed March 13, 2024.

15. Plantinga, Alvin. *Warranted Christian Belief*, Oxford University Press, Incorporated, 2000. *ProQuest Ebook Central*.180.

First, he asserts the importance of the capacity of our original cognitive equipment to have knowledge of God. He then claims the importance of Scripture and the movement of the Spirit. Clearly Plantinga believes in a healthy dose of reason in discourse about God. Reason is something that we may use to know God and understand Him better. In Plantinga's reformed religious epistemology, the Spirit plays a more vital role than the other thinkers have allowed for, however, he still asserts the importance of reason and scriptural study.

All six of these thinkers give reason to believe that thinking deeply about God is important for believers in their development and evangelism. We ought to follow in the examples of these great Christian minds and be prepared to step into the secular world equipped and confident to "make a defense to anyone who asks for a reason for the hope that is in" us (1 Peter 3:15). Even as some of the thinkers such as Augustine and Plantinga lean further towards a *sensus divinitatis* or illumination of the Spirit epistemology, it is important to note at what lengths they have considered this. These are authors who have written thousands of pages of dense philosophy in an attempt to understand who God is and how to best understand and be in community with Him. As a result, even those thinkers who are the least evidentialist exhibit a profound commitment to deep thought and theological study. This ought to be highly encouraged in the Christian community as it is invaluable to our development in relationship with God. We will conclude our study on religious epistemology with some objections to the centrality of reason to the Christian faith.

Chapter 4: Objections to the Rational Pursuit of Truth

Objection 1

More Reason and Evidence Decreases Faith

THE IDEA BEHIND THIS objection is that as more evidence is acquired and arguments are made in support of what one believes, there will be less reliance on faith. In this view faith is seen to be a good thing. As a result, anything that would harm or decrease one's faith must be a bad thing. For this reason, there are individuals who believe that they ought to stay away from argumentation and evidence in an attempt to preserve their faith.

In response, I propose that we do not want to abandon evidence and argumentation. If we extended this perspective, we would be required to wish that there was no evidence for our beliefs at all. An utter lack of evidence would force us to rely completely on faith rather than any evidence and would be seen by this view as a net good.

If there were no evidence, however, could we know anything at all? Even the Saints who uphold a spiritual view of knowledge appeal to external evidences to support their truth claims. Would it really be preferable if there were no witnesses for the Book of Mormon? What if all eleven who claimed to have seen the golden plates never had a witness of its reality? Further, what if Joseph never saw the plates and God merely put all of the ideas directly into his mind with no external connections to reality?

Certainly, this would not make a believer any better off. The ability to form and support beliefs with evidence is of unbelievable value. As has been discussed in the previous chapters, reason is a powerful tool to bring us into a fuller understanding of what is true. As esteemed Puritan clergyman Cotton Mather said, "Ignorance is the Mother not of Devotion but of HERESY."[1]

Another major flawed assumption of this objection is the concept that faith and reason are in opposition to each other. This is not the case. Rather, when in appropriate function they work alongside each other to increase our devotion to God.

Objection 2

Reason and Evidence Don't Convince People

This objection asserts that reason and evidence do not convince people to make new beliefs. It is unclear whether arguments, even when incredibly compelling, change a person's mind especially in the sphere of religion. Because argumentation changes no one's mind, there are people who believe that it ought to be neglected. Some of the LDS missionaries I have spoken with have quoted 1 Corinthians 2 to establish this point. In this passage, Paul says that he did not come with "plausible words of wisdom, but in demonstration of the Spirit and of power." The missionaries used this passage to conclude that we do not need reason or philosophy to share the gospel message. If Paul, says that he did not preach with "words of wisdom," why should we?

> **1 Corinthians 2:1–4**
>
> And I, when I came to you, brothers, did not come proclaiming to you the testimony of God with lofty speech or wisdom. ²For I decided to know nothing among you except Jesus Christ and him crucified. ³And I was with you in weakness and in fear and much trembling, ⁴and my speech and my message were not in plausible words of wisdom, but in demonstration of the Spirit and of power, ⁵so that your faith might not rest in the wisdom of men but in the power of God.

In this objection, there are two points that deserve response. I will respond to the roles of reason and faith in evangelism and then briefly to the passage from 1 Corinthians. First, I completely agree with the

---

1. Allen Carden, *Puritan Christianity in America: Religion and Life in Seventeenth-Century Massachusetts* (Grand Rapids, Mich: Baker Book House, 1990).186.

CHAPTER 4: OBJECTIONS TO THE RATIONAL PURSUIT OF TRUTH

first premise of the assumption. Reason and argumentation do not *make* anyone believe in anything. It is necessary to accurately understand the limitations of reason in leading a person to believe something. Reason does an excellent job leading people to observe and believe in mathematical proofs. Once an individual has walked through a mathematical equation for themselves, they reach a conclusion. 2+2=4. The reasoning is convincing. What we tend to mean in a religious sense is that reason cannot convince someone into faith. I agree with this and believe that this is because faith does not consist of mere mental assent. Faith is deeper. It is an actionable belief. Faith is putting one's trust into something. This conception of faith is dealt with in Hebrews 11. "By faith Noah, [. . .] constructed an ark." "By faith Abraham obeyed when he was called to go out to a place." "By faith he [Moses] left Egypt." "By faith people crossed the Red Sea as on dry land." It appears that the author of Hebrews is trying to convey that faith is not merely a believing word, but a trusting word. The belief must be there, but what makes it clear, what confirms it, is when that belief is acted upon.

One of my good friends Micah Long uses the following illustration when elaborating on this topic. There is an obstacle in many high ropes courses called the "Leap of Faith." This obstacle is constructed so that a participant gets harnessed in and climbs to the top of a wooden telephone pole that is about 20 feet high. When they reach the top, they stand on the pole without any support. The surface that they are standing on is about eight inches in diameter. Six feet in front of the person there is an object hanging such as a buoy. This is where the leap happens. While standing on a telephone pole that is eight inches in diameter, any breeze makes you feel as though you could be knocked off the pole (especially when you are 20 feet off the ground). Once the climber feels ready, they jump off the pole and try to touch the buoy hanging in front of them. After they leap out into the open air, they are caught by the rope on their harness and are lowered slowly to the ground.

Even though the participant is wearing a harness with a sturdy rope attached, standing twenty feet in the air on a tiny platform and jumping out into the void can be terrifying. In this illustration, the faith is what makes you jump. Some people require more assurance than others, but it is not the assurance that makes them jump. For instance, some people climb to the top and jump without the slightest hesitation. They needed very little additional assurance that they are safe. They just had faith.

On the other hand, there are some who are far more timid. When they climb to the top they feel the need to double and triple check their harness. They may wonder how much weight the rope can handle. They ask the course instructor if they are ready to catch them multiple times. They may follow every point that the rope contacts something, to make sure that there are no sharp edges which could sever the rope and drop them to their death. Only after thinking through all these things and checking their harness one more time will they jump off the pole. They did not jump from the pole because they were convinced with absolute certainty that nothing bad would happen. They just reached a point where they had acquired enough evidence to give themselves the level of confidence that they needed to take the "leap of faith."

This is how I believe reason can operate alongside faith. Reason, when used properly, is a supplement to faith. It can be used to add confidence in previously held beliefs and remove barriers for those who are not yet able to step out in trusting faith. Having more reason, true, does not convince a person to believe. However, it can build confidence and give people the comfort they need to choose to make the jump for themselves.

Second, I will address the passage in 1 Corinthians 2. First to note, Paul *does* use reason in his ministry. To demonstrate this, we need to look no further than verse 6 of the same chapter. Paul says, "Yet to the mature we do impart wisdom." There are two words here that are very important, "Yet" (δε) and "wisdom" (σοφιαν). First, the clause "Yet" implies that he is shifting his focus. In the previous five verses he is speaking of a different group of people. Presumably, these individuals are not the mature ones who he expects wisdom to be imparted to This brings us to the word "wisdom" what does Paul mean by this? The Greek word used for wisdom in this verse is "sophia" which translates to "wisdom, broad and full intelligence; used of the knowledge of very diverse matters." Verse 6 tells us that Paul intends broad and full intelligence to be given to the mature.

He goes on to say that the wisdom is "not a wisdom of this age or of the rulers of this age," Scholars typically believe this to be speaking of the very specific type of knowledge being taught in Corinth at the time. At this period in Corinth, the people were worshipping Pagan gods. Archaeological studies discovered temples to Egyptian, Greek, and Roman gods in Corinth. When Paul is speaking out against sharing the knowledge of the rulers of this age, he is referring to the beliefs in pagan gods. In addition, at the time in Corinth there was a culture of sophistry. It was not uncommon for speakers to take bribes to convince the public of whatever they were told to argue for.

With these cultural elements in mind, it is no question why Paul tells them that he is not preaching a wisdom of this age or of the rulers of this age. He is not coming with sophistry or another pagan deity. Rather, he is coming to bear witness of the true God. This interpretation clearly demonstrates that Paul is not against reason. In fact, it is quite the opposite! He is a champion of reason. He is a well-trained speaker who was deeply knowledgeable about what he taught and how to construct powerful arguments to share the truth with others. The book of Acts is full of passages of Paul going to *reason* with people in temples and marketplaces. When in Athens he even spoke in the aeropagus which was a cultural hub for sharing ideas. It was at this location where the trial of Socrates was held. Below is a brief list of the verses which demonstrate Paul's devotion to reason.

Acts 17:2

And Paul, as his manner was, went in unto them, and three sabbath days reasoned with them out of the scriptures.

Acts 17:17

Therefore disputed he in the synagogue with the Jews, and with the devout persons, and in the market daily with them that met with him.

Acts 18:1,4

After these things Paul departed from Athens, and came to Corinth; . . . (4) And he reasoned in the synagogue every sabbath, and persuaded the Jews and the Greeks.

Acts 19:8

And he went into the synagogue, and spake boldly for the space of three months, disputing and persuading the things concerning the kingdom of God.

Objection 3

Theology is too Heady and Difficult for Many People

This objection rightly points out that deep theological contemplation can be difficult and unpleasant. Many people do not find enjoyment in thinking deeply about theology or philosophy. These concepts can also be incredibly difficult for people to grasp. Just as some people (myself especially) experience extreme discomfort and lack of talent in the study of mathematics, there are individuals for whom philosophy and theology just do not 'click.' Because it is difficult and unpleasant people should refrain from embarking on this journey of intellectual effort, right?

Of course, this is not the way that we ought to approach difficult questions! Just as the old proverb says, "things worth having don't come easy." I have two responses to combat this notion. First, just because something is difficult to think about does not mean that it's not important. In fact, there may be a great deal of value in diving into problems that are difficult. It is precisely at the edge of our comfort zone, intellectual and otherwise, that we experience the greatest growth. Here we will affirm the value of the questions of theology and why we should think deeply about them.

In his book Pensees, Pascal presents an argument for Christianity that is now referred to as "Pascal's Wager."[2] The form of this argument is a weighing of pros and cons. Pascal points out that, when eternal paradise or damnation are on the line, earthly costs matter very little. What does it take, he asks, to become a Christian? Certainly, there are things that must be sacrificed to live a Christian lifestyle, but you stand to gain eternal paradise and escape the threat of eternal torment. On the other hand, if you assume that Christianity is not true, what does one stand to gain? There may be some temporary earthly pleasures, but one is risking eternal paradise and stepping into the danger of eternal condemnation. This simple approach of weighing the cost, highlights the value of considering one's religious questions carefully. I do not use Pascal's approach as a reason to believe Christianity is true. This is because it is not primarily interested in finding what is true However, his argument does make clear the value of these questions of faith.

---

2. Blaise Pascal and A. J. Krailsheimer, *Pensées*, Rev. ed, Penguin Classics (London : New York: Penguin Books ; Penguin Books USA, 1995).

CHAPTER 4: OBJECTIONS TO THE RATIONAL PURSUIT OF TRUTH

The question of whether what you believe is true is of eternal significance. If you fail to think deeply about this question you risk a blind march into Hell. Pascal's Wager makes a compelling case for all people to consider theological issues earnestly.

With that argument, we have established the importance of thinking deeply about theological issues. If our responses to issues of salvation are not accurate, we may lose our souls. The degree of rigor we exercise in answering these questions ought to be directly correspondent to the significance of their consequences.

Second, I think about this issue like upper-level math. In school I was awful at math. I did not enjoy it, was not good at it, and knew I would never use college algebra in my future. However, for some reason society has decided that it is necessary to teach all students upper-level math. The majority of these students will never have a need for college algebra, and many despise it. However, society has deemed it necessary for all people to think about high level math.

The same objections are frequently leveled against the study of theology. Many people do not enjoy it and find it too abstract or boring. Theology, however, is inherently useful. It deals with questions of eternal significance and helps to bolster one's faith. If we require our children to engage in the challenging, often unenjoyable work of mathematics which they may never again use, why do we not encourage the same rigor for studies of eternal value? In First Timothy Paul expresses it this way: "for while bodily training is of some value, godliness is of value in every way, as it holds promise for the present life and also for the life to come." (1 Timothy 4:8)

These topics, as was previously touched on, are among the most important that a person may ever consider. They have eternal significance. For these reasons, even if a person has a deep aversion and lack of proclivity towards thinking about theology, it ought to be encouraged and, perhaps, even required. If we are obligated to think deeply about high level math, we ought to think deeply about what we know to be of immensely more value; the beliefs that are foundational to the way we live our lives. These topics of essential value are what we will examine in the following chapters.

Part 2: **Theology**

Chapter 5: **Are Mormons Christians?**

As we continue our study, we will consider the question: "are Mormons Christians?" First, we must present a definition for what a "Christian" is. This can be a bit tricky to define. I could define Christianity as "all those who are saved and will take part in eternal life by the atonement of Jesus Christ." However, despite its apparent simplicity, this definition presents some challenges. Who exactly will be saved? What are the exact requirements of salvation? Are there a certain set of propositional beliefs that one must affirm to be saved? Does a person have to have a clear conception of the attributes of God? Can a person with an inaccurate view of who Christ is still accept His atonement? These questions are all fraught with ambiguities. As a result, for the definition in this part, I will judge whether the LDS community can be called Christians based upon their adherence or dissidence with traditional, orthodox Christian belief.

Thus, our working definition of "Christian" will be those who affirm the orthodox teachings of the Church. "Orthodox," of course, will also be a problematic term. I will be considering the beliefs which have been most unanimously affirmed by Church tradition to fulfill the orthodoxy requirement.

Are Mormons Christians? The Latter-Day Saints "unequivocally affirm themselves to be Christians. They worship God the Eternal Father in the name of Jesus Christ."[1] They claim to be Christians because they believe that they share a common set of beliefs with Christianity such as worship of God the Father in Jesus' name. If we define Christians as "believers and followers of Christ" then Latter-Day Saints fit the description well; after all,

---

1. "Are 'Mormons' Christian?,".

their church is named after Christ. However, there are many scholars that would protest this categorization.[2] The primary reason for this is that there are a number of theological distinctions between LDS beliefs and those of orthodox Christianity. These differing beliefs are not merely outlying issues, but essential doctrinal deviances. Because of this, our theological definition of adherence to orthodox Christian doctrines will be used to demonstrate that the LDS community cannot be considered "Christians." In the following chapters we will examine four main points where LDS teaching and Christianity are at odds. These are: the conception of God, views of Jesus, the mode of salvation, and personal eschatology.

On the Oneness of God

The First major difference between LDS and Christian theology is their conceptions of God. The vast differences between the beliefs will be expounded upon by considering several of the key divine attributes. A handful of the core differences include the following: The saints are polytheists and believe in many gods as well as the possibility of becoming gods themselves. They believe that God was once a man and is, therefore, changeable as He has not always been God. They do not believe in the eternal perfection of God. They do not see Him as a necessary, but rather as a contingent being. They see Him as co-eternal with matter. One of the most important resources for understanding the LDS conception of God is Joseph Smith's famous sermon, the *King Follett Discourse*. Quotes from this sermon will be shared below but I highly encourage investigators to read it in its entirety. It can be found in appendix A of this book. In this sermon, Joseph intentionally makes some revolutionary and wildly unorthodox claims about the nature of God. Towards the beginning of his speech, he explains that his intention is to "find out the character of the only wise and true God, and what kind of a being He is; [. . .]" After stating his intent, he proceeds to give his revelations.

> God himself was once as we are now, and is an exalted man, and sits enthroned in yonder heavens! That is the great secret. If the veil were rent today, and the great God who holds this world in its orbit, and who upholds all worlds and all things by His power, was to make himself visible—I say, if you were to see him

---

2. "Is Mormonism Christian?,".

CHAPTER 5: ARE MORMONS CHRISTIANS?

today, you would see him like a man in form—like yourselves in all the person, image, and very form as a man; [. . .]

It is necessary we should understand the character and being of God and how He came to be so; for I am going to tell you how God came to be God. We have imagined and supposed that God was God from all eternity. I will refute that idea, and take away the veil, so that you may see. These ideas are incomprehensible to some, but they are simple. It is the first principle of the gospel to know for a certainty the character of God, and to know that we may converse with Him as one man converses with another, and that He was once a man like us; yea, that God himself, the Father of us all, dwelt on an earth, the same as Jesus Christ Himself did; and I will show it from the Bible. [. . .]

Here, then, is eternal life—to know the only wise and true God; and you have got to learn how to be gods yourselves, and to be kings and priests to God, the same as all gods have done before you, namely, by going from one small degree to another, and from a small capacity to a great one; from grace to grace, from exaltation to exaltation, until you attain to the resurrection of the dead, and are able to dwell in everlasting burnings, and to sit in glory, as do those who sit enthroned in everlasting power.[. . .]

But they shall be heirs of God and joint heirs with Jesus Christ. What is it? To inherit the same power, the same glory and the same exaltation, until you arrive at the station of a god, and ascend the throne of eternal power, the same as those who have gone before. [. . .] The head God called together the Gods and sat in grand council to bring forth the world. The grand councilors sat at the head in yonder heavens and contemplated the creation of the worlds which were created at the time.

These excerpts make several unorthodox claims about the nature of God. The very first concept that will be appealed is the idea that there are many gods. The above quotations from Smith's sermon are held as doctrine by the LDS church. He says, "you have got to learn how to be gods yourselves, and to be kings and priests to God, the same as all gods have done before you." In another place he speaks of the creation of the world and teaches that "[t]he head God called together the Gods and sat in grand council to bring forth the world." Both quotations make clear the LDS view that there are many gods.

First, in the beginning, there was a council of gods necessary to organize the matter and form the world.

Second, Joseph commits to the doctrine that we may become gods "the same as all gods have done before you." These teachings boldly articulate a plurality of gods. This polytheism is in blatant contradiction with Scripture and orthodox Christian tradition. Further, it has ruinous implications for other divine attributes. In order to expose the misalignment that this teaching has with true Christianity, I will appeal to Scripture, great works of Christian theologians, and a couple of philosophical arguments.

Christianity has been a monotheistic religion since its very inception and foundation in Jewish tradition. This can be shown by a prominent Jewish prayer, the *Shema*, which is found in Deuteronomy 6:4. "Hear, O Israel: The LORD our God is one LORD:" This prayer is ancient and can be traced to the very earliest records in Jewish tradition. The book of Deuteronomy is believed by Christians and Saints to be written by Moses[3] somewhere near the 15th or 16th century BC. This means that 1,500 years before Christ, the Israelites were practicing monotheism. This doctrine has not changed since the very beginnings of recorded Jewish practice and continues to be affirmed throughout the Bible, but rarely as passionately as in the book of Isaiah. Below are some verses for consideration that definitively uphold monotheism as the only Christian perspective.

Deut. 4:35

To you it was shown, that you might know that the Lord is God; there is no other besides him.

Deut. 32:39

See now that I, even I am he, and there is no god beside me.

2 Sam. 7:22

Therefore you are great, O Lord God. For there is none like you, and there is no God besides you, according to all that we have heard with our ears.

Nehemiah 9:6

You are Lord, you alone. You have made heaven, the heaven of heavens with all their host, the earth and all that is on it.

---

3. "Introduction to the Book of Deuteronomy,".

CHAPTER 5: ARE MORMONS CHRISTIANS?

Isaiah 43:10

Ye are my witnesses, saith the LORD, and my servant whom I have chosen: that ye may know and believe me, and understand that I am he: before me there was no God formed, neither shall there be after me.

Isaiah 45:21–22

Who hath told it from that time? Have not I the LORD? and there is no God else beside me; a just God and a savior; there is none beside me. ²²Look unto me, and be ye saved, all the ends of the earth: for I am God and there is none else.

Isaiah 44:6

Thus saith the LORD the King of Israel, and his redeemer the LORD of hosts; I am the first and I am the last; and beside me there is no God.

Isaiah 44:8

Fear ye not, neither be afraid: have I not told thee from that time, and have declared it? Ye are even my witnesses. Is there a God beside me? Yea, there is no God; I know not any.

Mark 12:29

Jesus answered, "The most important is, Hear O Israel: The Lord our God, the Lord is one.

1 Cor. 8:4–6

We know that an idol is nothing in the world, and that there is none other God but one. ⁵For though there be that are called gods, whether in heaven or in earth, (as there be gods many, and lords many,) ⁶But to us there is but one God, the Father of whom are all things, and we in him; and one Lord Jesus Christ, by whom are all things and we by him.[4]

These verses clearly commit themselves to the oneness of God. There is no God but one. When I share this doctrine in meetings with my LDS friends, they make a couple of objections. Often, they claim that they also believe in only one God. This objection is typically voiced something like

---

4. See also: Deut. 4:39, 1 Kings 8:60, Joel 2:27, Isaiah 45:5-6, Isaiah 45:18, 1 Tim. 2:5, James 2:19, Eph. 4:6, Rom. 3:30, Gal. 3:20

"for us, there *is* only one God, and we worship only our Heavenly Father." This objection may appear to resolve the tension between Scripture and Joseph's teaching at first, but quickly falls apart.

Two verses which I believe make the doctrine of the oneness of God absolutely and unmistakably clear are Isaiah 43:10 and 44:8. Isaiah 43:10 states that before our God there "was no God formed and neither shall there be after me." The LDS conception of God says that there are many gods and that we may become gods one day. God says clearly in this verse that before Him there were *no gods* and that there will be *none* after Him. If this does not conclusively confine the realm of possibilities to one God only, Isaiah 44:8 certainly does. "Is there a God beside me? Yea, there is no God; I know not any."

In this verse our almighty God says that He does not even *know* of any other gods. This prompts at least three possibilities. One, God is not all-knowing and there are other gods that he does not know about. Two, God knows that there are other gods but intentionally deceives us telling us that there are none. Three, there are no other gods. Both Christians and Latter-Day Saints believe that God is omniscient. That is, we believe that He "knoweth all things." (2 Nephi 2:24) We also agree that He is truthful with us and does not lie (Numbers 23:19). In light of this, there is one conclusion available to us.

Because of the weight of Scripture entailing this conclusion, it would be impossible to hold a Christian worldview and to believe in a multiplicity of gods. Scripture refutes this heresy clearly and vehemently.

Let's move on to classical theological arguments for the oneness of God. One of the first points to be made from a theological perspective is the agreement of tradition. As mentioned earlier, the Church has remained consistent on her monotheistic stance since her roots in Judaism. This can be demonstrated by the many thinkers and councils who affirmed this view. The Nicene Creed, which was adopted as early as 325 AD, opens with the lines "We believe in one God the Father almighty, maker of all things, both visible and invisible."[5] The Westminster Shorter Catechism, written in 1647, echoes this doctrine in its response to question 5. "Q. Are there more Gods than one? A. There is but one only, the living and true God."[6] This view was also held by early Church fathers

---

5. Nicene Creed Andrew Ewbank Burn 1909

6. *The Westminster Shorter Catechism: With Scripture Proofs* (Edinburgh: Banner of Truth Trust, 2008).6.

and theologians. In the opening to his influential work *Monologion*, medieval era theologian Anselm (1033–1109) affirms:

> If anyone does not know, either because he has not heard or because he does not believe, that there is one nature, supreme among all existing things, who alone is self-sufficient in his eternal happiness, who through his omnipotent goodness grants and brings it about that all other things exist or have any sort of well-being.[7]

Here Anselm supports the belief that there is one unique entity who is supreme. He asserts this entity to be God and goes on to make many other arguments that have been significant in the historical development of Christian thought.

An LDS investigator may object that there may be many gods who are all equally powerful. They all became gods and organized the matter to form their own planets. Are they not all equally great? The response to this objection is found in a study of contingent beings. Joseph makes the case that all who are gods (including our Heavenly Father) became gods through the process of exaltation. Joseph says: "We have imagined and supposed that God was God from all eternity. I will refute that idea, and take away the veil, so that you may see." Joseph clearly denies that God is a necessary being by proposing the doctrine that He was not always God. He goes on to say:

> God himself was once as we are now, and is an exalted man, [. . .] and you have got to learn how to be gods yourselves, [. . .] the same as all gods have done before you, namely, by going from one small degree to another, and from a small capacity to a great one; from grace to grace.

Joseph Smith teaches that there is a god-forming process. All gods began as men and through good works, or going from "grace to grace," they became gods. I might briefly note that in LDS theology, no people were created out of nothing. Rather, people existed in an immaterial state as eternal souls until they were placed in bodies. This doctrine is also taught in the King Follett sermon. "There never was a time when there were not spirits; for they are co-equal [and co-eternal] with our Father in heaven." These unembodied spirits, co-eternal with God, are not yet gods

---

7. Anselm et al., *Monologion and Proslogion: With the Replies of Gaunilo and Anselm* (Indianapolis, Ind: Hackett, 1996).10.

but merely bear the potential for this end. This god-forming process, called exaltation, commences when God places spirits into bodies.

If this is the case for all gods before, as Joseph states, we are driven to ask; which god put our God into his body and started His exaltation process? Would that god not be greater? If our god is dependent on another being for his god-ship then that being must, by necessity, be greater. What about that god? Who started his exaltation? Another god before him? What about before him? Where does this process end? There are two responses to this question.

The first answer is that there was a first God who is a necessary being greater than all others because he alone is God from all eternity to all eternity. (Psalms 90:2) He did not require any other being to put him in a body and begin his exaltation. He is "Alpha and the Omega, the first and the last, the beginning and the end. (Rev. 22:13) All things emanate from and find their being in Him. (Acts 17:28) His eternal god-ness is a greatness which he uniquely possesses. He is the being of which no greater can be thought. He is the true God, any alleged others which are dependent upon a prior being are lesser beings.

The second possible answer is that there is an infinite regress of gods. In this perspective, there was no beginning, and this process has been going on for all of eternity. There is no first God because we may always find a god before him. Though somewhat challenging to wrap one's head around, this response initially appears to be effective. However, a thoughtful investigation exposes its faults.

My counterargument to this point is based upon the impossibility of counting to an actual infinity. If you started counting from 1, how long would it take before you reach infinity? Of course, you would never reach infinity. By progressive, numerical succession it is impossible. The same applies for counting down from infinity. If you begin at infinity and count backwards, how long will it take you to reach the number 1 or even 1 million? Again, it is impossible. This same reasoning can be applied to the eternal past of gods. Starting to count from an eternal past we could never progress forward to a specific time. However, we do seem to be at a specific time, the present. Therefore, there cannot be an infinite past. Because there is no eternal past, we must return to the first answer. There is a finite past, and it is reliant upon a necessary being who we all hold to be the one and only true God.

For all of the reasons that we have explored in this chapter the LDS and Christian communities have irreconcilably different views on this subject. The LDS church believes that there are many gods and that we may become them one day. On the other hand, Christian tradition asserts, as it always has, that there is one God only. Though the saints consider themselves Christians because of their worship of Christ, they fail to align with doctrinal traditions held by virtually all of Christianity. Because of this, we must ask if they can be called Christians at all. As we proceed, we will consider other differences between LDS and Christian views on the person of Christ.

Chapter 6: **Who is Jesus?**

THE UNDERSTANDING OF THE nature of Christ is the place where the LDS community claims that it shares the most similarity with Christianity. Indeed, this is where they claim the title of their church. Although they identify by the name of Christ, they do not share the same Christology as orthodox Christianity. The Christ that they believe in is substantively different than the Christ of orthodox Christianity. Many of these features of differentiation are smuggled in by their dissolution of the Trinity. This point will be addressed over the course of this chapter. Affirmation of the Trinity is one of the most dearly held Christian beliefs and without it there are many challenges. Much of the problem that this chapter deals with is the fact that Jesus is one with God. This, both the LDS community and the Christian community appear to agree on. It is the details surrounding this belief that provide the most prominent differentiation.

As previously stated, the LDS community claims that they are also Christians. Their belief in and worship of Christ is their most cited reason for this belief. After all, Christians are Christ followers; the Saints follow Christ so they must be Christians, right? Unfortunately, I am compelled to say that this is not the case. While they do worship under the same name, they do not worship the same person.

For example, if I were to ask you if you knew Tim, you would reasonably respond with "who?" or "which one?" While it is plausible that you know a Tim or at least know *of* one, it is far less likely that you know *my* Tim. Tim is my identical twin brother, married to a woman named Taryn, and pastors a Church in Kansas City, Missouri. While we might both truthfully say we are friends of "Tim" it is likely that we would be speaking of different people.

The same is true when we speak of being followers of Christ. This is obfuscated by the fact that it is not customary to ask people which Christ they follow because it is assumed to be the same. However, when speaking with the saints, it is important to clarify. Are we speaking of the spirit brother of Satan, a created being, who has not always been God or are we speaking of the Christ of orthodox Christianity? This Christ has been God from all time, is one with God the Father as one of the three persons in the divine Trinity and is superior to all including Satan. These are two vastly different views of who Christ is. With this in mind, we can see that it is important to consider which Christ is being worshipped in the same way you might ask which "Tim" I am referring to.

To address this important question of who Christ is and how the LDS conception departs from that of orthodox Christianity we will consider the LDS views of Jesus and the Trinity and contrast them with the Christian doctrines of the Trinity and Christ's own claims about who he is. The Trinity is a complex doctrine which theologians have spent thousands of years and tens of thousands of pages elaborating upon. We will not attempt to provide direct proofs or functional models of the Trinity here. Instead, we will look to three main items that affirm the orthodox Christian view of who Jesus is. These are: logical alternatives, Jesus' claims about himself from Scripture, and some of the conclusions reached by the early Church. After we touch upon these topics, we will look at the most common LDS objection to the Trinity and offer a response.

An important LDS document that is sometimes referenced to give people an idea of what the church believes of Jesus is called *The Living Christ*.[1] This is a one-page essay that presents an overview of the character of Jesus Christ. This very tame summary contains little which would be objectionable to the typical Christian reader. Its claims include that "He [Jesus] was the Firstborn of the Father, the Only Begotten Son in the flesh, the Redeemer of the world." These all sound consistent with sound Christian teaching. The only truly significant difference to be noted between this essay and traditional Christianity is the claim that Jesus "also ministered among his "other sheep" (John 10:16) in ancient America." Even this belief, however, does not necessarily paint a different character of Jesus. Where, then, do the unorthodox Christological

---

1. The Church of Jesus Christ of Latter-day Saints, "The Living Christ,".

doctrines come from? To answer that question, we will review some LDS Church essays and an article from the LDS apologetics organization FAIRLatterDaySaints.

First, the LDS Church teaches that Jesus is distinct from the Father in substance. This doctrine is taught in many places in LDS doctrine and is not a teaching that they attempt to obscure. Below is an excerpt from the Church essay *What Latter-Day Saints Believe About Jesus Christ*.

> Latter-Day Saints believe that the simplest reading of the New Testament text produces the simplest conclusion — that the Father, the Son and the Holy Ghost are separate and distinct personages, that They are one in purpose. We feel that the sheer preponderance of references in the Bible would lead an uninformed reader to the understanding that God the Father, Jesus Christ and the Holy Ghost are separate beings.[2]

This distinction in substance is the first prominent distinction between LDS teaching and that of orthodox Christianity.

First, we explore the fact that Jesus is believed to be the literal offspring of God. In an essay entitled *Does The Church of Jesus Christ of Latter-Day Saints Teach That God Had SEX with Mary?*[3] FAIRMormon discusses the conception of Christ. The most notable point of the essay is that no conclusion to this question was reached! The article ends with the quote "the LDS Church simply has no official position concerning the mechanics of how the Son was begotten of the Father and conceived in Mary's womb."

While it is true that the Church holds to no clear position on this topic, their lack of response when confronted with their own sources that point to the plausibility of God having sex with Mary is questionable. There are a handful of sources which appear to teach this questionable doctrine. Here I will provide just three.

Teachings of Ezra Taft Benson

> "The LDS Church proclaims that Jesus Christ is the Son of God in the most literal sense. The body in which He performed His mission in the flesh was sired by that same Holy being we worship as God, our Eternal Father."[4]

---

2. "What Latter-Day Saints Believe About Jesus Christ,".

3. "Did God Have Sex with Mary?," *FAIR* (blog).

4. Ezra Taft Benson, *The Teachings of Ezra Taft Benson* (Salt Lake City, Utah : Bookcraft, 1988).Utah\\uco\\u8239{}: Bookcraft, 1987.

CHAPTER 6: WHO IS JESUS?

Gospel Principles

"Thus, God the Father became the literal father of Jesus Christ. Jesus is the only person on earth to be born of a mortal mother and an immortal father."[5]

The Mormon Puzzle

"The official doctrine of the Church is that Jesus is the literal offspring of God. He's got 46 chromosomes: 23 came from Mary, 23 came from God the eternal father."[6]

Is Jesus, then, a demigod? My intention in sharing these selected quotes with you is not merely to evaluate potentially frivolous LDS teachings about Jesus. While this topic may be amusing, I want to make clear the fact that the LDS Church teaches that Jesus came from God. Not necessarily as a created being (because the LDS Church does not believe that God can create any 'souls'[7]) but as a being distinct from the Father. He is a son of the Father in the most literal sense. This is further illustrated in the Church's essay *How can Jesus and Lucifer be spirit brothers when their characters and purposes are so utterly opposed?*. This essay affirms the LDS teaching that Jesus and Satan are spirit brothers as both are believed to be offspring of Heavenly Father. "Both the scriptures and the prophets affirm that Jesus Christ and Lucifer are indeed offspring of our Heavenly Father and, therefore, spirit brothers."[8]

These couple of points are enough to find numerous significant differences between the Christ of the Latter-Day Saints and the Christ of orthodox Christianity. The LDS Jesus is one of multiple Gods. He is a literal son of the Father this means that his divinity came from his Father by inheritance. This is described in the LDS Church essay *The Life of Christ*. "He inherited divine powers from His Father. From His mother He inherited mortality and was subject to hunger, thirst, fatigue, pain, and death."[9] The natural conclusion to this teaching is that He must be of a lesser substance than the Father because He came into

---

5. Church of Jesus Christ of Latter-day Saints, *Gospel Principles*, 2009th ed. (Salt Lake City, Utah: Church of Jesus Christ of Latter-Day Saints, 2009).64.

6. Stephen E. Robinson, interview in *The Mormon Puzzle*, DVD, North American Mission Board, Southern Baptist Convention, 1997.

7. "King Follett Discourse,".

8. "How Can Jesus and Lucifer Be Spirit Brothers When Their Characters and Purposes Are so Utterly Opposed?,".

9. "Chapter 11: The Life of Christ,".

being by the Father. Finally, as a mere spirit son of the Father he is of the same essence as the devil. Jesus and Lucifer, in this worldview, are believed to be brothers.

With these distinctions in mind, we ask ourselves are the Saints Christians? They follow Christ, but is this the same Christ as that of traditional Christianity? It appears to me that we answer this question with a resounding "No." In order to further elaborate this, we will proceed to present and justify the Christian perspective.

As I said above, I have no intention of providing a comprehensive argument for the Trinity, rather, I will do my best to affirm this teaching succinctly.

First, we need to consider the possible options of Jesus' divinity. The way I see it there are at least three main options. (1) Jesus is not divine and, therefore, not one with God. (2) Jesus is divine and not one with God. (3) Jesus is divine and one with God. We made very clear last chapter that there is only one God. This is foundational. Because there is one God only and no others, it is impossible that Jesus is God and not one with God the Father. Jesus and Heavenly Father cannot be separate beings, and both remain divine. Scripture, reason, and tradition have not left that option open to us. Either Jesus is divine and one with God or He is not divine at all.

Both the LDS Church and Christian tradition hold Jesus' divinity. Because of this, there is no need to argue the point. The common belief of Jesus' divinity is mutually held and neither community is willing to deny it. With this second option removed, we find that the only option remaining is that Jesus is God and is also *one* with God.

Let us not forget the foundational premises for our trinitarian argument. One, Jesus is divine. Two, there is only one God. If we disagree with the doctrine of the Trinity, we deny one of these premises. Both communities hold tightly to Jesus' divine nature. As a result, if there is still some uncertainty about this doctrine it is likely caused by a denial of the second premise. If this is the case, I encourage the reader to review the previous chapter. The Trinity is a mystery of church doctrine. Admittedly, the presence of three persons in one being is difficult to grasp.

How do we understand this? We will review the way that this doctrine is elaborated in Scripture and tradition.

First let's look at the scriptural reasons to believe in the doctrine of the Trinity. There are numerous verses which confirm that the Father, Son, and Holy Spirit are one.

CHAPTER 6: WHO IS JESUS?

If there is only one God, then every time that Jesus asserts his divinity, he is either lying or affirming his oneness with the Father. Below are some verses which help us to understand the Trinity.

John 1:1

In the beginning was the Word, and the Word was with God, and the Word was God.

John 10:30

[30] I and the Father are one."

John 17:21

That they may all be one, just as you, Father, are in me, and I in you, that they also may be in us, so that the world may believe that you have sent me.

Colossians 1:15–17

He is the image of the invisible God, the firstborn of all creation. [16] For by him all things were created, in heaven and on earth, visible and invisible, whether thrones or dominions or rulers or authorities—all things were created through him and for him. [17] And he is before all things, and in him all things hold together.

Colossians 2:9–10

For in him the whole fullness of deity dwells bodily, [10] and you have been filled in him, who is the head of all rule and authority.

Philippians 2:5–6

Have this mind among yourselves, which is yours in Christ Jesus, [6] who, though he was in the form of God, did not count equality with God a thing to be grasped,

John 10:33

The Jews answered him, "It is not for a good work that we are going to stone you but for blasphemy, because you, being a man, make yourself God.

John 5:18

This was why the Jews were seeking all the more to kill him, because not only was he breaking the Sabbath, but he was even calling God his own Father, making himself equal with God.

John 14:9–11

Jesus said to him, "Have I been with you so long, and you still do not know me, Philip? Whoever has seen me has seen the Father. How can you say, 'Show us the Father'? [10] Do you not believe that I am in the Father and the Father is in me? The words that I say to you I do not speak on my own authority, but the Father who dwells in me does his works. [11] Believe me that I am in the Father and the Father is in me, or else believe on account of the works themselves.

Titus 2:13

Waiting for our blessed hope, the appearing of the glory of our great God and Savior Jesus Christ,

These verses present a strong case for the belief that the Father and the Son are one. John 10:30 states this explicitly. Colossians 2:9 states that "in him the whole fullness of deity dwells bodily." If the *fullness of deity* is contained in Jesus, He must be fully God. There may be some ways that scholars and apologists attempt to interpret these verses to demonstrate the idea that Jesus and the Father are wholly separate. However, I believe that they fail to create cases that do so successfully. This is even more the case when the verses are evaluated alongside all of those that affirm that there is only one God.

The Jesus of Tradition

With these verses presented, we begin to look at Church tradition on the topic of Jesus' oneness with the Father and the early Church's view of the Trinity. Before we dive into this evidence, it is important to identify its value. There are some, especially within the LDS community who try to make the case that the Trinity was merely a late development of Christian thought. They assert that this doctrine did not make its appearance until the 3rd or 4th century AD with the Council of Nicea.[10] I want to

---

10. Daniel C. Peterson and Stephen D. Ricks, "Comparing LDS Beliefs with

demonstrate that this is not the case. Rather, trinitarian thought has been present since the very beginnings of Christian tradition. While it may not have been explicitly clarified in definite terms until Nicea, it was implicit in the teachings of the apostles and the early Church Fathers. I am going to build an argument for this by presenting the beliefs of four early Church Fathers: Ignatius, Irenaeus, Clement, and Athanasius.

To highlight the antiquity of the doctrine of the Trinity, I will provide a timeline that details important dates and elaborates their significance. Jesus was crucified in 33 AD.[11] The apostle John was reported by Irenaeus to have been with the Christians in Asia "up until the times of Trajan"[12] which is the expected date of his exile. Using the beginning of Emperor Trajan's rule, we can identify this time as around 98 AD.[13] In addition, another early Church Father who we will not discuss further, Polycarp, was thought to have known John personally.[14] Polycarp was martyred by burning in 155 AD.[15] This relationship between John and Polycarp was written of by Irenaeus who also knew Polycarp and wrote around 175 AD.[16] With this brief timeline of a few key characters of the early church, it is clear how closely linked the enduring Christian tradition is with its origins. We can trace many of our doctrines through Church history all the way back to the apostles and ultimately to Christ. The thoughts that were shared by the Fathers who we list here were the contemporary theories and were defended heroically by the leaders of the early Church.

As these analyses will demonstrate, trinitarian thought was not a spontaneous creation of the 4th century at the council, but rather, is rooted deeply in Church origins. This is shown by the continuity of sources from Jesus, to the Apostles, to the early Church fathers, and to the ecumenical councils that declared and clarified the doctrine. We begin by looking at St. Ignatius' beliefs.

First-Century Christianity," accessed March 18, 2024.

11. "April 3, AD 33: Why We Believe We Can Know the Exact Date Jesus Died," The Center for Biblical Studies, April 8, 2020.

12. Irenaeus, "Against Heresies," Book II, Chapter 22, section 4.

13. "Trajan,".

14. Paul Hartog, "John or Paul: Who Was Polycarp's Mentor?" Tyndale Bulletin 61, no. 1 (2010): 1–14.

15. "Martyrdom of Polycarp | Description, Importance, Date, & Facts | Britannica,".

16. "What Do We Know of the Life of John the Apostle after the Day of Pentecost?,".

Ignatius: (50–117 AD)

Saint Ignatius was an incredibly influential early Church Father. His primary goals of teaching were to emphasize the reality of Christ's humanity and to combat the Judaizers who rejected the authority of the New Testament. He was martyred for his faith by wild beasts in the Roman colosseum. The exact date of his execution is a topic of some debate. Using the writings of another early church father, Eusebius, it may be placed during the reign of Trajan which was approximately 98–117 A.D. As such, he is an incredibly early source as he is one of the earliest Church Fathers after the apostles. This makes him, a significant[17] author, and his writings give us valuable insight into the mind of the early church. Mark Hanson from Maranatha Baptist University presents Ignatius' views on this subject as follows.

> By examining all the epistles Ignatius wrote to the different churches, small pieces of his broader theology emerge. Ignatius clearly notes the importance of the Father, Son, and Spirit, but he also details that Christ was completely God: "To the church ... elected through the true passion by the will of the Father, and Jesus Christ our God." "For our God, Jesus Christ was, according to appointment of God conceived in the womb of Mary ... God Himself being manifested in human form for the renewal of eternal life."[18]

We see a link between Ignatius' theology and the doctrine of the Trinity. He is monotheistic, holding to the belief that God is God alone. In addition, he affirms Jesus' divinity. By holding these beliefs together, we can see the beginnings of trinitarian thought even in the writings of the earliest church fathers.

Irenaeus: (125–202 AD)

Irenaeus was a Bishop in Gaul and a student of the early Church Father Polycarp. His life and work are dated to around 125–202 AD. He is most well-known for his work *Against Heresies* in which he provided defenses for the Christian beliefs. He was also an emphatic opponent of

---

17. "Saint Ignatius of Antioch | Biography, Writings, & Martyrdom | Britannica," March 14, 2024.

18. "Tracing the Thread of Trinitarian Thought from Ignatius to Origen | Maranatha Baptist Seminary," accessed March 18, 2024.

Gnosticism.[19] When analyzing his beliefs, there is argument to be made that he had pre-trinitarian leanings as well. One Marquette University author writes:

> Irenaeus distinguishes the three entities in their eternal unity through attributing to them different functions in the economy. God/Father is the source of the creative and redemptive work, while Logos/Son and Sophia/Spirit enact the work. However, the logic of Irenaeus' argument demands that the same quality of divinity be shared among all three figures. Their equal divinity provides the Son and the Spirit the power to enact the will of the Father in the economy. The result is a developed Trinitarian theology that posits three distinct entities named Father, Son, and Spirit, eternally united through one divine and spiritual nature.[20]

As is demonstrated by this author's study, here is yet another incredibly early source that articulates beliefs which are the foundation of the future doctrine of the trinity. We next consider the beliefs of Clement of Alexandria on this topic.

Clement: (150–215 AD)

Clement of Alexandria was a "Christian Apologist, missionary theologian to the Hellenistic (Greek cultural) world, and second known leader and teacher of the catechetical School of Alexandria."[21] He was born in Athens around 150 AD and died between 211–215 AD. He is well known within the scholarly Christian community as a prominent early Church Father and his writings are treasured by many. In chapter 1 of book 5 of the *Stromata*, one of Clement's famous writings, he articulates a belief structure about the Godhead which sounds very trinitarian.[22]

> Nor is the Father without the Son; for the Son is with the Father. And the Son is the true teacher respecting the Father; and that we may believe in the Son, we must know the Father, with whom also is the Son." "Son and Father, both in One, O Lord . . . the Alone Father and Son, Son and Father, the Son, Instructor and

19. "Irenaeus | Theopedia,".
20. Jackson Jay Lashier, "The Trinitarian Theology of Irenaeus of Lyons," n.d.
21. "Saint Clement of Alexandria | Biography, Apologist, Works, & Facts | Britannica,".
22. "Tracing the Thread of Trinitarian Thought from Ignatius to Origen | Maranatha Baptist Seminary,".

Teacher, with the Holy Spirit, all in One, in whom all is all, for whom all is One.[23]

In reading this work I would find it very difficult to walk away without the assumption that he has some early conception of the Trinity. He proposes, in this quote, all things necessary to the doctrine. He addresses the distinctness of each person, their unique roles, and then proceeds to affirm that they are all one.

Thus far we have presented the conceptions of the Trinity by three of the most notable early Church Fathers. We could go on to list agreement and further articulation of these beliefs from numerous others including Justin Martyr, Tertullian, Origen, Hippolytus, Polycarp,[24][25] etc. However, for brevity's sake we will exclude them from this analysis. I encourage you to investigate their beliefs on this subject as well. The three fathers that we have looked at here were pre-Nicene. That is, they were teaching before there was a formalized and canonized articulation of the Trinity. This all changed with the Church Father, Athanasius.

Athanasius: (297–373)[26]

Athanasius was a theologian born in Egypt around 297 AD. During his mid-teen years, he went to study at a famous catechetical school which boasted teachers such as Clement and Origen.[27] We see prominently here the succession of doctrinal thought. Clement taught at this institution and his ideas directly affected students such as Athanasius. Athanasius went on to be an essential supporter of the Trinity. Indeed, he was one of the greatest proponents of this doctrine and debated against Arius in support of Jesus' divinity.

Arius was a teacher who had become famous for his denial of the divinity of Jesus.[28] Arius and his followers held that Jesus was truly the Son of God and was the highest *created* being. However, He could not be

---

23. Clement of Alexandria, "Stromata," 5.1.

24. James Richardson, "Quotes from the Early Church Fathers: On the Trinity," Apostles Creed, February 27, 2015.

25. Coleman Ford, "Trinitarianism in the Early Church," The Gospel Coalition.

26. "Saint Athanasius | Biography & Facts | Britannica," accessed May 8, 2024.

27. "Athanasius, Champion of the Trinity," Chalcedon, November 1, 2008.

28. "Athanasius' Defense of the Incarnation | Reformed Bible Studies & Devotionals at Ligonier.Org | Reformed Bible Studies & Devotionals at Ligonier.Org," Ligonier Ministries.

God Himself because He did not possess the same nature as God. During the early 300s AD, there was immense conflict over the topic about the nature of the persons of the Trinity. During the council of Nicea in 325 AD, which Athanasius attended,[29] the Arian belief, of Jesus not being divine, was condemned as a heresy. This was the first ecumenical council. It was initiated by Emperor Constantine in direct response to the Arian conflict. The council concluded that Jesus was "homoousios"[30] which means that He and the Father are "of the same substance."

This had and continues to have important implications for the beliefs of the Church. The idea that Jesus is *of the same substance* with the Father makes clear that he is fully God. Not only is he divine, but he is *one* with God in perfect unity. At this council the Nicene Creed was formed, and the doctrine of the Trinity was affirmed.[31] The beginning of this creed reads as follows:

> I believe in one God,
> the Father almighty,
> maker of heaven and earth,
> of all things visible and invisible.
> I believe in one Lord Jesus Christ,
> the Only Begotten Son of God,
> born of the Father before all ages.
> God from God, Light from Light,
> true God from true God,
> begotten, not made, consubstantial with the Father;
> through him all things were made.

Key conclusions that were reached here include that Jesus is "consubstantial with the Father." From this point on, virtually all of Christianity has affirmed the doctrine of the Trinity. It is a difficult and beautiful topic, and many theologians have spent thousands of pages on its explanation. It is a crucially important element in the Christian faith. While some have asserted that it was a spontaneous creation at the council of Nicea, it has here been demonstrated that trinitarian ideas have been around since the very beginning of the faith. It is important to emphasize

---

29. "10 Things You Should Know about Athanasius," Crossway, January 7, 2018.

30. Andy Witchger, "Arianism, Athanasius, and the Effect on Trinitarian Thought," n.d.

31. "Homoousios | Definition, History, & Importance | Britannica,".

this point. The monotheistic and trinitarian perspective of the Godhead was not created. It was affirmed. This is traceable from the Scripture, the earliest writings in Christian tradition, through the Church Fathers, and into contemporary Christian belief.

Objections to the Trinity

Now that we have expounded upon the Trinity we proceed to two further points of interest. The first is addressing the most common LDS objection to the Trinity. The Saints, when addressing this doctrine, often look to the baptism of Jesus and Joseph Smith's visions as evidence that the persons of the Trinity are three separate beings.

> **Matthew 3:13–17.**
>
> [13] Then Jesus came from Galilee to the Jordan to John, to be baptized by him. [14] John would have prevented him, saying, "I need to be baptized by you, and do you come to me?" [15] But Jesus answered him, "Let it be so now, for thus it is fitting for us to fulfill all righteousness." Then he consented. [16] And when Jesus was baptized, immediately he went up from the water, and behold, the heavens were opened to him, and he saw the Spirit of God descending like a dove and coming to rest on him; [17] and behold, a voice from heaven said, "This is my beloved Son, with whom I am well pleased."

One can easily see where the confusion comes from when this argument is made. In this passage there are clearly three differentiated persons in separate locations. We see Jesus in the water being baptized, the Holy Spirit in the form of a dove, and God the Father as the voice from Heaven. It could appear that this is the smoking gun in the case for the Trinity. One might exclaim, "See! Clear scriptural evidence that proves that they are separate. They are clearly three gods who are one in purpose." Additionally, when we consider the LDS exegesis strategy that was quoted earlier recommending aways taking the simplest reading of Scripture there is no doubt where this conclusion might come from. It appears to be the most reasonable conclusion to be found from reading this passage.

In addition to the baptism accounts, Saints cite Joseph's first vision account in which he claims to have seen multiple personages (depending on which first vision account you refer to). While this does seem convincing, there are, multiple responses that we may level against this objection.

First, and probably most importantly, the appearance of three separate beings poses no actual threat to the doctrine of the Trinity. The orthodox position is not unitarian. We do not believe that there is only one God present in one person, the Father. As touched upon above, we believe in three persons in one being. Like Athanasius said, while Jesus is, in fact, a distinct *person* from the person of God the Father, He is "homousion" or *of one substance* with the Father. This being said, while we believe in "one substance," we also believe that there are three distinct persons. Because of this, it is not unreasonable that we should see all three together in the same setting.

Second, let's consider the "simplest reading" strategy. If this is the best approach to be used for interpretation of Scripture, what shall we do with other verses such as the following? John 10:30 "I and the Father are one." John 10:9 "I am the door . . . " If we adopt this strategy for John 10:30, then we have manifestly contradictory results. Jesus cannot be one with the Father and also a separate being. In addition, if we look at the other two verses listed above, a simplistic interpretation will lead us to some strange conclusions. Is it wise to say that Jesus is actually a door? It appears that this is not the case. There are plenty of verses in the Bible that, if read simplistically or literalistically will lead to contradictory or bizarre results. Because of this, it is important to engage in deep study and practice effective strategies for understanding scripture. Remember, even the Bible asserts that it is difficult to understand. (Acts 8:30–31) In light of this, it is important to find responsible strategies for reading scripture.

Third, there is some material in the Book of Mormon that appears very trinitarian. There are those who disagree with this perspective; however, it is rather difficult to get around the numerous verses that appear to support trinitarian doctrine.[32] In addition to the verses that remain in the current editions of the Book of Mormon, there were some verses that were edited from the original 1830 edition. This is peculiar because they shift from a trinitarian view to one that is more in line with Joseph's later theology. For "the most correct of any book on earth,"[33] it is rather odd that it ought to be edited from its original

---

32. "Question: Did Joseph Smith Begin His Prophetic Career with a 'Trinitarian' Idea of God? - FAIR," accessed May 14, 2024.

33. *History of the Church*, 4:461.

edition. Notably, the editing was not just grammar or formatting, but included new words that cause doctrinal shifts. Below are some LDS Scriptures that include a trinitarian view followed by a side-by-side table containing some of the edited verses.

Alma 11:38–39

Now Zeezrom saith again unto him: Is the Son of God the very Eternal Father? [39]And Amulek said unto him: Yea, he is the very Eternal Father of heaven and earth, [. . .] he is the beginning and the end, the first and the last;

Alma 11:44

Before the bar of Christ the Son, and God the Father, and the Holy Spirit, which is one Eternal God, to be judged according to their works.

Ether 4:12

I am the same that leadeth men to all good; he that will not believe my words will not believe me- that I am; and he that will not believe me will not believe the Father who sent me. For behold, I am the father, I am the light, and the life, and the truth of the world.

These three verses which are in the current edition of the Book of Mormon have clear trinitarian readings. They claim that the Son *is* the eternal Father and that the Father, the Son, and the Holy Spirit are "one Eternal God." While these verses do not represent the current stance of the LDS Church on the Trinity, they do provide a compelling case that, at some point, there was trinitarian theology within the Book of Mormon. The next verses were altered from the original version to make the trinitarian reading less apparent.[34] I believe that these altered verses present an even more robust case for trinitarian origins in LDS theology. I have italicized the words added in the modern edition for ease of comparison.

---

34. "Changes to Latter-Day Scripture," Institute for Religious Research, July 1, 2011.

CHAPTER 6: WHO IS JESUS?

1830 Edition	Current Edition
"And he said unto me, Behold, the virgin which thou seest, is the mother of God, after the manner of the flesh." *1 Nephi 3 (p.25)*	"And he said unto me: Behold, the virgin whom thou seest is the mother of *the Son of* God, after the manner of the flesh." *1 Nephi 11:18*
"And I looked and beheld the virgin again, bearing a chi[l]d in her arms. And the angel said unto me, behold the Lamb of God, yea, even the Eternal Father!" *1 Nephi 3 (p.25)*	"And I looked and beheld the virgin again, bearing a child in her arms. ²¹And the angel said unto me: Behold, the Lamb of God, yea even *the Son of* the Eternal Father!" *1 Nephi 11:20-21*
"And I looked and beheld the Lamb of God, that he was taken by the people; yea, the Everlasting God, was judged of the world;" *1 Nephi 3 (p.26)*	"And I looked and beheld the Lamb of God, that he was taken by the people; yea,, the *Son of the* everlasting God was judged of the world;" *1 Nephi 11:32*
"shall make known to all kindreds, tongues, and people, that the Lamb of God is the Eternal Father and the Saviour of the world;" *1 Nephi 3 (p.32)*	"Shall make known to all kindreds, tongues, and people, that the Lamb of God is *the Son of* the Eternal Father, and Savior of the world;" *1 Nephi 11:40*

Above are four verses from 1 Nephi that were all edited in later editions of the Book of Mormon. As is clear from the side-by-side comparison, the words "the Son of" were added to each of these verses where they were previously excluded. In each of the originals there is a clear case made that Jesus *is* the everlasting Father. This wording presented some issues for future LDS doctrine. Because of this, they had to be changed. In the original edition, dictated by Joseph Smith and translated by the power of God, there were apparent errors that the LDS community felt the need to correct. This is curious considering Joseph's high view of the Book of Mormon, as mentioned earlier, "the most correct book of any on earth." The fact that these verses were changed betray that some believed that they contained substantial problems. These verses were adjusted to progress and change along with the corresponding LDS theology.

For the reasons laid out, we find no convincing objections to the trinity from the LDS sources. This doctrine has been affirmed throughout this chapter. Trinitarianism is the orthodox interpretation of reason, Scripture, and tradition and was present within the initial LDS Scripture as well. By providing a compelling support for the Trinity we have also defended the common Christian understanding of the character of Christ and differentiated His character from the LDS understanding of it. This is of great value in our comparative study because Christology is one of the most fundamental tenets delineating orthodox belief. Indeed, this is a place where the LDS Church claims that we share much common ground. We have demonstrated that our views are quite divergent. We again present the question, are the Latter-Day saints Christians? We continue to answer this question by diving into the views of salvation espoused by the LDS Church and how they differ from those of orthodox Christianity.

Chapter 7: **Comparing LDS and Evangelical Soteriology**

IN THIS CHAPTER, WE touch on a topic of vital importance, the study of salvation. This study is a central principle in both LDS and Christian teaching. Both communities share as one of their core commitments the desire and command to teach the gospel of Jesus Christ and His plan for humanity. This is the most valuable message that has ever been given to man and it is crucial that we understand it properly so that we may have a knowledge of the saving truth and be able to share that truth with others (1 Timothy 2:4).

Although both Evangelical Christians and Latter-Day Saints share the purpose of spreading the gospel to the ends of the earth, we have very different understandings of what this gospel looks like. Saints and Christians (Catholics aside) have drastically different views of what it means to be saved, what the hope of salvation is, and how one is saved. These differences will be outlined below. We will begin this study by understanding what it means to be saved in the LDS belief system. Following this exposition, we will contrast the LDS beliefs with those presented by evangelical Christianity.

To understand LDS soteriology, we must ask what they mean by "being saved." When you look at salvation in the LDS perspective, 6 definitions arise. These are:

1. Salvation from physical death
2. Salvation from sin
3. Salvation to be born again

4. Salvation from ignorance
5. Salvation from the second death
6. Salvation in the form of eternal life/exaltation

For the purposes of this study, I focus primarily on salvation from sin, second death, and eternal life/exaltation as these are most conducive to understanding the divergence of LDS and Christian teaching. I will handle these three definitions separately. First, we will consider salvation from sin by the atonement of Christ. Second, we will examine salvation from second death and the hope of eternal life/exaltation.

Salvation from Sin:

The adherents of LDS theology, like Christians, agree that humanity needs liberation from sin. Beyond this, The LDS perspective strays from the main body of Christian orthodoxy. They claim that sin came into the world as a result of the free agency of Adam and Eve as they chose whether or not to obey God. In the garden, Adam and Eve lived in innocence and could have lived forever. However, the Saints propose that, in these circumstances, Adam and Eve could not experience true joy because there was no sadness. In a similar way, they lacked the ability to become truly good because they lacked any kind of testing that would help them to grow. One of the primary resources for LDS missionaries, *Preach My Gospel* elaborates on this teaching.

> Satan tempted Adam and Eve to eat the forbidden fruit, and they chose to do so. This was part of God's plan. Because of this choice, they were cast from the garden and out of God's physical presence. This event is called the fall. Separation from God's presence is spiritual death. Adam and Eve became mortal, subject to physical death, or separation of the body and spirit. They could now experience disease and all types of suffering. They had moral agency or the ability to choose between good and evil. This made it possible for them to learn and progress. It also made it possible for them to make wrong choices and to sin. In addition, they could now have children, so the rest of God's spirit children could come to earth, obtain physical bodies, and be tested. Only in this way could God's children progress and become like him.

This passage includes some peculiarities of LDS doctrine. We will address a number of these later, however, for now it is enough to consider the origin of sin and the problem it creates for mankind. One notable doctrinal difference is that the Saints believe that man is not condemned by Adam's sin but only by their own sins. The fall of Adam and Eve still brought mortal death into the world, and all of the other problems that come along with the fall, but they make it clear that humans are not condemned by the result of Adam or Eve's actions. Every man is condemned only for his own sin. This clarification on the doctrine of original sin has little effect on man's need of Salvation as Saints also recognize the universality of sin. As Romans 3:23 states, "All have sinned and fall short of the glory of God." This sin, the Saints believe, requires some form of justification because no unclean thing can dwell with God.

> **1 Nephi 10:20–21**
>
> Therefore remember, O man, for all thy doings thou shalt be brought into judgement.[21] Wherefore, if you have sought to do wickedly in the days of your probation, then you are found unclean before the judgment-seat of God; and no unclean thing can dwell with God; Wherefore, ye must be cast off forever.

The filth of our sin keeps us from being able to enter the presence of God. This problem is the source of the one of the most prominent questions in the monotheistic religions. How can man reconcile the distance between himself and his God? The Christian response is that this is achieved only through the atonement of Jesus Christ. This perspective is also shared by those in the LDS church with some important deviances from the Christian model.

Up to this point, the LDS and Christian traditions are found to share numerous commonalities. We both hold to the belief that all of humanity is fallen and in desperate need of a way to become worthy to be in the presence of God. Further, we agree that the method to enter into the presence of God is through the atonement of our Lord and Savior Jesus Christ. LDS Scripture highlights the necessity of an atonement for the sins of man.

> **Alma 34:9–10**
>
> For it is expedient that an atonement should be made; for according to the great plan of the Eternal God there must be an atonement made, or else all mankind must unavoidably perish; yea, all are hardened; yea, all are fallen and are lost, and must

perish except it be through the atonement which it is expedient should be made. For it is expedient that there should be a great and last sacrifice; yea, not a sacrifice of man, neither of beast, neither of any manner of fowl; for it shall not be a human sacrifice; but it must be an infinite and eternal sacrifice.

With clarity, we know that the infinite and eternal sacrifice spoken of in this passage is Jesus. The messianic passage from around 74 B.C. continues:

Alma 34:11–12

Now there is not any man that can sacrifice his own blood which will atone for the sins of another ... ^{12} But the law requireth the life of him who hath murdered; therefore there can be nothing which is short of an infinite atonement which will suffice for the sins of the world.

No man can take the punishment for the sins of another. However, because Christ lived the perfect life, He is able to take on the sins of the world. He was the perfect sacrifice. His atonement applies to all mankind, but the extent of saving power is applied differently to different people. If we return, for a moment, to the six definitions of salvation outlined earlier, we can find one of the ways in which Christ's atonement has universal effect. Definition 1 was salvation from physical death. Christ's atonement makes it possible that all men will be resurrected. That is, though all men will die a physical death, their souls will be reunited with their bodies and presented at the final judgement.[1]

Alma 10:42,44

Now, there is a death which is called a temporal death; and the death of Christ shall loose the bands of this temporal death, that all shall be raised from this temporal death ... ^{44}Now this restoration shall come to all, both old and young, both bond and free, both male and female, both the wicked and the righteous; ... but every thing shall be restored to its perfect frame ... and be arraigned before the bar of Christ the Son, and God the Father and the Holy Spirit, which is one Eternal God, to be judged according to their works, whether they be good or whether they be evil.

---

1. Bruce R. McConkie, *Mormon Doctrine*, 2d ed. (Salt Lake City, Utah: Bookraft, 1979).671.

Aside from this salvation from physical death, there is still a need for salvation from sin which causes the second, spiritual death. This death is separation from the presence God. Christ's atonement alone is not enough to save a person from this kind of death within the LDS framework. It is true that Christ's sacrifice did make it *possible* for those who believe to be saved from their sins, but his death and resurrection alone is insufficient to save one from this second death. The third article of faith in the *Pearl of Great Price* states "We believe that through the atonement of Christ all mankind may be saved, by obedience to the laws and ordinances of the Gospel."

Although Christ's atonement is absolutely necessary for salvation, it is not the only or all-sufficient requirement. The atonement must be taken hold of. For the Saints, this is accomplished by obedience to the ordinances and doctrines of the Church. The LDS doctrinal resource *Gospel Principles* further explains these concepts. "Christ did His part to atone for our sins. To make His Atonement fully effective in our lives, we must strive to obey Him and repent of our sins." Here we begin to see a more significant distinction between the doctrines that make up Christian and LDS soteriology. This is found in conflict over the sufficiency of Christ's life, death, and resurrection.

The steps for salvation for the Saints are faith, repentance, baptism, laying on of hands to receive the Holy Ghost, and enduring to the end. These steps are laid out within Articles of faith 1:4. If one abides by these steps they may be saved from their sins. This, in combination with obedience to gospel ordinances, can lead to exaltation. For the Saints, Exaltation is the ultimate goal of salvation. We will touch upon this more a little further on, but first we consider each of the five steps to salvation.

Faith

For the saints, faith is considered to be a knowing word. This has already been briefly addressed earlier. They uphold an interpretation of Hebrews 11:1 which states that "faith is the assurance of things hoped for, the evidence of things not seen" to understand that faith is seemingly intellectual. This is echoed in Alma.

Alma 32:21

> And now as I said concerning faith- faith is not to have a perfect knowledge of things; therefore if ye have faith ye hope for things which are not seen, which are true.

Under this definition, faith is a word nearly synonymous with believing. It is considered a virtue in the LDS community to have a strong faith that rests not necessarily upon firm evidence or teaching, but rather the personal revelation of the Holy Ghost. This faith, although primarily a noetic term, must also drive one to action. If an individual truly believes in Christ and His teachings, one will follow them. "Having faith in Jesus Christ means relying completely on Him—trusting in His infinite power, intelligence, and love. It includes believing His teachings."[2]

In Joseph Smith's *Lecture Third* contained in *Lectures on Faith*, a collection of teachings which became accepted as LDS Scripture in 1835, Joseph further elaborates this topic. These lectures are sometimes arranged in a catechetical, question and answer, format. Question 5 of this lecture inquires:

"How many things are necessary for us to understand, respecting the Deity and our relation to him, in order that we may exercise faith in him for life and salvation?" He answers his own question that there are three things necessary. He proceeds in the answer to Question 6 to enumerate these three. "First, that God does actually exist. Secondly, correct ideas of his character, his perfections, and attributes. And thirdly, that the course which we pursue is according to his mind and will."[3] This is the first foundation for LDS salvation.

As a brief side note, it may be worth considering that Joseph asserts the essential nature of having a "correct ideas of his [God's] character." This, he claims, is of such great significance that it is a prerequisite of salvation. Recalling the previous pages in which we contrasted the LDS conception of God with that of orthodox Christianity, we may question how many Saints have these "correct ideas" of God's character. Joseph teaches if they fail to have this right, they do not possess the necessary elements to exercise faith in Him.

---

2. "Faith,".

3. Joseph Smith, *Lectures On Faith: Restoration Edition*, 2020th ed. (United States: Restoration Scriptures Foundation, 2020).

Repentance

The second step for salvation is repentance. As Chapter 19 in *Gospel Principles* states, "Faith in Jesus Christ naturally leads to repentance."[4] This is a necessary step that all people must take to be saved from their sins (Moses 6:57). This call to repentance is found throughout the LDS canon. Also, within this chapter are listed numerous actions which demonstrate the genuineness of one's repentance. The most prominent of these are the recognition of our sins (Alma 42:30), confessing them (D&C 61:2), forsaking them (D&C 58:43), and obedience to God's commandments (D&C 1:31–32). If one participates in these elements of true repentance, they may be saved.

> **Moses 6:57**
>
> Wherefore teach it unto your children, that all men, everywhere, must repent, or they can in nowise inherit the kingdom of God for no unclean thing can dwell there or dwell in his presence . . .
>
> **Mosiah 4:10**
>
> And again, believe that ye must repent of your sins and forsake them, and humble yourselves before God; and ask in sincerity of heart that he would forgive you and now, if you believe all these things see that ye do them.

Baptism

The next step of salvation for a member of the LDS Church is baptism. The first two doctrines that we discussed above, faith and repentance, are considered principles which are true beliefs or teachings. Baptism is the first ordinance of the gospel. "An ordinance is a rite or ceremony."[5] This is the third step in the salvation process. Once a person has faith and is truly repentant, they must be baptized. Having completed these three steps, they may be saved by the atonement of Christ.

---

4. Church of Jesus Christ of Latter-day Saints, *Gospel Principles*, 2009th ed. (Salt Lake City, Utah: Church of Jesus Christ of Latter-Day Saints, 2009).

5. Church of Jesus Christ of Latter-day Saints, *Gospel Principles*, 2009th ed. (Salt Lake City, Utah: Church of Jesus Christ of Latter-Day Saints, 2009).115.

D&C 20:37

And again, by way of commandment to the church concerning the manner of baptism—All those who humble themselves before God, and desire to be baptized, and come forth with broken hearts and contrite spirits, and witness before the church that they have truly repented of all their sins, and are willing to take upon them the name of Jesus Christ, having a determination to serve him to the end, and truly manifest by their works that they have received of the Spirit of Christ unto the remission of their sins, shall be received by baptism into his church.

2 Nephi 31:5

And now, if the Lamb of God, he being holy, should have need to be baptized by water, to fulfill all righteousness, O then, how much more need have we, being unholy, to be baptized, yea, even by water!

The LDS Church affirms the necessity of baptism to wash us clean of our sins. In addition to its requirement, the Book of Mormon and continued revelations of the Church have revealed stipulations for what constitutes a legitimate baptism. These include the dictate that baptism should be performed by immersion (D&C 20:74) and that children should not be baptized until they have reached the age of accountability which, in the LDS Church, is 8 years old. Once a child has reached the age of 8 years, they have become fully accountable for their actions and the condition of their eternal soul. At this age children may and should be baptized (Moroni 8).

The Gift of the Holy Ghost

Once a person has been baptized, they are ready for the fourth step of the salvation process, receiving the gift of the Holy Ghost. This gift is reserved for individuals who have already expressed their faith in Christ by having faith, repenting, and being baptized into the Church and may only be given through elders of the Church. Even when an individual follows the ordinance, by having hands laid on them being prayed for by eligible elders, there is no guarantee of them actually receiving the gift. The Spirit comes to those who keep their thoughts and actions pure and earnestly desire His presence. The gift of the Holy Ghost helps to lead elders into what is right through quiet promptings of the heart. He is also recognized to be the force that brings individuals outside of the Church to the belief that the Book of Mormon is true.

The sum of these steps leads a person to salvation under the belief system of the LDS Church. If one follows these steps and holds genuine faith in the beliefs required, they may receive salvation from sin. The final element required in the life of a Saint is endurance to the end. If a person does not remain within the Church and does not maintain their faith in Christ, then they will not remain saved. Only by holding to these principles and ordinances can one be saved from eternal death. This brings us to the second part of our analysis of LDS soteriology.

We will now look to the other two definitions of salvation that were previously emphasized. These two were #5 and #6; Salvation from the Second Death and Exaltation. What happens to the souls that have been saved or those which remain unsaved? What does the afterlife look like in an LDS framework? The teaching from the LDS Church on these topics differs widely from what is representative of orthodox Christianity.

Salvation from Second Death

According to LDS theology there are four destinations for an eternal soul: three kingdoms and the outer darkness. (D&C 88) The LDS doctrine of three kingdoms of heaven comes from Joseph's interpretation of a passage in 1 Corinthians.

> **1 Corinthians 15:41–43**
>
> There is one glory of the sun, and another glory of the moon, and another glory of the stars; for star differs from star in glory.[42] So is it with the resurrection of the dead. What is sown is perishable; what is raised is imperishable.[43] It is sown in dishonor; it is raised in glory. It is sown in weakness; it is raised in power.

Joseph interprets this passage to teach that the glory of the sun, moon, and stars, are emblematic of three distinct levels of Heaven. The deceased are sorted into their peculiar level of Heaven or Hell based upon their works during their mortal life.[6] These three kingdoms, in order of decreasing glory, are the Celestial, Terrestrial, and Telestial kingdoms. The fourth destination for a soul is the "Outer Darkness." This is a place

6.

reserved for "Satan, his angels, and the sons of perdition—those who have denied the Son after the Father has revealed Him[.]"[7]

The "sons of perdition" are those who have committed the unpardonable sin. This is typically known as blasphemy against the Holy Ghost. Joseph Smith speaks about these individuals in his *King Follett Sermon*.

> All sin shall be forgiven, except the sin against the Holy Ghost, for Jesus Christ will save all except the sons of perdition. What must a man do to commit the unpardonable sin? He has got to deny the plan of Salvation; He has got to say that the sun does not shine while he sees it with his eyes open; he has got to receive the Holy Ghost, deny Jesus Christ when the heavens are open to him, know God, and then sin against him. After a man has sinned the sin against the Holy Ghost, there is no repentance for him.[8]

As the passage above elaborates, in order for a man to truly commit the unpardonable sin he must deny God after having full knowledge of Him. Smith analogizes this saying that it would be as though a man saw the sun shining right in front of him, but steadfastly denied its existence. This principle is further detailed by President Spencer W. Kimball who says in his book *The Miracle of Forgiveness*. "The sin against the Holy Ghost requires such knowledge that it is manifestly impossible for the rank and file to commit such a sin."[9]

The result of this is that virtually no one is thrown into Outer Darkness. Saints would hold that even dictators of extraordinary evil may end up in the telestial kingdom as opposed to joining the Devil and the Sons of Perdition in Hell. As very few humans will be cast into outer darkness, the LDS personal eschatology becomes almost universalist in nature. Christ's atonement saves men from their sins and is efficacious for their resurrection to judgement. In this judgement, almost no one will be judged worthy of outer darkness. Consequently, almost all will attain to at least one of the levels of heaven.

---

7. "Hell,".

8. "King Follett Discourse,".

9. Spencer W. Kimball, *The Miracle of Forgiveness* (Salt Lake City, Bookcraft, 1969).123.

Telestial:

The telestial kingdom is the lowest kingdom of glory and is compared to the splendor of the stars. This kingdom is for those who "did not receive the gospel or the testimony of Jesus either on earth or in the spirit world." This kingdom will contain many people. D&C 76 provides detail about what the telestial kingdom will look like.

> **D&C 76 103–106, 109**
>
> These are they who are liars, and sorcerers, and adulterers, and whoremongers, and whosoever loves and makes a lie. [104]These are they who suffer the wrath of God on earth. [105]These are they who suffer the vengeance of eternal fire. [106]These are they who are cast down to hell and suffer the wrath of Almighty God, until the fulness of times, when Christ shall have subdued all enemies under his feet, and shall have perfected his work;[. . .] [109]But behold, and lo, we saw the glory and the inhabitants of the telestial world, that they were as innumerable as the stars in the firmament of heaven, or as the sand upon the seashore;

As this passage states, those who have inherited the telestial kingdom will be placed in hell for punishment until Jesus has conquered evil for good. Once Jesus has claimed His victory, these individuals will be placed in their kingdom of glory. Those who make it into this kingdom are essentially everyone who has not committed the unpardonable sin.

Terrestrial:

The terrestrial kingdom is the second level of glory. This kingdom is compared to the glory of the moon. The people in this kingdom are those who did not receive the gospel in their mortal life but did in their spirit life. One of the reasons for individuals in this category not accepting the gospel in their mortal life is because of the "craftiness of men." (D&C 76:75) Alternatively, these are the saints who received the gospel but were "not valiant in the testimony of Jesus;" (D&C 76:79). We may assume that this means that these individuals failed to endure to the end. Instead, they fell away from the true Church at some point during their lives. A more complete description of this kingdom of glory can be found in Doctrine and Covenants 76 from verses 71–80.

Celestial:

The celestial kingdom is the greatest and is compared with the glory of the sun. This kingdom is by far the most complicated and is undoubtedly the kingdom which receives the most attention from both LDS and LDS-critical scholars and apologists. This kingdom of glory is split up into three parts; each ascending in glory (D&C 131:1). The highest of these kingdoms is what is known as "exaltation." The individuals who attain exaltation become equal to God Himself in glory.

> **D&C 132:20**
>
> Then they shall be gods, because they have no end; therefore shall they be from everlasting to everlasting, because they continue; then shall they be above all, because all things are subject unto them. Then they shall be gods, because they have all power, and the angels are subject unto them.

In order to attain this level of glory there are many requirements that must be fulfilled. These are all enacted during one's mortal life; "this life is the time for men to prepare to meet God;" (D&C 34:32). In order to make it to, the highest level, exaltation, one must be married for all of eternity within the Church (D&C 131:2–3). If a person keeps the other ordinances but fails to accomplish the ordinance of marriage, they cannot enter into exaltation and become gods themselves. Rather they will be ministering angels to God for the rest of eternity.

> **D&C 132:16–17**
>
> Therefore, when they are out of the world they neither marry nor are given in marriage; but are appointed angels in heaven, which angels are ministering servants, to minister for those who are worthy of a far more, and an exceeding, and an eternal weight of glory.
>
> [17]For these angels did not abide my law; therefore, they cannot be enlarged, but remain separately and singly, without exaltation, in their saved condition, to all eternity; and from henceforth are not gods, but are angels of God forever and ever.

As is articulated in this passage, the covenant of eternal marriage is required for reaching the highest level of the celestial kingdom and becoming gods. Many Saints will not attain to godhood themselves due to the rigor of what is required. Godhood aside, there are numerous requirements for making it into any level of the celestial kingdom. God "judge[s] all men according to their works, according to the desire of their hearts." As God judges humanity, he determines who is and is not worthy of reaching the celestial kingdom. The requirements for this are laid out in *Gospel Principles* Chapter 47.

Ordinances

1. Baptism
2. Receive the laying on of hands to become a member of the Church and receive the gift of the Holy Ghost
3. Receive the Melchizedek Priesthood
4. Receive a temple endowment ("[T]he temple endowment is literally a gift from God whereby He bestows sacred blessings upon you."[10])
5. Must be married for all eternity either in this life or the next. (This requirement is exclusive to exaltation.)

Other Commands

1. Love God and our neighbors.
2. Keep the commandments.
3. Repent of wrongdoings.
4. Search out kindred dead and receive saving ordinances on their behalf.
5. Attend our Church meetings as regularly as possible.
6. Love our family members and strengthen them in the ways of the Lord.
7. Have family and individual prayers every day.
8. Teach the gospel to others by word and example.
9. Study the scriptures
10. Listen to and obey the words of the prophets.

If an individual manages to keep all of these ordinances and commands, then they may be eligible for the celestial kingdom. There are,

---

10. "About The Temple Endowment,".

however, some exceptions to these stipulations. Doctrine and Covenants 137 clarifies these cases.

> **D&C 137:7–8,10**
>
> All who have died without a knowledge of this gospel, who would have received it if they had been permitted to tarry, shall be heirs of the celestial kingdom of God;
>
> [8]Also all that shall die henceforth without a knowledge of it, who would have received it with all their hearts, shall be heirs of that kingdom;[. . .]
>
> [10]And I also beheld that all children who die before they arrive at the years of accountability are saved in the celestial kingdom of heaven.

This passage describes that there is a kind of salvation by intent that may take place for taking some to the celestial kingdom. That is, if there are individuals who could not receive the gospel because of, for example, an early death or from never having been exposed to the doctrines, those people may be saved because God knows that they *would* have accepted this gospel if they were given the opportunity.

Another category is children under the age of eight years old. As discussed previously, this is the age that the LDS Church claims as the age of accountability. Prior to this age, all children will be taken to the celestial kingdom because they could not be accountable for their actions good or bad. The final category of those who may be saved without fulfilling the exact requirements themselves are the dead relatives of current Saints. The saints believe that they can perform temple ordinances such as baptism on the behalf of their deceased ancestors and, by completing these ordinances, their ancestors may achieve a higher level of glory.

The celestial kingdom is that which all saints strive for. The ultimate goal of the LDS faith is exaltation, to become gods themselves like Joseph says that they may be in his famous *King Follett Sermon*. According to LDS theology, if one remains faithful to God and to the ordinances of the Church it is possible for them to receive this gift.

Above, we have discussed the soteriological beliefs of the LDS Church. I have intentionally refrained from presenting a more thorough level of detail on each of the points of this subject as I believe that this gives a sufficient sketch of what is required for salvation and what that salvation means to a member of the LDS Church. This, I believe, is a good starting point for informed conversations regarding LDS soteriology.

Chapter 8: **A Response to LDS Soteriology**

IN THE LAST CHAPTER I presented a generalized overview of LDS soteriology. In this chapter I will articulate responses to their approach. I believe that the plan of salvation, as the Saints believe it, is deeply flawed. As this has been the decisive conclusion of my research, I feel it necessary to address these beliefs in a critical light. It truly upsets me to say that I do not believe that the LDS gospel is a saving one. I have often shed tears in prayer over the Latter-Day Saints because I do not hold confidence in their salvation. The depth of my feeling is, by no means, a justification for my beliefs. Indeed, the strength of my feelings has no bearing on the accuracy of my conclusions. My love for the LDS community and my genuine concern for them is, however, the inspiration of my passion for this research and writing. While I present my critique, I want readers to understand that it is out of love and not disdain for the Saints. In his first letter to the Corinthians, St. Clement said:

> Be contentious and zealous brothers, about the things relating to salvation. You have looked into the holy scriptures, which are true, which were given by the Holy Spirit. You know that nothing unrighteous or falsified is written in them.[1]

Clement underscores the importance of this issue. When considering things that have an impact on our salvation, we must be zealous and

---

1. Rick Brannan, ed., *The Apostolic Fathers: A New Translation*, Lexham Classics (Washington: Lexham Press, 2017).42.

test everything against Scripture. Following this model, I will address some of my concerns with the LDS teachings on salvation.

There is a strategy that Christian missionaries use when witnessing to Latter-Day Saints called the "Impossible Gospel." While this approach has been used by numerous individuals, it was coined "The Impossible Gospel" strategy by Keith Walker who is the founder of Evidence ministries. He is a missionary to Saints and Jehovah's Witnesses and has contributed greatly to Christian efforts to reach both groups.

The Impossible Gospel seeks to ask one primary question. *Are you comfortable in your position before God?* It goes on to demonstrate that Saints who firmly maintain their Church's doctrinal teaching cannot possess assurance of salvation (in the second death/exaltation sense). Once this problem is exposed, there is space to consider the true beauty of Jesus' sacrifice.

It is likely not necessary for us to convince the Saints of the trustworthiness of their canon of scriptures and modern revelations. Members of the LDS Church are very familiar with Joseph's claim that the Book of Mormon is "[. . .]the most correct of any book on earth, and the keystone of our religion, and a man would get nearer to God by abiding by its precepts, than by any other book." In addition to this, the Saints sustain contemporary revelation through their prophet. Everything this prophet may say is considered to be canon. This is reflected in multiple places throughout LDS tradition including: D&C 21:5 "For his word ye shall receive, as if from mine [God's] own mouth, in all patience and faith." See also: *Journal of Discourses 13:95* where Brigham Young, the second prophet for the church, said "I have never yet preached a sermon and sent it out to the children of men, that they may not call scripture."[2]

For a Saint, an incredible amount of confidence can be placed in the words of Scripture and the living prophet. The authority of the Church is absolute in matters of doctrine. As a result, though LDS scholars may engage in rigorous evaluation of their beliefs, they are in complete submission to Church leadership which alone possesses the authority to define and clarify LDS doctrine. Sister Elaine Cannon summarized this point in a way that has become ubiquitous in LDS discussion: "When the prophet speaks, sisters, the debate is over."[3] For this reason, I will appeal

---

2. *Journal of Discourses Volume 13*, accessed November 11, 2023,95.

3. Church of Jesus Christ of Latter-day Saints, *Ensign of the Church of Jesus Christ of Latter-Day Saints* ([Salt Lake City] Church of Jesus Christ of Latter-day Saints, 1971).180.

CHAPTER 8: A RESPONSE TO LDS SOTERIOLOGY

to LDS sources, which they cannot deny, to demonstrate the emptiness of the LDS gospel. A person who wishes to dispute the case made by the *Impossible Gospel* may contend with how these sources are interpreted, but not the authority behind them.

We open the case by repeating the notion that no one can be saved unless they repent. As addressed in the last chapter, everyone is sinful and must repent in order to be saved from their sins through the grace of our Lord and Savior Jesus Christ. This is laid out in the Book of Moses.

> **Moses 6:57.**
>
> Wherefore teach it unto your children, that all men, everywhere, must repent, or they can in nowise inherit the kingdom of God, for no unclean thing can dwell there, or dwell in his presence.

With the necessity of repentance in mind we look to Moroni for the next step.

> **Moroni 10:32**
>
> Yea, come unto Christ, and be perfected in him, and deny yourselves of all ungodliness; and if ye shall deny yourselves of all ungodliness, and love God with all your might, mind and strength, then is his grace sufficient for you, that by his grace ye may be perfect in Christ; and if by the grace of God ye are perfect in Christ, ye can in nowise deny the power of God.

This verse shows the prerequisite for the grace that may be bestowed on believers. We notice specifically here the conditional case made by Moroni. "*If* you shall deny yourselves of *all* ungodliness[. . .] *then* is his grace is sufficient for you[.]" Moroni proposes that in order to receive God's grace in a way that is "sufficient for you" you must deny yourself of all ungodliness. This prompts another important question. What does *all ungodliness* look like? Is His grace sufficient for us if we deny ourselves of a lot or even most ungodliness? Not according to Moroni. Moroni says that we must deny ourselves of the entirety of our ungodliness.

At a *General Conference in March of 2015* Member of the quorum of the 12 apostles, Neal A. Maxwell, said the following: "Jesus declared the need for us to deny ourselves of all ungodliness thus including both large and small sins." After this statement we see that for God's grace to be sufficient we must deny ourselves of all sin. A similar notion is echoed in one of the most prominent verses on LDS soteriology,

2 Nephi 25:23.

For we labor diligently to write, to persuade our children, and also our brethren, to believe in Christ, and to be reconciled to God; for we know that it is by grace that we are saved, after all we can do.

Again, in this verse we obtain an insight into the requirement for salvation from an LDS perspective. This verse is more than a little reminiscent of *Ephesians 2:8-9* "For by grace you have been saved through faith. And this is not your own doing; it is the gift of God, [9]not a result of works, so that no one may boast." In direct conflict with verse 9 of Ephesians, 2 Nephi 25:23 holds that we are saved by grace "after all we can do." *Articles of Faith* 1:3 describes what one must do. "Through the Atonement of Christ, all mankind may be saved, by obedience to the laws and ordinances of the gospel," namely, Faith, Repentance, Baptism, and the Laying on of hands for the gift of the Holy Ghost.

Note that in Articles of Faith 1:3, obedience to both the laws and the ordinances are prerequisites for salvation. Obedience to the law essentially means no longer sinning, as described in Moroni 10:32, but also includes obedience to the *Word of Wisdom* and other LDS commands.[4] Joseph Fielding Smith, who served as the Prophet from 1970–1972, adamantly affirmed the essential nature of obedience saying: "we most emphatically declare that all men must obey these laws if they would be saved."[5]

Considering this, what do we suppose that Nephi means when he says, "all we can do?" Certainly, this injunction extends past obedience to laws and ordinances alone. It is safe to say that I have never lived a day where I have done *all* I could do. In a lecture Keith Walker asks "if you prayed for five or ten minutes this morning, could you not have prayed for six or eleven?" When we apply this logic to every area of our lives it begins to paint a depressing picture. If we have not done *all* we can, if we have not denied ourselves *all* ungodliness, we cannot be saved.

When faced with this bleak outlook on the state of our eternal souls some will certainly feel the need to respond that: "We are incapable of living this way and certainly God does not expect this level of devotion from us!" After all, surely God would never expect something from us

---

4. Church of Jesus Christ of Latter-day Saints, *Gospel Principles*.111.

5. Joseph Fielding Smith, *Doctrines of Salvation Volume 2 - Joseph Fielding Smith*, 1954,305.

CHAPTER 8: A RESPONSE TO LDS SOTERIOLOGY

that is impossible for us to accomplish. In response to this intuition, the Book of Mormon prophet Nephi states:

1 Nephi 3:7

And it came to pass that I, Nephi, said unto my father: I will go and do the things which the Lord hath commanded, for I know that the Lord giveth no commandments unto the children of men, save he shall prepare a way for them that they may accomplish the thing which he commandeth them.

Nephi here teaches that God does not give commands that he knows we cannot accomplish. As a result, the commands of Moroni 10:32 and 2 Nephi 25:23 remain inescapable. If God has commanded perfection, (3 Nephi 12:48) you can and must be perfect. There is another important element that we read about in LDS theology. We can be saved *from* our sins but not *in* our sins. That is, we can only be saved of sins that we have repented of.

Alma 11:37

And I say unto you again that he cannot save them in their sins; for I cannot deny his word, and he hath said that no unclean thing can inherit the kingdom of heaven; therefore, how can ye be saved, except ye inherit the kingdom of heaven? Therefore, ye cannot be saved in your sins.

We ask then, what is the difference between being saved in sin and being saved from sin? The major difference between these two conditions is whether or not the person is repentant. According to LDS theology, a person may be saved of past, repented sins, but cannot be saved from those sins which they continue to commit. It is those who are repentant who are saved by the grace of God.

D&C 1:31–33.

For I the Lord cannot look upon sin with the least degree of allowance; [32]Nevertheless, he that repents and does the commandments of the Lord shall be forgiven; [33]And he that repents not, from him shall be taken even the light which he has received; for my Spirit shall not always strive with man, saith the Lord of Hosts.

As with many other terms that are shared between Christians and members of the Church of the Latter-Day Saints, "repentance" is defined differently by Saints and Christians. There are multiple steps to repentance of sins in the LDS view. According to *Gospel Principles*, these are: recognizing them, feeling sorrow for them, forsaking them, confessing them, making restitution for them, forgiving others, and keeping God's commandments.[6] Only if we adhere to all of these principles can we be found truly repentant.

The most important definition of Repentance in the LDS corpus is in D&C 58:43.[7] "By this ye may know if a man repenteth of his sins -behold, he will confess them and forsake them." The confession requirement is similar to what we see in Christianity, however, the "forsaking" differs quite significantly. While Christians agree that true repentance leads us to turn away from our sins, we also understand that we can never be perfect and continue to sin despite our best efforts. In the LDS conception, merely turning from sin is insufficient. One must *forsake* it. The common definition of this word is exactly how it is used in the LDS circles. To forsake is to abandon completely, never to return.[8] This is affirmed in *Preach My Gospel*. "If we sincerely repent, we turn away from our sins and do them no more."[9] Neil L. Andersen, a member of the Quorum of the Twelve Apostles agrees saying: "Whatever our weapons of rebellion, let us bury them and never again return to them. Let us forsake our sins."[10]

Such is the requirement for salvation in the LDS view. In order to be saved from one's sin, one must repent. This includes perfect obedience and forsaking sin. Though we strive with all our might, can any of us truly say that we have passed even a day without committing a single sin? Faced with the incredible weight of this burden, we ask, what of those who have repented and proceed to sin again? President Russell M. Nelson invites Saints to "discover the joy of daily repentance."[11] However daily repentance within the LDS view appears to be false repentance. If one repents and sins again, they have failed to forsake their sin. Thus, the requirements of repentance were not met and they did not truly repent in the first case.

---

6. Church of Jesus Christ of Latter-day Saints, *Gospel Principles*, 2009th ed. (Salt Lake City, Utah: Church of Jesus Christ of Latter-Day Saints, 2009).74.

7. D&C 58:43, This is also confirmed elsewhere in the LDS canon such as Mosiah 4:10 and D&C 93:1.

8. "Repentance and Forgiveness,".

9. Church of Jesus Christ of Latter-day Saints, *Gospel Principles*.64.

10. Spencer W. Kimball, *The Miracle of Forgiveness* (Salt Lake City, Bookcraft, 1969).53.

11. "The Joy and Gift of Repentance—Recent Messages from Prophets and Apostles,".

CHAPTER 8: A RESPONSE TO LDS SOTERIOLOGY

As such, the very practice of daily repentance indicates a failure to be truly repentant. Furthering a Saint's despair over sin, in D&C 82:7 Joseph dictates: "sin no more; but unto that soul who sinneth shall the former sins return." Elaborating on this principle the President Spencer Kimball details:

> Those who feel they can sin and be forgiven and then return to sin and be forgiven again and again must straighten out their thinking. Each previously forgiven sin is added to the new one and the whole gets to be a heavy load. Thus when a man has made up his mind to change his life, there must be no turning back.[12]

Ex-LDS Scholar, Corey Miller, summarizes Kimball's writing saying: "Kimball makes clear that all former sins -all former payments made on the mortgage- return if one does not reach moral perfection."[13] For the Saint, then, if after repentance they sin again, all the former sins return. Their condition is as though they had never repented in the first place. Further, every subsequent "repentance" demonstrates the illegitimacy of the last. As a result, they have never truly repented and are doomed, by their own gospel to die without grace.

This is an unbelievably hard pill to swallow. We know that we are incapable of living a life of absolute perfection. Can any of us live a day without committing any sin, any single infraction against the perfect standard of Christ? Can any of us say that we are capable of achieving the moral perfection that is required for Christ's atonement to be efficacious for us?

How confident can we be that after repenting of any sin, we will never commit it again at the risk of losing our salvation? This risk is truly frightening because if we commit a sin after repenting of it, it becomes as though we had never repented in the first place. Under these requirements for salvation, it does not matter that Christ died for us or that we have faith in him. None of us will have what it takes to be saved if we define repentance according to the LDS perspective.

For these reasons we see a distinct difference between Christian understandings of how one achieves salvation and those for the LDS. In the

12. Kimball, *The Miracle of Forgiveness*.170

13. Corey Miller et al., eds., *Leaving Mormonism: Why Four Scholars Changed Their Minds* (Grand Rapids, Michigan: Kregel Publications, 2017).and representatives of the LDS church often encourage this perspective. Despite points of agreement, major differences exist on foundational theological matters (for example, the Trinity50.

LDS view, the grace of Christ is still absolutely necessary. It is, of course, true that the saints believe that they are saved by the grace of God and His grace only. However, in order to be saved we must become worthy recipients of that grace. This is only done if we repent of our sins and are obedient to the commands given to us. As we addressed, these commands are impossible to follow as they require of us absolute perfection.

The very things which men have proven unable to do, cease sinning and live perfectly, are exactly what is required of them for salvation. Indeed, if men could have lived perfectly the atonement would not have been necessary at all. In this way, the atonement is powerless to aid those who have greatest need of its saving power.

This is an impossible gospel. The LDS Church claims that to be saved you can and must be perfect. In perfection, you may claim to be repentant, and the atonement will cover your sins. However, if you sin again, you never truly repented and are still in your sins. The only way to be saved from sin is to stop sinning. This, we are incapable of doing which renders the atonement for sins impossible.

Chapter 9: **A Call to Sola Fide**

It is difficult to come to grips with what was taught in the last chapter. The LDS Church teaches an impossible gospel. By it no one can be saved.

There is hope to be found in the true gospel as it is taught in the Bible. I want to spend the next few pages expounding on the protestant doctrine of *Sola Fide*. Under this view it is not our perfection nor our good works that save us. We are saved by faith alone through Christ alone. These doctrines are called *Sola Fide* and *Sola Christi*. I believe that this approach to the process of our salvation is most in alignment with Scripture and I will endeavor to demonstrate the same throughout this chapter.

In the last chapter we dispatched of the notion that one is able to earn their righteousness. This is especially apparent under the LDS perspective. What then are we to do? How can we be saved? The answer is that we are saved by a righteousness that is not our own which we take hold of not by works, but by faith and faith alone. We hold that we are not saved by our own righteousness. When believers are judged by God He does not view those He has saved with the righteousness that they have *earned*. Rather, He views them with the righteousness of Christ.

Sin requires sacrifice to repair the damage it causes our relationship with our Heavenly Father. As taught in Romans 6:23, the just punishment for our sin is death. "For the wages of sin is death, but the free gift of God is eternal life in Christ Jesus our Lord." Not only are we sinful, justly meriting God's wrath, we are not good enough to merit an eternity with God in heaven. None of our righteous actions contribute anything when we are set before the judgement seat of God. Evangelical theologian Francis Shaeffer elaborates on this principle. "How many buckets of good works would it take to fill the infinite gulf that exists between God and us because of our sin?" In *Philippians* 3, Paul makes a point of the worthlessness of human righteousness when compared with that found in Christ. He says:

> **Philippians 3:4,6–8**
>
> So I myself have reason for confidence in the flesh also. If anyone else thinks he has reason for confidence in the flesh, I have more:[. . .] ⁶As to zeal, a persecutor of the church; As to righteousness under the law,⁷ blameless. But whatever gain I had, I counted as loss for the sake of Christ. ⁸Indeed, I count everything as loss because of the surpassing worth of knowing Christ Jesus my Lord. For his sake I have suffered the loss of all things and count them as rubbish in order that I may gain Christ.

How are we then to reconcile ourselves to God despite our infinite distance from his perfection and our inability to perfect ourselves?

The answer is that we can be saved by nothing other than the righteousness of Christ. This righteousness we are connected to by nothing other than faith. First it is important to consider how we are saved by Christ alone. When we are saved, we do indeed become new by the regeneration of the Spirit (2 Cor. 5:17), however, we do not suddenly become perfected. It is not as though once we possess a genuine faith we are instantaneously perfect and just recipients of salvation in and of ourselves. Rather, when one possesses a true and living faith, our Heavenly Father looks upon us with the righteousness of Christ. Thus, it is not our righteousness that saves us, but Christ's righteousness "imputed" to us. This doctrine of the imputation of Christ's righteousness explains how we can be saved despite our imperfect state. When we are in Christ, there are two exchanges that occur. Christ takes the punishment that we deserve for our sins and we receive the righteousness of Christ. In this way, God's wrath is averted, and we are made righteous. Thus, we are reconciled to God. Here I provide some references that make this teaching clear.

> **1 Corinthians 1:30**
>
> And because of him you are in Christ Jesus, who became to us wisdom from God, righteousness and sanctification and redemption.

2 Corinthians 5:21:

He made Him who knew no sin to be sin on our behalf, so that we might become the righteousness of God in Him.

1 Peter 2:24:

He himself bore our sins in his body on the tree, that we might die to sin and live to righteousness. By his wounds you have been healed.

Philippians 3:9

And be found in him, not having a righteousness of my own that comes from the law, but that which comes through faith in Christ, the righteousness from God that depends on faith-

Isaiah 53:5

But he was pierced for our transgressions; He was crushed for our iniquities; upon him was the chastisement that brought us peace, and with his wounds we are healed.

Former LDS Apologist Michael Flournoy writes:

> In 2016 I was trying to overcome the Impossible Gospel argument, and it was more than I could handle. Desperate and discouraged, I prayed for God to give me something to beat the argument that was making me doubt my faith. God is faithful, and he opened my eyes to something I wasn't expecting. An alien concept entered my mind. "What if the righteousness required isn't mine?" I searched The Book of Mormon and the Bible for an answer, and what I found surprised me. Over and over again, the books taught that it was Christ's righteousness that justifies the sinner. The idea made sense. I was the heir of an eternal debt, and what could pay it besides the infinite, imputed righteousness of Christ?[1]

Flournoy acknowledges the true source where our salvation comes from. As Scripture states, it does not come from us but from Christ's righteousness counted to us.

Acts 4:12

And there is salvation in no one else, for there is no other name under heaven given among men by which we must be saved.

---

1. Michael Flournoy, *Falling Into Grace*, n.d.

We note carefully that this verse declares that there is *no other name* by which we may be saved. I cannot be saved in my own name, nor by any other, but only by the name of Christ. Elder Bruce R. McConkie elaborated this principle of dependence:

> No man has power to save himself anymore than he has power to resurrect himself. [. . .] No matter how righteous a man might be, no matter how great and extensive his good works, he could not save himself. Salvation is in Christ and comes through his atonement. God through Christ reconciles man to himself.

Salvation is found in Christ alone. His righteousness is imputed to us and our sin was imputed to Him. Many saints may agree with this model of salvation. However, what is likely to cause more dissension is how we receive the righteousness of Christ. What causes His righteousness to be imputed to us? This is where our doctrinal differences will become even more apparent. Following in the tradition of the doctrine of Sola Fide, I extend that we are saved by faith alone apart from any good works.

We have already noted that it is not our works that save us. Further, I want to show that our good works are not what connect us to the righteousness of Christ. We are saved by faith alone apart from any works of the law.

Ephesians 2:8–9:

> For by grace you have been saved through faith. And this is not your own doing; It is the gift of God, ⁹not a result of works, so that no one may boast.

After Paul's powerful explanation of the gospel message nothing further must be said! In these two verses Paul has sufficiently answered those who believe in a salvation of faith and works. We are saved by grace through faith he says. Further, he says this is a gift and not of works. This stance is confirmed in many other places throughout the New Testament.

Romans 11:6:

> But if it is by grace, it is no longer on the basis of works; Otherwise grace would no longer be grace.

Galatians 2:16:

> Yet we know that a person is not justified by works of the law but through faith in Jesus Christ, so we also have believed in Christ

CHAPTER 9: A CALL TO SOLA FIDE

Jesus, in order to be justified by faith in Christ and not by works of the law, because by works of the law no one will be justified.

Romans 3:28:

For we hold that one is justified by faith apart from works of the law.

Titus 3:5–7:

He saved us not because of works done by us in righteousness, but according to his own mercy, by the washing of regeneration and renewal of the Holy Spirit, ⁶whom he poured out on us richly through Jesus Christ our Savior, ⁷so that being justified by his grace we might become heirs according to the hope of eternal life.

Romans 4:2–5

For if Abraham was justified by works, he has something to boast about, but not before God. ³For what does scripture say? "Abraham believed God, and it was counted to him as righteousness." ⁴Now to the one who works, his wages are not counted as a gift but as his do. ⁵And to the one who does not work but believes in him who justifies the ungodly, his faith is counted as righteousness.

These verses teach a powerful lesson on the topic of our salvation. We are not saved by our own righteousness but by the righteousness of Christ. Further, the righteousness of Christ is not counted to us because of our works, but rather because of our faith. As stated in Ephesians 2 this is the result of a generous gift of God. It was His grace that saved us, not our striving to please Him.

After listing these verses, some will undoubtedly throw James 2:17 and 24 into the debate. James 2:17 says: "So also faith by itself, if it does not have works, is dead." James 2:24 continues: "You see that a person is justified by works and not by faith alone."

Those who want to contend with the doctrine of Sola Fide using these verses try to make the case that these couple of verses contradict and disprove all of those I listed above. Are we to take all of the verses that I have just listed and reinterpret them on the account of these two? Let us not confuse the fruit of good works for the tree of faith. Many people attempt to use James 2:17 to support the idea of works as part of the faith as though faith were not a distinct entity from its works. In his book *The Freedom of a Christian*, Martin Luther presents the analogy of faith and works as that of a fruit tree.

> Christ says in Matthew 7:18: "A good tree cannot bear bad fruit, nor can a bad tree bear good fruit." It is clear that the fruit does not bear the tree nor does the tree grow on the fruit. In reality the reverse is true: the tree bears the fruit and the fruit grows on the tree. It is necessary that the tree is prior to the fruit. The fruit does not make the tree good or bad but the tree itself is what determines the nature of the fruit. In the same way a person first must be good or bad before doing a good or bad work. For one's works do not make one good or bad, but it is the essence of the person that determines whether a work is good or bad. [. . .] A work does not make the person either a believer or unbeliever. Works do not make a person a believer and they do not make a person righteous; However, faith does make a person a believer and righteous, and faith does good works as well.[2]

Luther does well to provide the distinction between faith and works. He elaborates on the idea that faith and works are distinct. The works do not come before the faith and are not what create it. Rather, faith comes first and is the impetus for any ensuing good works.

Some apologists for a faith and works approach will stand on the previous verses from James 2 and present James 2:24 as the final nail in the coffin of Sola Fide. However, rather than assume that James is in contradiction with Paul and the rest of the New Testament, I refer to the work of R.C. Sproul to give a general overview of this verse's proper exegesis. He points out that James is saying, not that a man is justified before God by his works, but that his claim to faith is shown to be genuine as he demonstrates the evidence of that claim of faith through his works. To simplify, before men we must be "justified by our works" because except by our works no one will see evidence of a saving faith.

Thus, James 2 does not provide a satisfactory refutation to the doctrine of Sola Fide. Instead, we are left with the truth that we are saved by the grace of God through Christ's righteousness which we are united to by faith alone. Reformed Pastor and Theologian Charles Spurgeon articulates this doctrine with typical eloquence in a sermon he delivered Feb. 5th, 1914.

---

2. Martin Luther and Mark D. Tranvik, *The Freedom of a Christian* (Minneapolis: Fortress Press, 2008).75.

That is the state into which faith brings a poor, last, guilty, helpless, good-for-nothing Sinner. The man may have been everything that was bad before he believed in Jesus, but as soon as he trusted Christ, the merits of Christ became his merits, and he stands before God as though he were perfect, "without spot, or wrinkle, or any such thing," through the righteousness of Christ. Note, however, as we have noticed the state of justification, the means whereby we reach it. "Being justified by faith." The way of reaching this state of justification is not by tears, nor prayers, nor humblings, nor working, nor Bible-reading, nor church-going, nor Chapel-going, nor sacraments, nor priestly absolution, but by faith, which faith is a simple and utter dependence and believing in the faithfulness of God, a dependence upon the promise of God, because it is God's promise, and is worthy of dependence.[3]

If you have never considered your path to salvation through this doctrinal framework, I encourage you to read through the New Testament with this approach in mind. I believe that the recognition that we are saved by faith alone gives us cause for joy and peace. We have peace through the recognition that it is not our strivings that make us right with God. We rejoice in what Christ has accomplished for us.

Prior to his experiences with God that lead to the reformation, Martin Luther would spend hours every day in confession confessing every single sin that he could remember having committed. Luther was in constant fear and agony over the state of his eternal soul with an acute awareness of his sinful nature. His confessions were so lengthy and thorough that it became a great annoyance to Johan Staupitz, his primary authority figure in the monastery. Following his encounters with God and his careful study of the Scriptures Luther discovered that we are saved by faith and not by works. This revelation caused him to find great peace, joy, and confidence in Christ. This same comfort can be found by all those who accept this beautiful gift of God's grace for what it is. This is the true gospel. God became man and died to save sinners who were incapable of saving themselves. This salvation comes not by any effort of ours, but by the grace of God which has been extended to us as a free gift in the form of the sacrifice of his Son.

---

3. "C. H. Spurgeon: Spurgeon's Sermons Volume 60: 1914 - Christian Classics Ethereal Library,".

Romans 5:6–10:

For while we were still weak, at the right time Christ died for the ungodly. [7]For one will scarcely die for a righteous person though perhaps for a good person one would dare even to die-—[8]but God shows his love for us in that while we were still sinners, Christ died for us. [9]Since, therefore, we have now been justified by his blood, much more shall we be saved by him from the wrath of God. [10]For if while we were enemies we were reconciled to God by the death of his son, much more, now that we are reconciled, shall we be saved by his life.

Romans 5:15

But the *free gift* is not like the trespass. For if many died through one man's trespass, much more have the grace of God and the free gift by the grace of that one man Jesus Christ abounded for many.

Notice in Romans 5:8 how Paul says that Christ died for us "while we were still sinners". This is yet another distinction from the suppositions of LDS theology. Christ did not die just to save those who have "repented," as they say, of all of their sin. His grace is not only sufficient once we have become perfect. Christ died for us while we were still in sin. We were *still* sinners. His love was so great that he would die for us even in our evil.

In Romans 5:15 Paul talks about our salvation from sin being a "free gift." In the original Greek, it is called *carisma*. The definition of this word is: "a favour with which one receives without any merit of his own." Notice, Paul is telling us that this gift of salvation is something we are to receive without any merit of our own. This is a comforting truth. By our own striving we can earn nothing but Hell. However, by the grace of God we have been granted life as a "free gift".

Those who have gone their whole lives believing in a salvation of faith and works are probably asking "Are you saying that we do not need good works?" I answer that this is true. We do not need good works for *salvation*. What then are good works for? May we sin all we please because we are under God's benevolent grace and not under the law? Paul preemptively responds to this objection in Romans 6.

Romans 6:1–2

What shall we say then? Are we to continue in sin that grace may abound? ²By no means! How can we who died to sin still live in it?

Romans 6:15

What then? Are we to sin because we are not under law but under grace? By no means!

Paul dispels the idea that our freedom from the law allows us to continue in sin. Rather, as he says in 6:2, we have died to sin. What then is the purpose of good works? We have established that they do not carry our salvation except as evidence of a saving faith. What are they for?

In an examination of the Westminster Confession of Faith, John Tweendale wrote an article for Ligonier ministries entitled *Good Works and the Christian Life* that outlines six reasons for good works. These are:

1. Good works demonstrate our gratitude to God for His saving work in our lives. (Col. 2:6)
2. Good works bolster our assurance of our faith. (1John 2:1–6)
3. Good works are a means for encouraging other Christians toward greater acts of Christ-centered love. (Heb. 10:24)
4. Good works are methods by which we embody the doctrine of God our Savior in our lives and ministry. (Titus 2:7–10)
5. Good works silence critics who devalue the goodness of biblical Christianity. (1 Peter 2:12,15)
6. Good works glorify God by displaying His work of love in our lives. (John 15:8–11)

These are all excellent reasons to continue in good works despite their lack of saving power. I want to extend that good works have an even greater value when not considered as necessary for salvation. In the former case, one may perform works as an escape of Hell or as an attempt to be worthy of Heaven. However, once we realize that it is not our works that save us, we are free to perform our works out of genuine love and gratitude for what God has done and not because of fear of an eternity in Hell. Certainly, if works are performed out of obedience it is a good thing, however, if works are performed out of the love in one's heart and a desire to please God, so much the better!

I pray that this chapter has been of value to you and that you find the peace, joy, and freedom that is possible with a biblical understanding of how God saves us from our sins. In my reading of former LDS apologists, this has been one of the most life-giving doctrines that they have found in Christianity. The true gospel is the most beautiful gift that we have been given and it is life altering when apprehended.

In the next half of this book we will cover the myriad of practical difficulties within the Book of Mormon. My urgent request, however, before we proceed is that you would deeply consider if the theology taught by Joseph Smith lines up with that taught by Scripture, reason, and church tradition. When you find that it does not, there is a place for you to turn; the arms of God's loving grace and mercy. 1 John 1:9 says "If we confess our sins, he is faithful and just to forgive us our sins and to cleanse us from all unrighteousness."

This is all it takes. We need only to confess and believe (Acts 16:31). We know we cannot earn our salvation. We know the depths of our sin and imperfection. If you are tired of trying to satisfy an impossible gospel, turn to God's grace. We cannot do it on our own, but God has already extended to us the gift of righteousness all we have to do is receive it by faith. I will close this chapter with a quote by New Testament scholar Thomas R. Schreiner from a book of his on this topic.

> Justification is by faith alone, but it isn't a faith that is alone, for true faith produces good works. Still, good works are not the ground or cause of salvation; they are the fruit of one's faith. The perfect righteousness of Christ is imputed to believers, so that their righteousness is not inherent but is theirs because they are united to Jesus Christ. At the final judgment God will declare publicly what was already the case in the lives of believers, i.e., that they are righteous by faith, and their works will verify (but will not be the foundation of) that declaration.[4]

---

4. Thomas R. Schreiner, *Faith Alone— the Doctrine of Justification: What the Reformers Taught . . . and Why It Matters* (Grand Rapids, Michigan: Zondervan, 2015).78.

Part 3: **Interior**

Chapter 10: Flaws Within the Book of Mormon

IN THE FIRST TWO parts of this book, we spent our time focusing on elements which were predominantly philosophical in nature. In Part One we explored religious epistemology and examined responsible methods for acquiring knowledge. We concluded that while there is some place for personal revelation, it has numerous deficiencies that make it unreliable for a grounding of one's faith.

Following our exposition on how we ought to go about acquiring religious knowledge, we explored the theological differences between the LDS tradition and that of orthodox, evangelical Christianity. Here we noted some deep points of contention between Joseph's religion and Christianity. While many of the same words are used in these two traditions, there is a lot of misunderstanding due to their broadly different meanings.

For the remainder of the book, parts 3 and 4, we are going to take a more practical approach to the beliefs of the saints. By this I mean, we will move on from discussing theology and philosophy and will address the credibility of Joseph and his BOM. There are many evidences, I believe, littered throughout the Book of Mormon and LDS tradition which demonstrate its inaccuracy and, its true authorship at the hands of Joseph Smith. In my treatment of them as we continue, I have categorized these points by whether they threaten the Book of Mormon's credibility internally or externally. Each of these evidences point to the fact that the Book of Mormon is not as reliable as it is thought to be by adherents of the LDS faith.

Joseph claimed this book to be the most accurate of any book ever written. The importance of its accuracy to LDS faith cannot be overstated. President Ezra Taft Benson notably said:

> The Book of Mormon is the keystone of testimony. Just as the arch crumbles if the keystone is removed, so does all the Church stand or fall with the truthfulness of the Book of Mormon.[1]

Here in part 3, I will begin by listing the elements within the Book of Mormon that ought to give an investigative reader reason to pause. I want to point out that many of the arguments that I will make in this second half of the book are not merely the products of "anti-Mormon" critics, but some have been leveled by members of the LDS church. Elder B.H. Roberts was one of these great scholars who presented many critical questions to the church leadership.

A large portion of the critical scholarship has been conducted by curious LDS church members either during or after their membership. Some of the most notable examples are Elder B.H. Roberts, Grant H. Palmer, Jeremy Runnells, John Dehlin, Jerald and Sandra Tanner, and Thomas Stuart Ferguson. These are just a handful of the *many* examples that could be listed. However, they succeed in demonstrating the fact that the critical research is not only written by individuals who have some agenda against the Church. It is speculated that B. H. Roberts never lost his faith despite being one of the most influential and scrutinous critics of LDS teaching and history.

A number of the arguments I make in the pages to follow may appear to be frivolous or unimportant the question of truthfulness of the BOM. It may seem that I am being overly scrutinous on details that are insignificant in the conversation between Christians and Latter-Day Saints. After all, the BOM teaches spiritual truths. What does it matter if there were elephants in the Americas?

While I am well aware that questions of this kind may appear unimportant, I am under the impression that they do bear a great deal of significance. The charge that so many missionaries give investigators in their meetings is to read the BOM and pray to see if it is not true. This discernment asks only one question. Is the BOM true or not? Smuggled into this question, however, are about ten thousand other questions. The question "Is the BOM true?" contains questions such as the following. Did ancient Jews sail to America? Were there elephants, horses, and goats

---

1. "Chapter 4: The Book of Mormon: Keystone of Our Religion,".

in the ancient Americas. Were the ancient inhabitants of the Americas skilled in working with steel? Did they fight with swords and ride in chariots? These are just a few of the questions that "is the BOM true?" causes one to ask.

If any of the historical assertions made by the BOM are not true, can it still be said that the BOM is true? What is the significance of the BOM being true? As Benson details, "all the Church stands or falls with the truthfulness of the Book of Mormon."

All of this to say, does it really matter if there are elephants in the ancient Americas? In a sense, no. But it another sense, the entire Church stands of falls with the answer to that question. These are the questions we will consider as we proceed.

Chapter 11: **Anachronisms**

IN THIS CHAPTER WE examine a category of items known as anachronisms which are littered throughout the Book of Mormon. An anachronism is "a thing belonging or appropriate to a period other than that in which it exists."[1] Within the text of the Book of Mormon there are certain artifacts known by modern science to be anachronistic.

To provide an example, if you jumped into a time machine, traveled back to ancient Greece, and found Plato with an iPhone, that would be an anachronism. The technology necessary to create an iPhone is known not to have existed during that time. As a result, it would be incredibly unlikely to find that artifact in ancient Greece. If you told someone this story, they might conclude that you were being deceitful on account of your anachronistic detail.

Consider further, the more anachronistic details included the more you decrease your credibility. If you told your friends that Plato was driving around in his Tesla, listening to Billy Joel, and texting on his iPhone the story becomes even less believable. This is what we find in an analysis of the Book of Mormon. Although none of those in the BOM are to this degree of absurdity, there are many artifacts which are known to be foreign to the time and place where the text places them. This leads us to a decreased confidence in the accuracy of Joseph's narrative. We will proceed to perform our textual study by examining just five of the many anachronisms in the BOM.

Before we begin, however, I want to make something clear. Undoubtedly, in response to this section LDS apologists will claim that there

1. Oxford Languages: Definition of "Anachronism"

were once many more anachronisms that have since been vindicated. First, this does not in any way provide a positive evidence for the BOM. Striking down critiques is not a form of positively proving validity. Second, the remaining anachronisms still provide considerable issues for the Church as obstacles to the credibility of the BOM. Even if all but five anachronisms are eliminated, there is no reason to believe that these five will also be resolved until they are. Each anachronism poses a unique problem until it is solved. Here are five such problems.

Animals:

We will begin by looking at some of the anachronistic animals that are found in the BOM. The BOM gives rich detail about the land its people groups inhabited. These details include a list of animals found by the Jaredite and Nephite peoples in the ancient Americas. There is, however, a problem in the account translated by Joseph Smith. Modern researchers have found that many of these animals did not exist in North America during the time specified within Joseph's narrative. To understand the following examination of these animals and their location in the archaeological past, it is important to understand where the BOM places them.

The initial people group that the BOM reports arrived in the Americas are called the Jaredites. This people came from the split at the Tower of Babel and purportedly arrived in the Americas around 2200 B.C.[2] This is the earliest event documented within the BOM and is found in the book of Ether; which is the earliest book in the BOM chronologically. This means that the earliest BOM descriptions of animal presence date to around 2200 B.C. Ether 9:17–19 is one of the most important passages for identifying the anachronistic animals in the BOM. It reads:

> **Ether 9:17–19**
>
> [17]Having all manner of fruit, and of grain, and of silks, and of fine linen, and of gold, and of silver, and of precious things; [18]And also all manner of cattle, of oxen, and cows, and of sheep, and of swine, and of goats, and also many other kinds of animals which were useful for the food of man. [19]And they also had horses, and asses, and there were elephants and cureloms and cumoms; all of which were useful unto man, and more especially the elephants and cureloms and cumoms.

2. "Book of Mormon Time Line,".

If any of the animals listed here can be demonstrated to have been extinct before 2200 B.C., or non-existent in the Americas at this time, they would be considered anachronistic because they would be foreign to the time period in which they have been described. If this is the case, the presence of those animals in the narrative would threaten the BOM's credibility. Rather than go through all of the animals listed in the BOM I will examine just three.

Goats are found in verse 18 quoted above as well as a couple of other places in the BOM (Enos 1:21 and 1 Nephi 18:25). They are placed in view right from the beginning of the timeline in the book of Ether. During the reign of King Emer, goats, many other animals, and characteristics of his prosperous reign are described. However, secular zooarchaeology has concluded that goats were not present in the Americas until the 1500s when they were brought by Spanish explorers and settlers.[3] This scientific conclusion casts a doubtful shadow over the probability that King Emer and the Jaredites had goats.

Elephants are also found in verse 19 above. These animals were, apparently, particularly helpful along with the cureloms and cumoms. Nobody claims to know for certain what cureloms and cumoms were supposed to be. In fact, on one LDS coloring page for students, they leave that animal as a blank for the child to draw whatever their imagination can conjure.[4] Elephants, on the other hand, did make it onto the coloring page. Despite their description in Ether 9, secular scholarship places their extinction in North America at around 8000 B.C.[5,6]

Horses are perhaps the most infamous animal addressed by LDS apologists and critics. Also listed in Ether 9:19, they are found far more commonly throughout the BOM. They appear in: 1 Nephi 18:25, 2 Nephi 12:7 and 15:28, Alma 18:9,10,12 and 20:6, 3 Nephi 3:22, 4:4, and 6:1, Enos 1:21.

Although they are clearly present in the BOM, modern science finds them to be surprisingly absent during the time period it describes. According to the academic consensus, North American horses went extinct approximately 11,000–13,000 thousand years ago and remained absent from the North American continent until they were reintroduced in the

---

3. Ryan, "Heritage Goats," *The Livestock Conservancy* (blog).
4. "Book of Mormon Animals," accessed May 19, 2024.
5. "Gone But Not Forgotten: Bring Back North American Elephants," ScienceDaily.
6. "Proboscidean | Evolution, Adaptations & Extinction | Britannica,".

15th and 16th centuries.⁷ ⁸ This is yet another animal that is found in the BOM and is unproven by the modern archaeological record.

For the sake of brevity, I leave the analysis of anachronistic animals in the BOM to these three. However, there are many others which remain in the debate, and which have an alleged presence in ancient America according to LDS doctrine, but which remain invisible from the searching eye of archaeological discovery. Before we proceed to examine other anachronisms, I want to respond to some of the most common objections to what I have laid out above.

Without a doubt, the most common response relies on a linguistic occurrence called loanshifting. This is when the meaning of a word is changed because of an influence from a different language. In the case of this study, LDS apologists claim that the term "horse" in the BOM does not actually refer to what we today call horses, but rather to deer or tapirs. The Nephites did not know the names for these animals and called them by the names they were familiar with- horses. Similarly, at the time, there were no words for the ancient American Mastadon (a type of mammoth). As a result, they were called elephants for simplicity of understanding.

This objection would be convincing. However, it fails to account for a couple of issues. The contextual definition of horses in the BOM precludes them from being deer or tapirs. As they are referenced in the BOM, they are domesticated creatures used for war with chariots (Alma 20:6). This is problematic as there is no record of deer ever being domesticated by the pre-Columbian Amerinds.⁹ With this in mind, loan shifting equally disrupts the credibility of the narrative. The BOM "horses" are treated, in the text, as horses and not deer. However, we know that there were no horses in America during the proper timeline. This artifact remains a disproof whether Joseph refers to horses or deer with the term "horses". Additionally, we consider the loan-shifting for elephants. A simplifying of the term for Mastodon does not help the fact that they did not exist during the period in which they were claimed. While a mastodon is more correct geographically, this has little impact on the accuracy of the timeline.

I have one final note on the proposal of loan shifting. If words were adjusted to make the text clearer to its readers, why were cureloms and

7. "The Surprising History of America's Wild Horses | Live Science,".

8. L Ara Norwood, "Vernal Holley, Book of Mormon Authorship: A Closer Look," n.d., 11.2.

9. Claude Bélanger, "Quebec History," accessed May 19, 2024.

cumoms not fixed? As addressed above, no one has any idea what these words refer to. If any of the animals need to be loan-shifted, it would be these two.[10]

Many of the animals mentioned in the Book of Mormon are anachronistic and provide powerful evidence for investigators trying to ascertain the truthfulness of the text. The next anachronism to be treated is metallurgy in the BOM.

Metallurgy:

Metallurgy has been addressed throughout the Book of Mormon. In this case, the problem is not so much the timeline of the metal use, but rather the location. For instance, while steel was in use in the ancient world, particularly the ANE (Ancient Near East), it was not known to be in use in the Americas during the time presented by the BOM narrative. Below are some of the verses that list the metals that were used by the Nephites.

> **Jarom 1:8**
>
> And we multiplied exceedingly, and spread upon the face of the land, and became exceedingly rich in *gold*, and in *silver*, and in precious things, and in fine workmanship of wood, in buildings, and in machinery, and also in *iron* and *copper*, and *brass* and *steel*, making all manner of tools of every kind to till the ground, and weapons of war- yea, the sharp pointed arrow, and the quiver, and the dart, entered the javelin, and all preparations for war. *[emphasis added]*
>
> **2 Nephi 5:15**
>
> And I did teach my people to build buildings, and to work in all manner of wood, and of iron, and of *copper*, and of *brass,* and of *steel*, and of *gold*, end of *silver*, and of precious ores, which were in great abundance. *[emphasis added]*
>
> **Ether 7:9**
>
> Wherefore, he came to the hill Ephraim, and he did Moulton out of the hill, and made swords out of *steel* for those whom he had drawn away with him; and after he had armed them with swords he returned to the city Nehor, and gave battle unto his

---

10. bwv549, "Who Is Doing the Loan Shifting?," A Careful Examination.

brother Corihor, by which means he obtained the Kingdom and restored it unto his father Kib.

As is shown above, the BOM repeatedly commits itself to the presence and use of gold, silver, copper, iron, brass, and steel. Some of these metals are not anachronistic. For instance, Copper is well-known to have been used in the pre-Columbian Americas. However, other metals do not fit into the geographical timeline of the Americas.

It is difficult to determine exactly where the Nephites or the Jaredites landed when they came to the Americas. The speculation is that they landed either in North America or in the Mesoamerica region. However, thus far, we have not uncovered enough evidence to validate a certain location (or any location for that matter) as a home for the wayward Israelites.

Metallurgy is a process by which metals are extracted, refined and alloyed. This process requires a level of technology that allows for containing and utilizing extreme temperatures. These high temperatures are used to melt metals to extract them from ores or mix them with other metals to increase certain features such as durability.

As briefly mentioned above, some metals fit with the historical record. It is known that American tribes, particularly those in South or Central America had the use of gold. They made beautiful art from it.[11] There is evidence of Copper use in North America as far back as 5000 BC.[12] It has been shown that there was metallurgy in the ancient Americas. Although it remained confined, for the most part, to South America. While this affirms the presence of metallurgy at the proper timeline, the location remains inaccurate. The LDS church does not hold that the ancient Jews who sailed to America became the Maya or the Aztecs. Rather, they became a different civilization in North America. For this reason, the metallurgy of Mesoamerica and North America remain of most interest to us.

As of yet, no evidence has been found of melting, smelting, or casting of metals in prehistoric North America.[13] Further, metallurgy was

---

11. Warwick Bray, "Gold-Working in Ancient America," *Gold Bulletin* 11, no. 4 (December 1978): 136–43.

12. R. P. Beukens et al., "Radiocarbon Dating of Copper-Preserved Organics," *Radiocarbon* 34, no. 3 (1992): 890–97.

13. Martin, S.R. (1999). *Wonderful Power: The Story of Ancient Copper Working in the Lake Superior Basin*. Great Lakes Books Series. Wayne State University Press. p. 136.

first introduced to Mesoamerica around 800 AD.[14] The reason this lack of metallurgy technology does not exclude the ancient American use of copper is because it is an easier metal to use. Copper is relatively soft and can be manipulated by hammering. As a result, smelting and other advanced metallurgy practices were not necessary to its use.

The lack of evidence for advanced metallurgical practices becomes problematic to BOM credibility for a couple of reasons. Most prominent of these, the majority of the metals listed require some combination of these practices for their manufacture. Steel, which is mentioned numerous times throughout the BOM is an alloy of iron (which must be smelted) and carbon in varying amounts.[15] Brass is an alloy of Copper and Zinc. However, it should be noted that occasionally in the ancient past Brass was sometimes used to describe Bronze, an alloy of Copper and tin.[16] It is possible that the ancient writers of the BOM used the term "Brass" to describe what was actually Bronze. In either case, "Brass" is a Copper alloy. As a result, the metals addressed in the verses above could not have been produced because of a missing technology.

Here the problem arises. We have no evidence indicating that smelting or alloying were being used to process metals in ancient North America. However, the metals listed throughout the BOM require these processes. In this instance, we find the BOM to be inaccurate. Perhaps in the future vindicating evidence will be found confirming the use of these metallurgical practices and the alloys listed in the text above. Until that time, however, these details remain harmful to the credibility of the BOM.

Swords:

The next anachronism for us to examine is swords. The BOM repeatedly describes the use of swords. However, swords were not native to the region or time period in which they are here described. Beyond mere absence of evidence of their use in Meso and North America, they could not have been made. This was addressed in our last topic on metallurgy. As a result, not only do we fail to see their existence from the historical

---

14. Dorothy Hosler, "Ancient West Mexican Metallurgy: South and Central American Origins and West Mexican Transformations," *American Anthropologist* 90, no. 4 (1988): 832–55.

15. "Steel | Britannica,".

16. "Brass | Definition, Properties, & Facts | Britannica,".

research, but we fail to see the possibility for their manufacture. Below are a handful of the verses in the BOM in which swords are mentioned.

Alma 17:7

Nevertheless they departed out of the land of Zarahemla, and took their *swords*, and their Spears, and their bows, and their arrows, and their slings; And this they did that they might provide food for themselves while in the wilderness.

Alma 57:9

And it came to pass that we did camp round about the city for many nights; but we did sleep upon our *swords*, and to keep guards, that the Lamanites could not come upon us by night and slay us, which they attempted many times; But as many times as they attempted this their blood was spilt.

Helaman 1:14

And it came to pass in the forty and first year of the reign of the judges, that the Lamanites had gathered together and innumerable army of men, and armed them with *swords*, and with cimeters and with bows, and with arrows, and with head-plates, and with breastplates, and with all manner of Shields of every kind.

Mormon 6:9

And it came to pass that they did follow up on my people with the *sword*, and with the bow, and with the arrow, and with the axe, and with all manner of weapons of war.

Mosiah 9:16

And it came to pass that I did arm them with bows, and with arrows, with *swords*, and with cimeters, and with clubs, and with slings, and with all manner of weapons which we could invent, and I and my people did go forth against the Lamanites to battle.

1 Nephi 4:9

And I beheld his *sword*, and I drew it forth from the sheath thereof; and the hilt thereof was of pure gold, and the workmanship thereof was exceedingly fine, and I saw that the blade thereof was of the most precious steel.

Ether 7:9

> Wherefore, he came to the hill Ephraim, and he did Moulton out of the hill, and made *swords* out of steel for those whom he had drawn away with him; and after he had armed them with swords he returned to the city Nehor, and gave battle unto his brother Corihor, by which means he obtained the Kingdom and restored it unto his father Kib.

The most striking evidence against the presence of swords in the BOM is the way LDS apologists treat the subject. It is agreed upon quite universally that the pre-Columbian Native Americans did not use swords, at least in the common understanding of what a "sword" is. I know of no LDS apologists who assert that there were, in fact, common swords in use in ancient America. Rather, the scholars attempt to find their way around this using ancient American artwork that depicts a weapon strikingly similar to a sword in use—although not as much in appearance.[17]

First, we note that there is no evidence for the typical steel swords that were present in much of the old world. The Nephites came from Jerusalem and, as a result, must already have had an understanding of what a sword was. During the period of the Judges, the Israelites began to explore more advanced metallurgy especially the use of iron.[18] Ancient Egyptians had swords as early as 1500 BC. Although originally made of brass they switched to iron beginning in 1300 BC.[19] The word "sword" is used over 300 times in the Old Testament and it appears to be used meaning a metal cutting weapon. We see that the Israelites had clear knowledge of what a traditional sword looked like. In addition to this, they had the metallurgy know-how to create them. Despite this, we find no evidence for metal swords in the ancient Americas. This is counterintuitive. Would we not expect to see them from a people who had been so exposed to their use and the technology for their manufacture?

As I mentioned above, the LDS apologists do have an answer to this lack of traditional swords. They propose that the word "sword" in this period refers to a weapon such as the Aztec Macuahuitl or Macana. This weapon has been shown depicted in Ancient American art and appears

---

17. "BYU Religious Scholar Analyzes Book of Mormon Swords at FairMormon Conference —Deseret News,".

18. "Weapons and Warfare in Ancient Israel," Grace Communion International.

19. Dan Howard, *Bronze Age Military Equipment* (Casemate Publishers, 2011).armor and chariots, how they were made and their tactical use in battle. Spanning from the introduction of massed infantry by the Sumerians (c. 26th century BC34.

CHAPTER 11: ANACHRONISMS

to have been used in the same manner that a sword would be. The macuahuitl was an elongated, flattened piece of wood with a handle on one end. The end opposite the handle was studded with sharp rocks, obsidian, or copper to form a blade.[20]

As mentioned previously, it is not believed that the early Jewish travelers were the furnishing populations for the Maya or the Aztecs. With this in mind, we question why the Macuahuitl is championed by the LDS apologists as a possible explanation for why swords are in the BOM. Their response, no doubt is fueled by the lack of any other evidence for ancient American swords in North or Meso America. Because of this, they propose that the peoples in the BOM used swords like these which at least were known to have existed in the same time period and the same general region of the world.

This anachronism is not, however, solved by the use of this ancient Aztec weapon. Below I will demonstrate that we ought to expect traditional swords from the BOM peoples. First, we look at 1 Nephi 4:9. It is true that this verse takes place while the Nephites are still in Jerusalem. As a result, it is not surprising that we find a steel sword in use. In this case the sword of Laban is not anachronistic.[21] However, it does cement the idea that the Nephites knew what steel swords were. We then shift our search to 2 Nephi 5:14–15. In this passage the Nephites are no longer in ancient Israel but have made it to the new world. Let us examine these verses.

> **1 Nephi 4:9**
>
> And I beheld his sword, and I drew it forth from the sheath thereof; and the hilt thereof was of pure gold, and the workmanship thereof was exceedingly fine, and I saw that the blade thereof was of the most precious steel.
>
> **2 Nephi 5:14–15**
>
> And I, Nephi, did take the sword of Laban, and after the manner of it did make many swords, lest by any means the people who were now called Lamanites should come upon us and destroy us; For I knew their hatred towards me and my children and those who were called my people. ¹⁵And I did teach my people

---

20. "Question: Did Swords Exist in Pre-Columbian America during the Book of Mormon Time Period? - FAIR,".

21. "How Could Laban Have Possessed a Sword of 'Most Precious Steel'?," Book of Mormon Central, January 29, 2018.

> to build buildings, and to work in all manner of wood, and of iron, and of copper, and of brass, and of steel, and of gold, and of silver, and of precious ores which were in great abundance.

These verses in 2 Nephi describe the Nephites creating swords "after the manner" of the sword of Laban. His sword, we see, had a "hilt of pure gold" and "the blade thereof was of the most precious steel." The Nephites in the above passage were working with the sword of Laban as the example. It is difficult to believe that they were using Laban's sword as a model and proceeded to create macuahuitls for themselves. This is especially unlikely when considered against verse 15. Just after the author describes them making swords, he lists the disciplines that his people were instructed in. Among these skills were working with steel and gold.

If the Nephites used the steel and gold sword of Laban as a model and were proficient in working with those same metals, why would we believe that they created macuahuitls? Further, if a culture has mastered the crafting of steel and iron, why would they bother with wood-base swords at all?

The conclusion I find at the end of this examination is that we ought to read the BOM as speaking of traditional swords. The Nephites knew what they were, how to make them, and had a model of one to work off of. This reading does not allow for the defense of the LDS apologists with ancient Aztec weaponry. We find that the mention of swords in the BOM deals another blow to its credibility.

Wheels:

The next anachronism to be examined is wheels. Of the five we discuss in this chapter, some may claim that this is the most tentative. This is because the word "wheel" is only used a single time within the BOM. This is in 2 Nephi 15:28 "and their wheels like a whirlwind." The reason we will exclude this verse from our evidence of the anachronism is because it is quoting Isaiah 5:28 and not actually giving a description of the infrastructure or culture of the Nephites.

With this confession that we cannot even use the only verse in the BOM that mentions wheels in our analysis of them as an anachronism how do we proceed? We find the implication of wheels from the many mentions of chariots. Chariots are littered throughout the BOM. We get the idea of wheels from them because chariots were typically a kind of wheeled cart used as an implement of war. Below are a couple of examples of the presence of Chariots in the BOM.

2 Nephi 12:7

Their land also is full of silver and gold, neither is there any end of their treasures; their land is also full of horses, neither is there any end of their Chariots.

Alma 20:6

Now when Lamoni had heard this he caused that his servants should make ready his horses and his Chariots.

Though I have only provided two verses, there is a frequent mention of Chariots in the BOM. If chariots refer to the wheeled carts, which I will demonstrate that they do, we reach a point where it appears undeniable that there were wheels. However, as wheels are not explicitly mentioned, the LDS apologists argue that they may not have been *wheeled* chariots. An article by FAIRLDS (Faithful Answers, Informed Responses, Latter-Day Saints, an LDS apologetics ministry) presents the argument that we do not know for sure that the oft-mentioned chariots had wheels. Rather, in a loan shifting kind of way, chariots could refer to something else. Secondly, they propose that even if wheels did exist it is doubtful that wooden wheels would survive the climate erosion so that we could see them today.[22] Hence, either, the wheels existed, but nature destroyed all evidence, or they did not exist because chariots do not actually refer to the wheeled carts that are seen throughout history in the rest of the world.

First, I want to affirm the idea that chariots do, in fact, indicate the use of wheels. Almost every time that chariots are used in the BOM horses are listed. This link between horses and chariots is the significant factor in supporting a wheeled view of chariots. We see this clearly when it is commanded that someone ought to make ready "his horses and chariots" as is done in Alma 20:6. If Chariots have no wheels what is the significance of them being so closely associated with horses? Additionally, chariots and wheels were well known in the old world. Wheels were thought to have been in use for pottery as far back as 3000 b.c.[23] Further chariots

---

22. Paul R. Cheesman, "The Wheel in Ancient America," *Brigham Young University Studies* 9, no. 2 (1969): 185–97.

23. Maria Bondar, "Prehistoric Innovations: Wheels and Wheeled Vehicles," *Acta Archaeologica Academiae Scientiarum Hungaricae* 69 (December 1, 2018): 271–97.

have been noted as far back as 2000 b.c.[24] The Nephites would have been familiar with both wheels and chariots. To assume that they would sail to the Americas and simply forget how to use the wheel or the chariot is a bit beyond what I can believe. For these two reasons, I believe that in the BOM, when it claims chariots, it must be speaking of the wheeled conveyance known throughout the ANE.

We look then to the objection that all of the wheels may have decomposed. This, at first seems more likely than the previous attempted refutation of the nature of this anachronism. However, it does not matter that all of the wheels would have decomposed because it would be expected that we see new wheels. It is not often that a culture comes across a technology as groundbreaking as the wheel and then forgets about it. No, it would be expected that the wheel would remain until it could be documented by Columbian explorers. However, there is no evidence of these wheels in America. If the Nephites came from a culture that was advanced—such as that of Jerusalem, it would be incredible to think that they stopped using the wheel to the point that all evidence of its presence disappeared.

With these points in mind, it appears very likely that the BOM must mean wheeled vehicles when it refers to chariots. This becomes problematic because there is no evidence for wheels in ancient America aside from toy models which have been discovered.[25] Despite the presence of wheeled toys, there is no evidence for larger scale wheels that could be used in a practical manner as is necessitated by the claim to chariots. This presents a problem for the BOM. We once again conclude that the BOM has included details which are foreign to its time and location and are threatening to its credibility.

---

24. P. F. Kuznetsov, "The Emergence of Bronze Age Chariots in Eastern Europe," *Antiquity* 80, no. 309 (September 2006): 638–45.

25. "Why It Took So Long to Invent the Wheel | Scientific American,".

Chapter 12: **Theological Anachronisms**

THE FINAL ANACHRONISM THAT I am going to address is by far the most difficult to make the case for. All of the others have been direct in their desolation of the archaeological case for the Book of Mormon. This final one, however, is unique because the exact elements that an investigator may find to be its weaknesses are called strengths by the LDS apologists.

This anachronism is based on the presence of New Testament Theology in writings from the Old Testament periods. Not only are there prophecies and descriptions of a similar kind as those found in the Old Testament, the BOM prophecies and doctrinal teachings are explicit and extraordinarily detailed in a manner which is anachronous to the time they were written. This is why I say that LDS apologists will call these prophecies and descriptions a strength of the Book of Mormon. The earlier and more detailed a prophecy, the more impressive it is. If the Book of Mormon contains specific prophecies that provide accurate information about NT theology in the 6th century B.C. it could be considered very convincing evidence for the credibility of the BOM.

On the contrary, my contention is that the BOM is not an early source. The so-called prophecies are indeed accurate, but only because they were not written before the events they describe occurred. The level of detail in these descriptions and prophecies as well as their alleged incredibly early date, to me, read as counterevidence to its credibility.

To elaborate upon this topic, I will choose three main doctrines (although I could add numerous others) to demonstrate that the level of specificity is anachronistic. In order of the following treatment, these three points will be: early preaching and descriptions of the gospel, prophecies of Jesus' death by crucifixion, and prophecies of the resurrection.

The Gospel:

The first doctrinal artifact within the Book of Mormon that we will analyze is the presence of preaching the gospel. Throughout the Book of Mormon, the gospel is preached emphatically. The gospel focus is so much a part of the book's identity that the second sentence of the introduction claims that it "contains the fulness of the everlasting gospel." Below I will list a handful of the places that the gospel is described or preached in the BOM. The pertinent issue is that these teachings are impossibly early.

Ether 4:3,18 *(Most generous estimate 600 B.C.)*

³And now, after that, they have all dwindled in unbelief; And there is no save it be the Lamanites and they have rejected the gospel of Christ; therefore I am commanded that I should hide them up again in the earth.

¹⁸Oh God therefore, repent all ye ends of the earth, and come unto me, and believed in my gospel, and be baptized in my name; For he that believe faith and is baptized shall be saved; but he that believeth not shall be damned; and signs shall follow them that believe in my name.

2 Nephi 2:6–9 *(588–570 B.C.)*

Wherefore, redemption cometh in and through the Holy Messiah; for he is full of grace and truth.⁷ Behold, he offereth himself a sacrifice for sin, to answer the ends of the law, unto all those who have a broken heart and a contrite spirit; and unto none else can the ends of the law be answered.⁸ [. . .] no flesh that can dwell in the presence of God, save it be through the merits, and mercy, and grace of the Holy Messiah, who layeth down his life according to the flesh, and taketh it again by the power of the Spirit, that he may bring to pass the resurrection of the dead, being the first that should rise.⁹ Wherefore, he is the firstfruits unto God, inasmuch as he shall make intercession for all the children of men; and they that believe in him shall be saved.

CHAPTER 12: THEOLOGICAL ANACHRONISMS

2 Nephi 25:13 *(559–545 B.C.)*

Behold, they will crucify him; And after he is laid in a sepulchre for the space of three days he shall rise from the dead, with healing in his wings; and all those who shall believe on his name shall be saved in the kingdom of God. Wherefore, my soul delighteth to prophecy concerning him, for I have seen his day, and my heart doth magnify his holy name.

Alma 21:9 *(90–77 B.C.)*

Now Aaron began to open the scriptures unto them concerning the coming of Christ, and also concerning the resurrection of the dead, and that there could be no redemption for mankind save it were through the death and sufferings of Christ, and the atonement of his blood.

Listed above are just a couple of places in the Book of Mormon that prophesy or teach the gospel message. The issue is the specificity of these teachings and their early date. The verses from Ether teach an explicit gospel message. The readers are told to repent, believe in the gospel, and be baptized in the name of Christ. Even allowing the most generous dating, this book was written six hundred years before Christ was even born. The *gospel* of Christ was not preached at all in the Old Testament. There were prophecies of a coming messiah, however, the exact process of this coming king was unclear. A salvation purchased by the sacrifice of Jesus was never explicitly stated.

The "atonement of his blood" spoken of in Alma 21:9 is not at all characteristic of ancient Jewish theology. The death of the coming savior would have taken many Jews by complete surprise—as it ultimately did. Many Jews expected Jesus to fulfill a role like King David and return them to a glorious kingdom under a messianic monarchy.[1] In stark contrast with the conquering king expectation, the notion that He would come and die as a sacrifice for our sins would have been verging on blasphemy. The atonement doctrine, as taught in the gospel, would have been irreconcilably foreign to the time the above passages were written.

Further, the name "Christ," based off the Greek word "χριστος" is nowhere even mentioned in the Old Testament. In spite of this fact, it is pervasive throughout the English translation of the BOM. No doubt, there are several linguistic and translation arguments to be leveled regarding

---

1. Robert P. Kraynak, "The Idea of the Messiah in the Theology of Thomas Hobbes," *Jewish Political Studies Review* 4, no. 2 (1992): 115–37.

this point. We will address similar translation-focused concerns further on. In any case, Ether presents an explicit New Testament gospel message at least six hundred years before Jesus was even born. While certain LDS advocates may find this compelling evidence for the Book of Mormon, I have another interpretation for this data.

Crucifixion:

The second doctrinal anachronism I want to analyze is the early and very specific claims of Jesus' crucifixion. It is true that Jesus' death is prophesied in the Old Testament. We may look to Psalm 22:16 "They have pierced my hands and feet-" or to Isaiah 53:5 "But he was pierced for our transgressions; He was crushed for our iniquities;" however, crucifixion is not mentioned explicitly. Indeed, the words crucify, crucified, or crucifixion do not appear in the Old Testament. However, we find explicit BOM prophecies detailing that Jesus would be killed on a cross.

> **1 Nephi 11:33** *(600–592 B.C.)*
>
> And I, Nephi, saw that he was lifted up upon the cross and slain for the sins of the world.
>
> **1 Nephi 19:13** *(588–577B.C.)*
>
> And As for those who are at Jerusalem, sayeth the prophet, they shall be scored by all people, because they crucified the God of Israel, and turned their hearts aside, rejecting signs and wonders and the power and glory of the God of Israel.
>
> **2 Nephi 6:9** *(559–545 B.C.)*
>
> Nevertheless, the Lord has shown unto me that they should return again. And he also has shown unto me that the Lord God, the Holy One of Israel, should manifest himself unto them in the flesh; And after he should manifest himself they should scourge him and crucify him, according to the words of the angel who spake it unto me.
>
> **Mosiah 3:9** *(124 B.C.)*
>
> And lo, he cometh unto his own, that salvation might come unto the children of men even through faith on his name; and even after all this they shall consider him a man, and say that he hath a devil, and shall scourge him, and shall crucify him.

CHAPTER 12: THEOLOGICAL ANACHRONISMS

These passages above, as well as many others throughout the BOM prophesy that Jesus would be put to death by crucifixion. I mentioned above that there are biblical prophecies about the death of Christ, however this level of specificity in the prophecies is highly suspect.

This is especially the case for one key reason. Crucifixion was not even invented until around the 6th century B.C. It was initially used by the Assyrians and the Babylonians and then by the Persians. However, the origins of crucifixion look different than what Jesus experienced and what the prophet Nephi saw in 1 Nephi 11:33. In the original process, "victims were usually tied, feet dangling, to a tree or post; crosses weren't used until Roman times,"[2] Another ancient crucifixion style was the kind used for Haman's execution in the book of Esther. He was impaled on a giant stake.[3] Both of these forms of crucifixion would have been known to the Jews. However, crucifixion on a cross was not developed until the Romans began perfecting this form of execution in the 3rd century B.C.[4] This becomes problematic because the BOM authors prophesy of Jesus being crucified on a cross before this type of crucifixion even existed. Understandably, this argument will also lead to different conclusion for those reading with a predisposition towards or against the credibility of the BOM. After considering our final doctrinal artifact, I will make the case that these all constitute evidence against the BOM.

---

2. "Jesus Wasn't the Only Man to Be Crucified. Here's the History behind This Brutal Practice. | Live Science,".

3. "Was Haman Hanged, Impaled or Crucified? - TheTorah.Com,".2024, https://www.thetorah.com/article/was-haman-hanged-impaled-or-crucified.}","plainCitation":"'Was Haman Hanged, Impaled or Crucified? - TheTorah.Com," accessed May 19, 2024, https://www.thetorah.com/article/was-haman-hanged-impaled-or-crucified.", "noteIndex":24},"citationItems":[{"id":717,"uris":["http://zotero.org/users/11630472/items/4DBEUBTL"],"itemData":{"id":717,"type":"webpage","abstract":"The manner in which Haman's execution was depicted had real world consequences. | Dr. Abraham J. Berkovitz","title":"Was Haman Hanged, Impaled or Crucified? - TheTorah.com","title-short":"Was Haman Hanged, Impaled or Crucified?","URL":"https://www.thetorah.com/article/was-haman-hanged-impaled-or-crucified","accessed":{"date-parts":[["2024",5,19]]}}}],"schema":"https://github.com/citation-style-language/schema/raw/master/csl-citation.json"}

4. F. P. Retief and L. Cilliers, "The History and Pathology of Crucifixion," *South African Medical Journal = Suid-Afrikaanse Tydskrif Vir Geneeskunde* 93, no. 12 (December 2003): 938–41.

The Resurrection:

The final doctrinal anachronism to be evaluated is the resurrection of Jesus. This teaching is echoed continuously throughout the BOM and finds no place in OT teachings. Below are a couple of places that the prophecy of Jesus' resurrection appears in the BOM.

> **2 Nephi 2:8** *(588–570 B.C.)*
>
> [8] No flesh that can dwell in the presence of God, save it be through the merits, and mercy, and grace of the Holy Messiah, who layeth down his life according to the flesh, and taketh it again by the power of the Spirit, that he may bring to pass the resurrection of the dead, being the first that should rise.
>
> **2 Nephi 26:3** *(559–545 B.C.)*
>
> And after the Messiah shall come there shall be signs given unto my people of his birth, and also of his death and resurrection;
>
> **Alma 41:2** *(74 B.C.)*
>
> Behold, it is requisite and just, according to the power and resurrection of Christ,
>
> **3 Nephi 6:20** *(26–30. A.D.)*
>
> Concerning the redemption which the Lord would make for his people, or in other words, the resurrection of Christ; and they did testify boldly of his death and sufferings.

The BOM repeatedly prophesies the resurrection of Christ in specific detail. In one verse, it even mentions that he would lay in his "sepulchre" for three days prior to his resurrection. All these prophesies are extremely early and foretell a message spoken by no Old Testament writer. Some try to assert that Psalm 16:10 is and Old Testament prophesy about Jesus' resurrection "For you will not abandon my soul to Sheol or let your holy one see corruption." It appears that there is another interpretation of this verse, which would have been more likely apprehended by the ancient Jews. Dr. William Lane Craig provides that the view that death would be avoided all together.[5] In agreement with Craig, I believe that this verse addresses not the resurrection, but protection.

---

5. "Old Testament Prophecies of Jesus' Resurrection," The Good Book Blog - Biola University Blogs, September 20, 2019.

CHAPTER 12: THEOLOGICAL ANACHRONISMS

The absolute lack of OT description for the resurrection when compared to the explicit detail of BOM prophecy is enough to make one very suspicious. I believe that this comparison demonstrates that the BOM prophecies are anachronistic and harm the credibility of the BOM.

These, as I have stated, are not compelling evidence that the BOM is the word of God. Rather these artifacts demonstrate prophecy that was anachronistic to its time and can be explained away with relative ease.

The BOM prophecies are far more specific prophecies than are found in the Old Testament. Does this make them more compelling? Absolutely it does! That is, if they can be confirmed to be true prophecies. However, their specificity also makes them more suspect. For example, if a stranger told me he was going to predict what books I had on my bookshelf and rightly told me that I had Dostoevsky's *The Idiot*, I would be very impressed. On the other hand, if he told me he was going to predict what books I had on my bookshelf and proceeded to tell me every single book that I own I would be more than alarmed! Predictions of that specificity often indicate deception. Although, if confirmed a genuine prediction, I would be far more impressed than in the previous case. It is the same with the BOM. If the prophecies were less specific, they would be less impressive, but also more believable. As they possess brilliant, explicit detail it is understandable that readers would be skeptical about their origin.

This brings us to the early date of these prophecies. The BOM prophecies are incredibly early. Further, unlike the early OT prophecies, those found in the BOM are far more difficult to confirm because we have no record of the original writings of these prophecies to confirm their antiquity. The best information we have to confirm their early date is the introduction to each chapter in the BOM. The only manuscript of the BOM that is known to exist was that on the golden plates given to and then taken away from Joseph Smith in the early- mid 1800s. Because of this, we have no evidence confirming their early date. We have no testable evidence demonstrating that the prophecies were actually written prior to the events they describe.

The Old Testament prophecies, on the other hand, have a far more reliable basis on which to confirm their antiquity.

One evidence to support this is the dead sea scrolls. These scrolls were discovered in caves in the Middle East and have been dated all the way back to between the 3rd century B.C. and the first century C.E.[6] They

---

6. "The Dead Sea Scrolls | The Israel Museum, Jerusalem,".

contain every book of the Old Testament with the exception of Esther.[7] Among these scrolls is one known as "The Great Isiaiah Scroll" which dates back to approximately 100 B.C.[8] This manuscript contains all 66 chapters of the book of Isaiah, a book renowned for its messianic prophecies. The significance of this cannot be overstated. We have textual evidence of written prophecies concerning Christ, that date back to before He was even born. As a result, we have good evidence to support the idea that the OT prophecies were genuine prophecies. In the Dead Sea Scrolls, there is clear evidence supporting that the prophecies were written well before the events which were prophesied of. There is no similar supporting evidence for the BOM. We have no early documents which can be dated to before the described events.

The specificity of the BOM leads to great suspicion. Added to this, there is no tangible evidence that forces one to believe that the prophesies were written before their prophesied events. There are zero early manuscripts for the BOM. Lacking evidence to the contrary, it is reasonable to consider that Joseph, may have written the BOM long after the events occurred and merely included them in his narrative. It may be that Joseph, from the 1800s, had all the history of Jesus' life and placed it as "prophecies" within the BOM.

I understand that this argument will not be compelling to all—especially for those who hold a bias toward the BOM narrative. I recognize that the specificity and early dating are impressive if true. Rather than trying to convince further that these three doctrinal "anachronisms" (as I believe they are) are dis-evidence I request that the reader keeps in mind the argument as a possibility.

Though doctrinal anachronisms may not be supremely convincing on their own, I believe that they contribute to a cumulative case which calls into question the credibility of the BOM.

This concludes our treatment of anachronisms within the Book of Mormon. Before we move on to other credibility threatening artifacts, I want to make a couple of final comments on those that have furnished the previous pages. First, this was by no means a comprehensive study. I believe that even the small number of anachronisms that we have examined here are compelling and, please note, they are not even one third of those that could be addressed.

7. "6 Things You May Not Know About the Dead Sea Scrolls," HISTORY, May 12, 2023.

8. "The Great Isaiah Scroll MS A (1QIsa) | The Israel Museum, Jerusalem,".

Second, rather than being viewed as mere critiques, I believe that the presence of these anachronisms also leads us to a conclusion. More than merely undermining the believability of the narrative, I believe they direct us to the author. We will find more evidence that leads us to conclusions about the true authorship of the BOM in the pages that follow.

Third and finally, it is possible that these critiques may be annulled. It may be that archaeological evidence vindicates the BOM on these five issues the way it has done with certain others. Despite this possibility, we must understand that these remain puissant critiques until they are solved. Just because they may be solved does not mean that they have been already. Until they are, they remain as they are now, potent arguments against the reliability of the BOM.

Chapter 13: **Inaccuracies and Missing Evidence**

WE HAVE COMPLETED OUR examination of anachronisms. As we continue our study, we will look to other elements within the BOM that challenge its credibility. We will examine three main points of error within the BOM. These points will be its archaeology, DNA studies, and the many changes made to the BOM.

Archaeology:

The BOM is narrative contains many exhilarating stories. There are wars and political regimes. There are curses and miracles. Entire civilizations prosper and are destroyed. The question that must be considered is whether this depiction of the ancient north american world is represented in the archaeological record. We will look at numerous aspects of these stories which could confidently be expected to leave archaeological evidence. This will aid us in determining whether the accuracy and historicity of these narratives can be vouched for by modern scientific studies.

First we consider war. War is a dominant theme throughout the BOM and is considered to be of such importance that God commanded Nephi to keep a second set of plates to keep a record of the "wars and contentions of [his] people." (1 Nephi 9:4)[1] For a book of only five hundred and thirty-one pages, it has around a hundred instances of war or armed

---

1. Stephen D Ricks and William J Hamblin, "Warfare in the Book of Mormon," n.d.

CHAPTER 13: INACCURACIES AND MISSING EVIDENCE

conflict.[2] When studying the archaeology of war there are four items that archaeologists search for. These are settlement data, injuries in human skeletal remains, war weaponry, and iconography.[3]

The BOM mentions three out of four of these items with regularity. There are numerous accounts of bodies, weapons, and settlements. Iconography, however, is more difficult to ascertain. Certainly, literacy is present in the BOM, however it is unclear how much of this was passed to their daily cultural practices. Even without assuming a broad literacy amongst the BOM people one would expect to find some evidence of written material. If any written material from the BOM peoples was to be found, it would be obvious evidence as it would take the form of the same reformed Egyptian language used for writing on the plates translated by Joseph.

The lack of any notable literary fragments from the Nephite time period is especially interesting when considering the sophisticated literary culture of ancient Israel.[4] It would be surprising for the Nephites to leave ancient Israel and abandon their literate culture especially when they value so highly the preservation of their record by writing on the plates. That said, aside from the plates, we find little evidence of writing or iconography throughout the BOM. In an article for the famous LDS publication *Times and Seasons*, scholar Jonathan Green proposes Nephite literacy to be between one person per village to one person per household. He explicitly disagrees with a case for widespread Nephite literacy.[5] This lack of mentioned literacy could be an argument in critique of the BOM, however, because iconography is rarely mentioned in the text, it should not be used in an archaeological search for evidence or absence thereof. As a result, for our study on BOM archaeology we will exclude iconography from our search. We begin by examining some of the great wars listed in the BOM in search of the first of the three artifacts adopted for our investigation.

In terms of body count, the BOM contains some truly stunning numbers. Below are some of the references to these deadly wars. In an

---

2. John L. Sorenson, Appendix: Annals of the Nephite Wars, in "Seasonality of Warfare in the Book of Mormon and in Mesoamerica," in this volume.

3. Patricia M Lambert, "The Archaeology of War: A North American Perspective," *Journal of Archaeological Research*, 2002.

4. "Study Confirms Widespread Literacy in Biblical-Period Kingdom of Judah," ScienceDaily.

5. "Jonathan Green," *Times & Seasons* (blog), March 23, 2024.

article for Book of Mormon Central entitled *Why are There So Many War Chapters in the Book of Mormon?* There is a useful graph that outlines some of the most prominent battles.⁶

Omni 1:24

And behold, I have seen, in the days of king Benjamin, a serious war and much bloodshed between the Nephites and the Lamanites.

Alma 2:19

And it came to pass that the Nephites did pursue the Amlicites all that day, and did slay them with much slaughter, insomuch that there were slain of the Amlicites twelve thousand five hundred thirty and two souls; and there were slain of the Nephites six thousand five hundred sixty and two souls.

Alma 16:9–11

Nevertheless, after many days their dead bodies were heaped up upon the face of the earth, and they were covered with a shallow covering. And now so great was the scent thereof that the people did not go in to possess the land of Ammonihah for many years. And it was called desolation of Nehors;[. . .]

Alma 28:2–3

And thus there was a tremendous battle; yea even such an one as never had been known among all the people in the land from the time Lehi left Jerusalem; yea, and tens of thousands of the Lamanites were slain and scattered abroad. ³Yea, and also there was a tremendous slaughter among the people of Nephi;[. . .]

---

6. "Why Are There So Many War Chapters in the Book of Mormon?," Book of Mormon Central, August 3, 2016.political, and cultural ideologies were frequently enforced through war. As is true today, warfare in the ancient world took on ideological importance for both sides of a conflict. Much more than simply reporting these wars like a modern journalist, Mormon infused moral and theological significance into his war narratives. These accounts not only provide important information on the history of the Nephites and Lamanites, but also give modern readers a window into Mormon's thinking on how and why he presented the history of his people the way he did.","container-title":"Book of Mormon Central","language":"en","title":"Why are There So Many War Chapters in the Book of Mormon?","URL":"https://knowhy.bookofmormoncentral.org/knowhy/why-are-there-so-many-war-chapters-in-the-book-of-mormon","accessed":{"date-parts":[["2024",5,19]]},"issued":{"date-parts":[["2016",8,3]]}}}],"schema":"https://github.com/citation-style-language/schema/raw/master/csl-citation.json"}

CHAPTER 13: INACCURACIES AND MISSING EVIDENCE

Alma 44:21

Now the number of their dead was not numbered because of the greatness of the number; yea, the number of their dead was exceedingly great, both on the Nephites and on the Lamanites.

Alma 49:23

Thus the Nephites had all power over their enemies; and thus the Lamanites did attempt to destroy the Nephites until their chief captains were all slain; yea, and more than a thousand of the Lamanites were slain; while, on the other hand, there was not a single soul of the Nephites which was slain.

3 Nephi 4:21

And the Nephites were continually marching out by day and by night, and falling upon their armies, and cutting them off by thousands and by tens of thousands.

Mormon 6:11–15

And when they had gone through and hewn down all my people save it were twenty and four of us, (among whom was my son Moroni) [. . .] ten thousand of my people who were hewn down, [. . .] ¹²And we also beheld the ten thousand of my people who were led by my son Moroni.

¹³And behold, the ten thousand of Gidgiddonah had fallen, and he also in the midst.

¹⁴And Lamah had fallen with his ten thousand; and Gilgal had fallen with his ten thousand; and Limhah had fallen with his ten thousand; and Jeneum had fallen with his ten thousand; and Cumenihah, and Moronihah, and Antionum, and Shiblom, and Shem, and Josh, had fallen with their ten thousand each. ¹⁵And it came to pass that there were ten more who did fall by the sword, with their ten thousand each; yea, even all my people, save it were those twenty and four who were with me, and also a few who had escaped into the south countries, and a few who had deserted over unto the Lamanites, had fallen;

These verses indicate an incredible number of people who died as a result of war. I want to add that, to this number, I only included war deaths. There are numerous other passages where the BOM peoples fall to famine or other catastrophes. For instance, the famine (which was prayed for as a substitute for war) in Helaman 11 was said to have killed "by thousands" (Helaman 11:6). When we look at all the deaths, even those from war only, we see corpses in the hundreds of thousands.

I want to draw special attention to two of the verses above. Alma 44:21 said that the dead were not even numbered because of how many there were. This is surprising if we remember that in Alma 28:2 they numbered the dead in the tens of thousands. If they were willing to number to tens of thousands, how many bodies must there be that they could not even be numbered? The second passage that deserves attention is the verses in Mormon 6.

Mormon 6 outlines a phenomenal battle in which the entire Nephite population (excepting twenty-four people) is wiped out. In the verses above we find that at least 230,000 men involved in the fight lost their lives during this battle. This is similar to the estimated 200,000 casualties[7] of the 1521 siege of Tenochtitlan where Hernan Cortez fought the final battle that caused the fall of the Aztec empire. With regard to the historical context, this battle is of an incredible number and force. A battle such as described in Mormon 6, taking the lives of 230,000 individuals is *very* significant.

Wars of this size prompt one to expect at least some form of evidence for them. What kind of archaeological evidence would we expect to find from wars like the ones listed above? We might expect to find some bodies preserved with clear injuries in the skeletal remains. Some may object that decay would make it so that no remains would be discovered of the bodies from these wars on account of the long duration of time since they occurred. On the contrary, I believe that biblical archaeology has demonstrated quite the opposite to be true.

For instance, at the sight of Lachish in Israel, there was discovered a mass grave of some 1,500 individuals from the war of the siege of Sennacherib during the reign of king Hezekiah in 701 B.C.[8] As described in the introduction to Mormon 6, this war occurred around the time of 385 AD. If archaeologists were able to discover the mass grave with human remains from 701 B.C., it is likely that they would be able to find remains from a war that occurred over 1,000 years later.

---

7. Ross Hassig, *Mexico and the Spanish Conquest*, Modern Wars in Perspective (London ; New York: Longman, 1994).

8. Lawrence T Geraty, "ARCHAEOLOGY AND THE BIBLE AT HEZEKIAH'S LACHISH," n.d., 11.

CHAPTER 13: INACCURACIES AND MISSING EVIDENCE

Further, these bodies would be relatively easily identifiable as being those described in the BOM. This is because the Nephites are of Jewish origin. Initially they sailed to Mesoamerica from Jerusalem. If this is the case, all of the remains from the wars listed in the BOM (of which there are *many*) would leave behind bodies with the bone structure of Jewish peoples.

In fairness, I am not stating that we ought to find bodies to substantiate all of the wars within the BOM. Rather, that any evidence we find of the ancient American Nephite wars *would* leave the evidence of Jewish remains. As of yet, we have found no evidence of ancient Jewish remains in North America. Thus, if we look back to our three archaeological elements of war, we find that we cannot use injuries in human skeletal remains because there are no confirmed skeletal remains fitting the criteria to be examined.

We might also expect to find weapons and armor (the second element of war archaeology) from wars of this size. The book of Helaman lists among the armaments of the Lamanites swords, cimeters, bows, arrows, breastplates, headplates, and shields of every kind (Helaman 1:14). Mormon 6 lists bows, swords, axes, and "all manner of weapons of war". Many of these weapons, no doubt, would have been made of metal. As we discussed previously, according to the BOM, the ancient inhabitants of the Americas (especially the Nephites) had unbelievable talents with advanced metallurgy. With these descriptions of war, certainly there would be some form of archaeological evidence.

Further, we ought to note that the kinds of weapons that we expect are those that are formed from this advanced metallurgy as opposed to the macuahuitl as was earlier addressed. Despite such grand claims in the BOM of wars full of advanced weapons and armor, we have yet to come across any discoveries asserting this archaeological evidence. In terms of weapons and armor as evidence, there is none that has sparked enough of a conversation to adjust the secular views of ancient American archaeology. As a result, we find strike two out of three on the war archaeology evidences.

Apologists may respond that all of the evidence has perished by this time and that we are no longer able to see any of it. However, I find this incredibly unlikely. Scientists are constantly making new discoveries from periods far older than the war described in Mormon 6 at around 385 A.D. For instance, in 2015 archaeologists found a tomb from a warrior of the Mycenaeans. These were the peoples who were described in the works of Homer and lived during the Bronze age over 1,000 years ago. An article for the Smithsonian magazine describes the find.

> Archaeologists uncovered bronze basins, weapons and armor, but also a tumble of even more precious items, including gold and silver cups; hundreds of beads made of carnelian, amethyst, amber and gold; more than 50 stone seals intricately carved with goddesses, lions and bulls; and four stunning gold rings. This was indeed an ancient grave, among the most spectacular archaeological discoveries in Greece in more than half a century.

If we are able to discover artifacts from this period in ancient Greece or, as also noted above, from King Sennacherib's siege at Lachish, certainly we would be able to uncover at least some evidence from as recent as 385 A.D. As may be expected, there remains no evidence that can support the existence of the wars addressed in the BOM.

Further, we have to ask what the death of nearly a quarter of a million people entails sociologically. This is emblematic of a large society. Certainly, as discussed in our anachronisms section, there is no doubt that the Nephites had a blessed and prosperous culture. The kind of culture needed to support such a war would have been similar to that of the Aztecs in their golden age. This is right on track with the description given by the BOM authors. Here we will proceed to explore the third and final element necessary for considering war archaeology, settlement data.

We would expect to see evidence of ancient American settlements (likely bearing many Jewish characteristics) as another avenue to support the accuracy of the BOM's historical war claims. As mentioned in numerous places previously, the Nephite culture was seen to be *flourishing*. A nation/culture does not reach the heights of technological advancement foretold of in the BOM without leaving some kind of settlement remains. These assumptions are well attested within the BOM as well. Let us look at a handful of the places where the BOM details the impressive settlements that were constructed. Esteemed elder B.H. Roberts notes of the watch towers and fortresses within the BOM especially with regard to their similarity to the descriptions by a contemporary work on the ancient Americans. We will address this comparison a little further on but here we will utilize the same references that he presented.[9]

---

9. B. H. Roberts and Brigham D. Madsen, *Studies of the Book of Mormon*, 2nd ed (Salt Lake City: Signature Books, 1992).

CHAPTER 13: INACCURACIES AND MISSING EVIDENCE

Mosiah 11:12–13

¹²And it came to pass that he built a tower near the temple; yea, a very high tower, even so high that he could stand upon the top thereof and overlook the land of Shilom, and also the land of Shemlon, which was possessed by the Lamanites; and he could even look over all the land round about. ¹³And it came to pass that he caused many buildings to be built in the land Shilom; and he caused a great tower to be built on the hill north of the land Shilom, which had been a resort for the children of Nephi at the time they fled out of the land; and thus he did do with the riches which he obtained by the taxation of his people.

Mosiah 19:5,6

⁵And it came to pass that he fought with the king; and when the king saw that he was about to overpower him, he fled and ran and got upon the tower which was near the temple. ⁶And Gideon pursued after him and was about to get upon the tower to slay the king,

Mosiah 20:7–8

⁷Therefore they sent their armies forth; yea, even the king himself went before his people; and they went up to the land of Nephi to destroy the people of Limhi. ⁸And now Limhi had discovered them from the tower, even all their preparations for war did he discover; therefore he gathered his people together, and laid wait for them in the fields and in the forests.

Alma 50:1–6

¹And now it came to pass that Moroni did not stop making preparations for war, or to defend his people against the Lamanites; for he caused [. . .] that they should commence in digging up heaps of earth round about all the cities, throughout all the land which was possessed by the Nephites. ²And upon the top of these ridges of earth he caused that there should be timbers, yea, works of timbers built up to the height of a man, round about the cities. ³And he caused that upon those works of timbers there should be a frame of pickets built upon the timbers round about; and they were strong and high. ⁴And he caused towers to be erected that overlooked those works of pickets, and he caused places of security to be built upon those towers, that the stones and the arrows of the Lamanites could not hurt them. ⁵And they were prepared that they could cast stones from the

top thereof, according to their pleasure and their strength, and slay him who should attempt to approach near the walls of the city. ⁶Thus Moroni did prepare strongholds against the coming of their enemies, round about every city in all the land.

Alma 49:18

¹⁸Now behold, the Lamanites could not get into their forts of security by any other way save by the entrance, because of the highness of the bank which had been thrown up, and the depth of the ditch which had been dug round about, save it were by the entrance.

Helaman 16:1

¹And now, it came to pass that there were many who heard the words of Samuel, the Lamanite, which he spake upon the walls of the city.

Described in these verses are impressive feats of wartime engineering. The Nephites built watchtowers, fortresses with wooden walls, fortresses made of enormous mounds of earth, and other walls. In fact, it was described in Alma 49, that the mounds of earth dug by the Nephites were so high (and steep) that the only way for intruders to enter was by means of the entrance. The BOM describes great wars and it also describes the settlement structure to go along with the war stories. The BOM leaves us without any doubt that there were great fortresses and structures that existed. As the third element of our war archaeology, we ought to expect to find them and, in so doing, substantiate the BOM history claims. Certainly, settlement data is one of the most likely to be observable in the future. Few artifacts exist with such permanence as do buildings.

For instance, consider the ruins from ancient cities all over the world! Ancient Egypt with its pyramids, the Great Wall of China, Mexico with the ruins of Tenochtitlan, ancient Greece with the colosseum and other monumental structures, and Israel with many holy sites; these are all historical places able to be visited today! A quick internet search will provide a researcher with hundreds of images for each of these.

It may be granted that the advancement of the Nephites likely was not quite comparable to that of many of these other ancient cultures. As a result, we may expect less of a footprint to be left than was by these other ancient cultures. Further, the Nephite civilization was utterly destroyed

CHAPTER 13: INACCURACIES AND MISSING EVIDENCE

by the Lamanites.[10] It is reasonable to assume that beyond destroying just the population, the Lamanites took pleasure in ransacking the buildings and all other elements of Nephite culture. We must still note, however, that this would not *erase* the Nephites from the archaeological record. Rather, it would provide greater evidence of conflict which, as previously mentioned, has not yet been substantiated.

As has now been thoroughly noted, we must have a confident expectation that structural, archaeological remains from these peoples and their wars remains somewhere in Mesoamerica. This expectation is supported by the history presented by the BOM as well as the consistency in the preservation and discovery of the ruins from other great ancient nations. Strikingly, there is not currently a single ruin or remain that has been purported by modern academia to be of Nephite or Lamanite origin. As such, our expectation remains utterly unsatisfied.

I will note again that absence of evidence is not evidence of absence. Just because we have not yet found any archaeological evidence supporting the BOM does not mean that it does not exist and that we never will find any. Indeed, the LDS apologist will not hesitate to mention that the large majority of ancient America remains unexcavated. LDS Scholar Tad R. Callister quotes a non-LDS scholar, Edwin Barnhart saying "Less than one percent of Mesoamerica has been professionally surveyed." Callister then proceeds to accurately point out that it would be "foolhardy to unequivocally claim there were no horses, cattle, steel, or the like in the Book of Mormon lands and times when at least 98 percent of archaeological sites in ancient America remain unearthed."[11] I agree that it would be very foolish to assert with certainty, based upon an absence of evidence, that the anachronisms and expected artifacts listed in the previous pages simply could not and do not exist. I refuse to take such a close-minded approach.

However, I am also unwilling to abandon the scientific process entirely. This is one of the beautiful elements of the scientific model of research. It is innately humble. Science cannot *prove* anything with absolute certainty. Any theory or perspective acquired may be later disproven by conflicting and more compelling evidence. Any theory is subject to revision. This humble and open-minded approach should not lead us to abandon the system and act as skeptics, withholding

10. "Lamanite Identity,".

11. Tad R. Callister, *A Case for The Book of Mormon* (Salt Lake City, Utah: Deseret Book, 2019).56.

judgement on every belief and assuming everything to be outside of our powers of comprehension.[12] Rather, we ought to proceed with intellectual humility following the evidence wherever it may be. Following this principle, while it is true that we should not unequivocally hold that the BOM will never be vindicated by archaeology, we must also realize that it has not been *yet*. Further, until it has been supported by the appropriate methodologies, the more reasonable belief is to assent that perhaps these artifacts do *not* exist.

Another point worthy of note is that you may be unconvinced by the lack of evidence for one of two other reasons. First, you may assert that regardless of the scientific process, 1-2% of Mesoamerica is too small a sample size to accurately depict the reality of the whole. This is a fair critique and while this point may not be enough to definitively disprove the existence of these items in your mind, I would suggest that anyone with this perspective try to find a middle ground for themselves where they consider that the existence or lack thereof for these artifacts are both reasonable positions. For those convinced that this lack of evidence means nothing, I would suggest deeply contemplating what it would mean if it were true that these artifacts were non-discoverable and non-existent. Would it change your perspective on other beliefs? How long should one continue to hold out belief (in disagreement with the contemporary archaeology) that these evidences do exist?

The second reason that some may not be convinced by this evidence is because it is just one small issue, and your interrelated web of other beliefs allows you to suspend belief about this one item. This can also be a compelling answer. While the current archaeology from a small sample size of excavations may not treat favorably the BOM, there are so many other beliefs that you hold about the BOM that allow you to continue in firm belief that this too will eventually conform to your existing structure of beliefs. My response to those in this category is to acknowledge the uncertainty that you may experience with regard to this specific element of LDS studies. LDS archaeology is (at present) not something to be terribly proud of. In addition, my goal is not to provide a single point that rewrites an otherwise unflawed system of belief. Rather, I am trying to address various pieces of information which have led me (and many others) to our current positions with regard to the accuracy of the BOM. Perhaps this one point is not convincing on its own. That is a fair perspective to

---

12. Katja Vogt, "Ancient Skepticism," in *The Stanford Encyclopedia of Philosophy*, ed. Edward N. Zalta, Summer 2021 (Metaphysics Research Lab, Stanford University, 2021).

hold. However, in light of everything else that we have touched upon and will continue to, maybe this critical view of LDS archaeology will become a bit more understandable.

Chapter 14: Thomas Stuart Ferguson

I WANT TO CLOSE this section on LDS archaeology by briefly detailing the journey of a brilliant LDS scholar, Thomas Stuart Ferguson.

Thomas Stuart Ferguson is one of the most important minds in the study of LDS archaeology. I dare say, that one will not get very far into a conversation concerning this topic without his name popping up. He began his professional journey as a lawyer. Influenced by a fellow student at UC Berkely where he attended university, he always had a deep interest in archaeological studies, history, and culture particularly those focused on the potential confirmation of the "unique historical claims of the Book of Mormon."[1] Ferguson described himself as an individual with an "unusually strong testimony"[2] of the divine truth contained within the BOM. Ferguson's passion for the BOM and his interest in ancient Mesoamerican history led him to pursue the archaeological field more formally and with greater commitment than his career in law had previously allowed.

Ferguson proceeded to become the founder and first president of the NWAF (New World Archaeological Foundation). Interestingly, the primary intent of this foundation was not only to prove the BOM to be accurate, but an open-minded, academic, and historical inquiry into the Mesoamerica. Ferguson took an objective and academic approach. His openness to study was likely motivated by his great confidence in the accuracy of the BOM's historical account. The NWAF held both LDS and

---

1. Stan Larson, "The Odyssey of Thomas Stuart Ferguson," n.d., 39.
2. Larson.

Non-LDS members; each holding different theories regarding what the results of their studies would be.

Ferguson is largely responsible for propagating the Tehunantepec theory of LDS geography which narrows the likely dwelling the peoples described in the BOM from large swaths of North and South America primarily to central America. With this theory guiding him, he led numerous expeditions to Mesoamerica to excavate in search of evidence for the BOM. As stated above, his personal intentions were quite clearly to vindicate the historicity of the BOM through archaeological study and excavation. However, he also believed that the only way this was to truly be accomplished was if the studies were performed in a manner as objective as possible. He was once recorded saying "Let the evidence from the ground speak for itself and let the chips fall where they may."[3] We ought to have great respect for Ferguson's approach to his studies. He exercises an impressive integrity in his search for truth that I believe we can all strive to emulate in our own investigations.

While his approach to the study was somewhat free from religious affection, the funding of his project was not. The NWAF received funding from both, the LDS church and BYU which later acquired and renamed the foundation. This funding did not come easily, however, as Ferguson had to send multiple requests for the funding leveraging his confidence that the excavations being performed in central America would definitively prove the accuracy of the BOM and the prophetic status of Joseph Smith to a critical world.

While the work of Ferguson and his foundation was not explicitly in service the LDS church, it came with some very clear expectations. Ferguson was not an anti-mormon attempting to dismantle the accuracy of the LDS church through haphazard study. He was a man on a mission to *prove* the truth of his faith through meticulous and objective study, something he was incredibly confident would occur.

Due to a lack of funding following the work he completed in 1953, he requested the church, again, to provide funding for his important studies. The church, at first, denied this request. Ferguson responded to this denial with a letter reiterating his confidence in the great likelihood of the future and past success of his mission. He writes: "I know beyond a shadow of a doubt that certain of the locations discovered [in 1953] were occupied by Nephites during Book of Mormon times. The importance of

3. Larson.

the work cannot be overestimated. [. . .] Thus, Book of Mormon history is revelation that can be tested by archaeology."

Despite all of his confidence and hard work, Ferguson failed to find anything that would support his faith to his satisfaction. By the mid 1960's, though the NWAF had earned great respect for their numerous discoveries and contributions to the understanding of Mesoamerican history, there was no evidence that could clearly be linked to the truth of the history as described in the BOM.

An expert in the field of Mesoamerican studies at the time, Charles J. MacCurdy Professor Emeritus of Anthropology at Yale, Michael D. Coe, commented on the work performed by the NWAF.[4] He noted that the work that was accomplished by this foundation was truly fantastic and worthy of commendation. He praises Ferguson, the other founding directors, the archaeologists, and the LDS church for its wisdom in providing financial aid to support such valuable studies. In addition to these glowing remarks, he adds a description of what these studies did not accomplish. "The bare facts of the matter are that nothing, absolutely nothing, has ever shown up in any New World excavation which would suggest to a dispassionate observer that the Book of Mormon, as claimed by Joseph Smith, is a historical document relating to the history of early migrants to our hemisphere."[5]

Indeed, Ferguson himself came to a similar conclusion regarding what his archaeological studies had accomplished. Commenting on an essay that he wrote detailing some of the seemingly unsolvable problems with LDS archaeology he states, "the real implication of the paper is that you can't set Book of Mormon geography down anywhere- because it is fictional and will never meet the requirements of the dirt archaeology."[6] I will readily note that, as author Stan Larson points out, it was not archaeology alone that carried Ferguson to this kind of statement. Rather, it was a culmination of a couple of different issues with the LDS church, archaeology being one among them.

Even so, we see here an example of a man who was uniquely devoted to his faith to the point that he started an archaeological foundation to test the historical claims which he was certain were true. He was

---

4. "Michael Coe: Influential Archaeologist Helped Unlock Secrets of Mesoamerica," YaleNews, October 8, 2019.

5. "Mormons and Archaeology: An Outside View | The Dialogue Journal," April 27, 2018.

6. Larson, "The Odyssey of Thomas Stuart Ferguson."

operating under his own confidence as well as that of the church and, later on, BYU as well. Here, perhaps the most important LDS archaeologist, found that he was unable to support his faith through his studies and, as a result, was forced to abandon many of his previously held beliefs. This is because, there is no conclusive archaeological evidence to support the LDS narrative.

As we conclude our review of archaeology and proceed to the next couple of topics, I want to re-assert the fact that a lack of evidence does not definitively disprove. It should, however, raise some serious questions in a mind that is in pursuit of the truth. I encourage you as the reader to keep these things in mind as we continue to consider new information regarding the accuracy of the claims found within the works of Joseph Smith. As stated before, missing archaeology alone, or the anachronisms alone, or theology alone, may not be enough to make one truly stop and reconsider. However, I believe that there comes a point when the weight of these diverse arguments add up and become quite an impressive burden.

Chapter 15: **DNA Evidence**

THE BOM PRESENTS A unique view of ancient American history. This is one of its valuable selling points. It provides a new and sometimes clearer understanding of certain aspects of history. One of the most notable historical conundrums that it sets out to solve is the origin of the native Americans. The BOM presents a view that was somewhat popular during the early mid 1800s. This perspective held that the genetic stock of the ancient American Indians was from some Old-World civilization. In particular, the BOM makes the case that these ancestors were ancient Jews. With more specificity still, it may be assumed that these ancient Jews were, perhaps, members of the 10 lost tribes of Israel.

The ten lost tribes of Israel were of great interest during Joseph Smith's time. It was a point of curiosity where these lost tribes ended up upon their disappearance. In the history of ancient Israel, the original twelve tribes were split into two kingdoms, the northern kingdom of Israel and the southern kingdom of Judah. The kingdom of Judah was comprised of the tribes of Judah and Benjamin. The kingdom of Israel to the North contained the remaining ten tribes, Asher, Dan, Ephraim, Gad, Issachar, Manasseh, Naphtali, Reuben, Simeon, and Zebulun. These tribes become lost to the history of the world around the 7th century B.C. when their kingdom was invaded by the Assyrians.[1] As such, this became an intriguing mystery that many attempted to solve.

Within the BOM it is presented that ancient Jews built boats and sailed to the Americas. This they were compelled to do by God himself. He

---

1. Stanford M. Lyman, "The Lost Tribes of Israel as a Problem in History and Sociology," *International Journal of Politics, Culture, and Society* 12, no. 1 (1998): 7–42.

CHAPTER 15: DNA EVIDENCE

instructed their construction and guided their journey until they arrived.[2] This journey by sea is a fascinating topic and worthy of much study on its own. One may feel the need to consider with special scrutiny this voyage which some have speculated could have lasted between nine months and a full year.[3] In any case, Lehi and his family, who left initially from Jerusalem[4] around 605 B.C.[5] set sail and arrived at the promised land (America). For some time, the LDS church taught that these individuals were the primary ancestors of the native Americans.

Of course, in the BOM history the Jaredites made it to the promised land first, however, this entire civilization died off and could not have been a part of the genetic composition of the native Americans[6] This role was left to Lehi and his family. This was the initial group that prospered into the great nations of the Nephites and, after a curse, the Lamanites. As mentioned previously, the BOM is full of wars between the Nephites and the Lamanites. These culminated in the complete annihilation of the Nephites leaving only the Lamanites to be the ancestors of the Native Americans.

This has been the traditional view of the LDS church. It was widely believed and taught that the Native Americans descended almost exclusively from the Lamanites. There are some LDS apologists who may want to say that there is no statement from the church which definitively concludes that ancient Jews were the essential ancestors to the native peoples of America. Before we proceed to evaluate this claim, I want to point out a number of the resources that demonstrate this to be the case.

First, this perspective is clearly articulated by a statement in the introduction to older editions of the BOM. In these editions, the introduction read "all were destroyed except the Lamanites, and they are the principal ancestors of the American Indians." Of course, the introduction to the BOM was not a part of the plates which were translated by Joseph Smith. Rather, it first appeared in the 1981 edition of the BOM.[7] This detail was included in the introduction to the BOM, which means that

---

2. 1 Nephi 18:23

3. "The Longest Voyage: Lehi's Journey to the Promised Land | Meridian Magazine," Meridian Magazine | Latter-day Saint News and Views, April 7, 2016.

4. 1 Nephi 2:4

5. Jeffrey R Chadwick, "Dating the Departure of Lehi from Jerusalem" 57 (2018): 47.

6. Ether 15:29

7. "The Introduction to the Book of Mormon,".

it was intended to be a useful guide for those reading—instructing them how to effectively understand the historical narrative.

Second, consider a speech presented by Spencer W. Kimball at BYU in 1967. He quite strongly articulates the historical LDS position on the ancestry of the Native Americans.

> The Indian is a Lamanite. There are South American, Central American, Mexican, Polynesian, and other Lamanites running into millions who are not specifically called Indians though they are related Lamanites. The Lamanites are a mixture of many. Undoubtedly there is, in their veins, the blood of Nephi, Joseph, and Jacob as well as that of Laman, Lemuel, and Sam also of the Mulekites of Judah. They are not Orientals. They are from the near east. The 12 apostles who were associated with the prophet Joseph proclaimed this to the world. [. . .] We also bear testimony that the Indians, so called, of North and South America, are a remnant of the tribes of Israel. [. . .] It is not impossible that there could have seeped across the Bering Strait a little oriental blood as claimed by some people [. . .] But basically, these Lamanites, including the Indians, are the descendants of Lehi who left Jerusalem 600 years B.C.[8]

This description of the background of the Native Americans is concrete. It leaves little room for speculation as to what the orthodox LDS position is on the topic. An official Church essay confirms this perspective stating that the majority of early LDS believers were under the impression that "Near Easterners or West Asians like Jared, Lehi, Mulek, and their companions were the first or the largest or even the only groups to settle the Americas."[9]

The LDS scholar who founded the website *LDS Discussions* further explains the belief that the Americas were initially inhabited by the Jaredites, and following them, the descendants of Lehi using passages from the BOM.

> Based on the Book of Mormon, Nephi himself would probably be as surprised as anyone by this talk of the Promised Land being already overrun by other people when he arrived. God also seems to be unaware that he was sending his chosen people to a place that was already populated by previous settlers. He told

---

8. Spencer W. Kimball, "The Lamanite: Their Burden, Our Burden," *BYU Speeches* (blog).

9. "Book of Mormon and DNA Studies,".

Nephi, "it is wisdom that this land should be kept as yet from the knowledge of other nations; for behold, many nations would overrun the land, that there would be no place for an inheritance. . .and they shall be kept from all other nations, that they may possess this land unto themselves" (2 Nephi 1:8,9). He told the Jaredites that he would send them to "that quarter where there never had man been," to a land of promise "reserved for a righteous people." (Ether 2:5-7) In Helaman we read: "And it came to pass that they did multiply and spread, and did go forth from the land southward to the land northward, and did spread insomuch that they began to cover the face of the whole earth, from the sea south to the sea north, from the sea west to the sea east" (Helaman 3:8) Does this sound to you like they were merely filling small gaps among the occupants of a land that was already densely populated? No, they were explicitly told by God that the land was not already overrun by "others,".[10]

The same essay proceeds to note the elements not described within the BOM. Interestingly, it is pointed out that the BOM depicts *many* of the findings of those who arrived in the Americas. The animals, plants, and natural resources were described with clarity. What we do not find is description of other peoples. If those keeping the record were so meticulous in their record of everything else, it would be unlikely, or even shocking, for them to leave out other nations inhabiting the same land.

Many other accounts could be given supporting the fact that this was the belief of the LDS church. Suffice it to say, the belief that the Lamanites were the primary ancestors of the Native Americans is *well* instantiated in LDS thought as it appears to have been taught authoritatively. That is, until this belief came under attack by genetic tracing studies utilizing DNA.

The issue that occurred for the LDS teaching about Native American ancestry was based in the studies tracing their genetic background. If, the LDS account were true, DNA studies could definitively demonstrate that there are genetics from the peoples of the Ancient Near East within the DNA of the Native Americans. Indeed, if we hold to the strong position of the LDS teachings in the past, Native American DNA would be primarily that of ancient Jews (as the vast majority descended from the family of Lehi). However, this is not remotely the case.

---

10. "LDS Gospel Topics Essay: DNA and the Book of Mormon (Annotated)," LDS Discussions.

The prevailing perspective in the contemporary scholarship is that the native Americans were primarily descended from Asian backgrounds.[11] This perspective has been asserted in numerous studies[12] and appears to be quite well supported within the science of ancient population genetics.[13] What makes this even more interesting is that the LDS church has assented to this point. In the church essay *Book of Mormon and DNA Studies* it is conceded: "The evidence assembled to date suggests that the majority of Native Americans carry largely Asian DNA."[14] This is a major admission. After clearly teaching that the identity of the peoples of the ancient Americas was Jewish for virtually all of LDS history, it was admitted in a church essay that this is not the case.

This correction was perhaps even more strikingly shared in 2006 with an updated introduction to the BOM. We recall that from 1981 to 2005 the introduction asserted that the Lamanites were "the *principal* ancestors of the American Indians." In 2006, the corrected introduction reads "all were destroyed except the Lamanites, and they are *among* the ancestors of the American Indians." (Emphasis mine) This is a tremendous swivel. True, the substantive change is only one word. However, this one word represents a fundamental shift in LDS belief.

It is worthy of note that this topic contains a lot of room for discussion. The LDS apologists have numerous strategies that they use to rationalize how this change does not negatively affect the truth or historical accuracy of the BOM. At this point, rationalization is the only possible response as genetic study dismantles the historical LDS position on this topic.

As we conclude our study on the way that DNA studies have impacted our understanding of the accuracy of the BOM we will examine Joseph Smith's perspective on this issue compared to what has been discovered by contemporary research. In his letter 1842 to a John Wentworth, Joseph describes the history of ancient America as follows:

> In this important and interesting book [the Book of Mormon] the history of ancient America is unfolded, from its first

---

11. Vincenza Battaglia et al., "The First Peopling of South America: New Evidence from Y-Chromosome Haplogroup Q," *PLoS ONE* 8, no. 8 (August 21, 2013): e71390.

12. "Native American Migrations,".

13. Alessandro Achilli et al., "Reconciling Migration Models to the Americas with the Variation of North American Native Mitogenomes," *Proceedings of the National Academy of Sciences* 110, no. 35 (August 27, 2013): 14308–13.

14. "Book of Mormon and DNA Studies."

settlement by a colony that came from the Tower of Babel at the confusion of languages to the beginning of the fifth century of the Christian era. We are informed by these records that America in ancient times has been inhabited by two distinct races of people. The first were called Jaredites and came directly from the Tower of Babel. The second race came directly from the city of Jerusalem about six hundred years before Christ. They were principally Israelites of the descendants of Joseph. The Jaredites were destroyed about the time that the Israelites came from Jerusalem, who succeeded them in the inheritance of the country. The principal nation of the second race fell in battle towards the close of the fourth century. The remnant are the Indians that now inhabit this country.[15]

The perspective that Joseph Smith articulates here is in clear discord with what DNA research has concluded. Further, the results to these kinds of studies are only becoming clearer. People may now quite conveniently send DNA tests into commercial companies to discover their genetic background with shocking accuracy.[16] As contemporary studies continue to improve, the LDS community has little recourse other than to issue corrections to the beliefs that have been firmly held and taught by the Church through its Prophets, Seers, and Revelators.

---

15. Joseph Smith Jr, "The Wentworth Letter," accessed May 20, 2022.
16. "AncestryDNA® Test Accuracy | AncestryDNA® Learning Hub,".

Chapter 16: **Changes to the Book of Mormon**

WE HAVE JUST ADDRESSED one significant change to the text of the BOM. In the pages to follow, we will evaluate other instances of changes to the BOM. It may be surprising to some that there have been *any* changes. In truth there are a myriad of changes throughout the BOM some less egregious than others. Despite the apparently harmless nature of some of the smaller changes, we ought to keep two claims in mind as we proceed in our investigation.

First, let's bring back to mind Joseph's claim that the BOM is "the most correct of any book on earth, and the keystone of [their] religion."[1] This is quite a claim. Indeed, Joseph Smith includes the Bible within this comparison, insinuating that the Book of Mormon is more correct than the Bible.

This bold statement is likely somewhat explained by *Articles of Faith 1:8* found within the *Pearl of Great Price*. It reads: "We believe the Bible to be the word of God as far as it is translated correctly; we also believe the Book of Mormon to be the word of God."[2][3]

In this case, it is believed that, because the Bible was translated numerous times from the original languages to the current translation it may have acquired some errors along the way. The game of telephone is an instructive illustration for this view. The chain of translations from the originals to what we have today inevitably resulted in errors and

---

1. "Volume 4 Chapter 27," *BYU Studies* (blog), 4.
2. "Chapter 4."
3. Pearl of Great Price: Articles of Faith 1:8.

CHAPTER 16: CHANGES TO THE BOOK OF MORMON

changes which compromise the absolute infallibility of the text. This is the orthodox stance of the LDS Church. It is well worth correcting this misconception and defending the miraculous accuracy of Biblical translation and preservation as is quite easily done.[4] However, in the spirit of brevity I will refrain from doing so here and encourage readers to investigate this topic.

Unlike the Bible, the BOM was not passed down a long line of translators. Rather, it was translated by one man through "the gift and power of God."[5] As such, unlike Scripture which may fail the test of being translated correctly, the BOM is certainly the clear and unadulterated word of God. A little further on, we will delve into the process of translation used for the BOM and consider its implications. However, for now, it is valuable to remember that the BOM was claimed by Joseph Smith to be the most accurate book of all.

Joseph makes it absolutely clear that this work is not of his own authorship. Rather, it is universally asserted that he was merely the translator. One of the three witnesses, David Whitmer gives the following account regarding the way in which Joseph was conveyed the meaning of the characters on the golden plates. "Then, a spiritual light would shine forth, and parchment would appear before Joseph, upon which was a line of characters from the plates, and under it, the translation in English; at least, so Joseph said."[6] Here Whitmer reports that according to Joseph Smith, the English translation would appear before his eyes. He would then dictate this message and it would be recorded. Another early follower of Joseph, Joseph Knight Sr, describes that "he [Joseph Smith] would take a sentence and it would appear in Brite Roman Letters then he would tell the writer and he would write it then that would go away [and] the next Sentence would Come and so on."[7] It is only this kind of gift from God that

---

4. Josh McDowell, *Evidence That Demands a Verdict: Life-Changing Truth for a Skeptical World* (Nashville, Tennessee: Thomas Nelson, 2017).

5. Church of Jesus Christ of Latter-day Saints, *The Holy Bible: Containing the Old and New Testaments, Translated out of the Original Tongues: And with the Former Translations Diligently Compared and Revised ; by His Majesty's Special Command. The Book of Mormon : Another Testament of Jesus Christ. The Doctrine and Covenants of the Church of Jesus Christ of Latter-Day Saints. The Pearl of Great Price.*, 2015.

6. "Source:The True Latter Day Saints' Herald:15 November 1879:A 'Seer Stone,' Which Was Placed in the Crown of a Hat, into Which Joseph Put His Face, so as to Exclude the External Light - FAIR,".

7. Grant H. Palmer, *An Insider's View of Mormon Origins* (Salt Lake City: Signature Books, 2002).5.

could ensure the accuracy of the BOM. It remains untainted by the errors associated with human translation. The English translation would appear, sentence by sentence in front of Joseph's eyes.

Beyond the BOM itself being the most correct, it was revealed that Joseph's translation was correct! In 1829, Joseph Smith, David Whitmer, and Oliver Cowdery were praying, and an angel appeared holding the plates. Shortly after, a voice from heaven stated "These plates have been revealed by the power of God, and they have been translated by the power of God. *The translation of them which you have seen is correct*, and I command you to bear record of what you now see and hear. [emphasis mine]" It is unavoidably asserted from the very beginning of LDS history that the BOM and its translation are *correct*.

The second claim to keep in mind is the fact that there is no way that young Joseph could have written this book on his own. After all, he had very little education and would not have been able to write with such eloquence. This too, is considered a powerful argument by some of the truth and inspiration of the BOM. God used Joseph Smith, a boy of little learning to write His message of the restored gospel.

As we continue to look into the changes to the BOM. We will keep these two claims before us and evaluate them according to what new information is presented. The numerous changes that we are about to consider may fundamentally shift the way we ought to think about the method of translation and the accuracy of the BOM.

Much in the same way that Biblical scholars appeal to the early manuscripts from the original languages, we may appeal to the early edition of the BOM. If the BOM was as accurately translated as was claimed, it would be inerrant having no need for corrections or updates. However, it appears that this is not the case as there have been numerous changes from the first edition of the BOM to the editions which are in circulation today.

As is well documented, the BOM was first printed and published in 1830.[8] Since then there have been multiple new editions each which carry their own series of updates. There are some who wish to explain away these changes as flaws made by the printer. I want to emphatically state that this is not the case. Rather, they were all present in the initial manuscript which Joseph Smith provided to the printer. In fact, the printer, a John H. Gilbert called into question the grammatical errors which were

---

8. "Book of Mormon First Edition (1830),".

CHAPTER 16: CHANGES TO THE BOOK OF MORMON

present in the manuscript and asked if he should correct them. This offer was declined by Martin Harris after he consulted with Joseph Smith.[9] It is also easily confirmed that printer's errors were not the cause of the lack of proper grammar by comparison with the early printer's manuscript. The LDS Church now owns the printer's manuscript of the BOM after purchasing it from the Community of Christ Church (Formerly RLDS).[10] This was a handwritten copy of the BOM which was given to the printer by Joseph Smith to base the printing off of.

With this context in mind, we will proceed by comparing the 1830 edition of the BOM with the modern editions. If you would like to participate in this exercise, and see the changes for yourself, you can do so by searching for the 1830 edition of the BOM which is available for free online and comparing it with your personal copy of the BOM. Replicas of the 1830 edition are also available for purchase from LDS bookstores if you prefer to have a paper copy for your personal library. The information that I present below is borrowed from the incredible work created by Jerald and Sandra Tanner *3,913 Changes in the Book of Mormon*.

First, we will look at some verse changes which represent a shift in the LDS doctrine of the godhead. As I present these changes, I will quote the 1830 edition of the sentence and follow with the contemporary version for comparison. As the 1830 edition of the BOM does not have verses numbered, I will provide page and line numbers for your convenience in following along.

> "And he said unto me, Behold, the virgin which thou seest, is the *mother of God*, after the manner of the flesh." (pg. 25:5)

> "And he said unto me: Behold, the virgin whom thou seest is the *mother of the Son of God*, after the manner of the flesh." (1 Nephi 11:18)

> "And the angel said unto me, behold the Lamb of God, *yea, even the Eternal Father!*" (pg. 25:10)

> "And the angel said unto me: Behold the Lamb of God, *yea, even the Son of the Eternal Father!*" (1 Nephi 11:21)

---

9. Jerald and Sandra Tanner, *3,913 Changes in the Book of Mormon*, n.d.
10. "LDS Church Buys Printer's Manuscript of Book of Mormon for Record $35 Million," Deseret News, September 21, 2017.

> "And I looked and beheld the Lamb of God, that he was taken by the people; *yea, the Everlasting God*, was judged of the world;" (pg. 26:9)

> "And I looked and beheld the Lamb of God, that he was taken by the people; *yea, the Son of the everlasting God* was judged of the world;" (1 Nephi 11:32)

> "that *the Lamb of God is the Eternal Father* and the Saviour of the world;" (pg. 32:10)

> "that *the Lamb of God is the Son of the Eternal Father*, and the Savior of the world;" (1 Nephi 13:40)

Here are four examples demonstrating a shifting LDS theology of the Godhead. Of course, as we have addressed elsewhere, orthodox Christianity has always held to a trinitarian view of God. Joseph certainly had trinitarian influences from the time he was a child. It is not surprising that we should find verses which affirm the divine unity in the BOM. However, what is curious is that a perfect translation would later change to align with the doctrine of a plurality of Gods. If the BOM, the most correct book on earth, originally taught that Christ was "the Everlasting God" how could it be acceptable to change these words that God revealed?

We will now proceed to see some other striking examples of changes that were implemented in later editions of the BOM.

> "on learning from the mouth of Ammon that *king Benjamin* had a gift from God, whereby he could interpret such engravings;" (pg. 200:24"

> "on learning from the mouth of Ammon that *king Mosiah* had a gift from God whereby he could interpret such engravings" (Mosiah 21:28)

> "and for this cause did *king Benjamin* keep them, that they should not come unto the world until after Christ . . . " (pg. 546:5)

> "and for this cause did *king Mosiah* keep them, that they should not come unto the world after Christ . . . " (Ether 4:1)

In these examples, the name of the king was completely changed! In the first case, (Mosiah 21:28) the BOM timeline would indicate that

CHAPTER 16: CHANGES TO THE BOOK OF MORMON

king Benjamin should have been dead for "some time."[11] The Tanners provide an interesting comment by LDS scholar Dr. Sidney B. Sperry of BYU regarding this change. He states:

> The prophet Joseph Smith did change the reading in the Second (1837) Edition despite the fact that the original manuscript reads "king Benjamin" [. . .] Who was responsible for the reading "king Benjamin," in the first place? Was it an inadvertent slip of the tongue on the part of Joseph Smith as he dictated his translation to Oliver Cowdery, or did he translate correctly enough an original error on the part of Mormon? The last of these suggestions is probably the correct one, for the fact remains that the reading "king Benjamin" is an out-and-out error.[12]

This is a truly surprising interpretation of the facts. Dr. Sperry goes so far as to assume that the inaccuracy was original to the plates themselves! If this is true, the divine record, contained a blatant contradiction as, historically, king Benjamin had been dead for quite some time. Further, Joseph Smith "deliberately altered this to eliminate the contradiction."[13]

Below we consider the three times that the word 'cherubim' appears in the BOM. Bruce R. McConkie points out interesting evidence in favor of the BOM concerning this word. He rightly points out that the plural form for the singular 'cherub' is 'cherubs' in English and 'cherubim' in Hebrew. McConkie further states that it is used properly as 'cherubim' in the BOM whereas it is improperly translated as 'cherubims' in the King James Bible. The Tanners point out, this translation of 'cherubims' would be the rough equivalent of saying 'geeses' as opposed to the already plural 'geese.' Below I have quoted the three times the word 'cherubim' appears in the BOM.

> "What does the scripture mean, which saith that God placed cherubim and a flaming sword on the east of the garden," (Alma 12:21)

> "he placed at the east end of the garden of Eden, cherubim, and a flaming sword which turned every way," (Alma 42:2)

> "the Lord God placed cherubim and the flaming sword, that he should not partake of the fruit-" (Alma 42:3)

---

11. Jerald and Sandra Tanner, *3,913 Changes in the Book of Mormon*, 913.
12. Jerald and Sandra Tanner, 91.
13. Jerald and Sandra Tanner, 91.

As shown here, McConkie is correct, in a sense, in the modern BOM the word is written as 'cherubim' however, this is not the case in the 1830 edition where, in all three occurrences, it is written as 'cherubims' as documented below.

> "What does this Scripture mean, which saith that God placed Cherubims and a flaming sword on the east of the garden of Eden," (pg. 256:39)

> "he placed at the east end of the garden of Eden, Cherubims, and a flaming sword which turned every way," (pg. 336:40)

> "the Lord God placed Cherubims and the flaming sword, that he should not partake of the fruit;" (pg. 338:1)

The same linguistic error appears with the word Seraphim. In current editions of the BOM it is written properly whereas in the 1830 edition it is erroneous.

> "Above it stood the seraphim; each one had six wings;" (2 Nephi 16:2)

> "Above it stood the seraphims: each one had six wings;" (pg. 91 chapter IX:3)

> "Then flew one of the seraphim unto me, having a live coal in his hand," (2 Nephi 16:6)

> "Then flew one of the searphims unto me, having a live coal in his hand," (pg. 91 chapter IX:13)

In this way, the very detail of Hebrew grammar which McConkie claims as notable evidence in support of the BOM is found to be disevidence. McConkie notes the significance of Joseph's translation departing from the KJV. This would indicate that he was not copying from a faulty KJV translation but making one of his own. What McConkie failed to notice, however, is that in Joseph's first manuscript, this exact error is present, coincidentally matching the translation errors of the KJV Bible edition which Joseph would have been most familiar with.

In addition to these somewhat understandable grammatical errors which were evident in the KJV Bible, the BOM is full of less excusable affronts to proper English. In order to keep my treatment of these topics brief I will list only one verse illustrating each of the select grammatical errors.

CHAPTER 16: CHANGES TO THE BOOK OF MORMON

First, we see improper use of the word 'no' as opposed to the word 'any'.

> "have not sought gold nor *no* manner of riches of you..." (pg. 157:1, Mosiah 2:12)

This error occurs at least 6 times in the 1830 edition.

Second, we see a mix up between uses of the words 'done' and 'did'. For example:

> "and this he *done* that he might overthrow the doctrine of Christ." (pg.140:Ch.IV:6, Jacob 7:2)

This error occurs at least 8 times in the 1830 edition.

Third, there are numerous improper uses of the word 'for'.

> "the Lamanites did gather themselves together *for* to sing..." (196:19, Mosiah 20:1)

This error occurs at least 10 times.

Fourth, the article 'a' is sometimes misplaced in sentences.

> "As I was *a* journeying to see a very near kindred..." (pg. 249:10, Alma 10:7)

This error occurs at least 13 times.

Fifth, the words 'is' and 'are' are frequently switched around.

> "the tender mercies of the Lord *is* over all..." (pg. 7:25, 1 Nephi 1:20)

This error occurs at least 16 times.

Sixth, there is somewhat frequent misuse of 'was' and 'were'.

> "and in this year there *were* continual rejoicing..." (pg. 414:27, Helaman 3:31)

This sort of error occurs at least 37 times.

Seventh, there are corrections of the words 'who'/'which'.

> "And the Son of God was the Messiah, *which* should come..." (pg. 23:20, 1 Nephi 10:17)

This occurs almost 80 times in the book of 1 Nephi alone.

Eighth, in a note potentially less grammatical than stylistic, the word 'that' was removed from the BOM many times.

> "And after *that* he had preached unto them . . . " (pg. 21:9, 1 Nephi 8:37)

This deletion of the word 'that' occurs more than 75 times in 1 Nephi alone.

We could list numerous other kinds of grammatical errors, but I believe that the eight that have been presented thus far are adequate. The 1830 edition of the BOM is *riddled* with all kinds of errors which, as was noted previously, are not the result of scribal errors. No, these were present in the printing manuscript given to the printer and approved. Dr. Sperry above noted (in elaboration on one of the errors) that the error could have been original to the golden plates themselves. However, is it not incredibly unlikely that many of these errors would have been from the plates? Indeed, these grammatical errors are, in some cases, rather unique to English. It would be unlikely that the ancient Reformed Egyptian language could be so clearly translated word for word that these exact grammatical errors would be present.

With this in mind, what are we to conclude? It is on the basis of this issue that the prominent LDS scholar B.H. Roberts held to a different view of translation than has traditionally been propagated in the LDS community. The LDS scholars who try to reconcile this issue propose the theory that God gave Joseph Smith the ideas which Joseph articulated in his own words. These were captured by his scribe. It appears that if we are to hold to the divine inspiration of the BOM this is the theory that must be adhered to. The traditional theories do not effectively combat the problems presented by the English in the 1830 edition.

Roberts found the perspective that the plates were translated word for word by the power of God to be untenable considering the nature of the grammatical flaws in the text. If it is to be believed that the prophet Joseph Smith merely read what was before his eyes on the Urim and Thummim and contributed nothing more, then the divine instruments would be the cause of the inaccuracies and flaws. Roberts finds this position to be outside the realm of faithful possibility. He notes: "This is to assign responsibility for errors in language to a divine instrumentality, which amounts to assigning such error to God. But that is unthinkable, not to say blasphemous."

He further notes that "such errors in grammar and diction as occur in the translation are just such errors as might reasonably be looked for in the work of one unlearned in the English language." and a little further on: "but the awkward, ungrammatical expression of the thoughts is, doubtless, the result of the translator's imperfect knowledge of the English language...."

Here we have evaluated many of the errors and changes which are present in the BOM. As we have now presented a sampling of these, we return to considering our initial two premises. First, that the BOM is the most correct book. Second, that a young Joseph Smith would never have been able to write it considering his little education.

To consider the first question of the superlative correctness of the book we ask, is the honest reader willing to maintain this position? The book certainly cannot be called 'correct' in a grammatical sense. However, one may say that the exact wording does not matter, rather, it is the doctrine and not the words of the BOM which demonstrate its accuracy. Even so, we considered changes that appear to be an intentional deviation from previous edition's description of the Godhead. Beyond this, there were multiple instances in which a king was named who had been dead for some time. This is a clear error. No matter what translation theory one holds, this error is inescapable. Either it was an inaccuracy which God communicated to Joseph Smith through the instruments, or it was a slip of the tongue on his part. In either case, the BOM fails to hold its grasp on infallibility. With this in mind, I ask the reader, how correct is the BOM?

Secondly, one of the most common arguments proposed by LDS missionaries for the validity of the BOM is the fact that Joseph Smith had little education and would have been utterly incapable of writing this book. I wonder if they would remain so confident in this evidence if they were well acquainted with the 1830 edition. I am of the opinion (along with B.H. Roberts) that any reader of this original printing would not be at all surprised to hear that it was penned by someone of little education. Admittedly, the stories and doctrines held within the BOM do inspire admiration for the strength of the mind capable of relaying them, however the elocution is less than impressive and certainly demonstrates no godly eloquence.

The LDS Church holds firmly that the BOM is God-Inspired and the most correct book of any on earth. In these pages, I believe that I have presented enough information to bring into question that perspective. We examined the historical and archaeological evidences within the

BOM and considered how they stack up alongside contemporary science. We examined DNA evidence and the claims that were made regarding the heritage of the Native Americans. Finally, we considered the many changes throughout the BOM from the 1830 edition to the present. Certainly, if one were to imagine what a God-Inspired book would look like, this would fail to pass the test. There appears to be a mountain of evidence which call into question the accuracy of the BOM, and it is only growing. Here we have only touched upon a select handful of what I find to be the most compelling examples from critical scholarship.

With this study completed, it is time to proceed to consider the actual process of Joseph's translation of the BOM and his other works.

Part 4: **Exterior**

Chapter 17: Joseph's Claims of Translator

AT THIS POINT, WE have become well acquainted a number of the flaws within the BOM. We have considered artifacts currently known not to have existed in America at the time described by the BOM. We have also evaluated the incredible historical claims made and their lack of support by archaeological data. The similarity between these elements is that in both, the BOM describes something which is simply known (or found) not to exist in the current historical record. In addition, we looked into the DNA studies which have effectively eliminated the traditional LDS beliefs regarding the peopling of the Americas. We then completed our investigation by looking into the extensive changes found within the BOM. At this point, the question arises; "How could Joseph, Smith, a young man of twenty-four,[1] with little to no education, have written this phenomenal story all on his own in only 65 days?"[2] Surely this task would be impossible if not for the power of God. The only way this could occur is if God gave Joseph Smith the golden plates and the power to translate them. This is, at least, the perspective of many of the Saints.

In the pages to follow, I plan to provide an answer to a handful of questions posed by this perspective. First, I want to evaluate the claim that the only way such a project would be possible is if Joseph Smith were translating these plates by the power of God. As it turns out, Joseph may have had a different approach to translating and a different skill level at this discipline than may be expected by an orthodox LDS believer.

1. "Joseph Smith,".
2. "How Long Did It Take Joseph Smith to Translate the Book of Mormon?,".

To begin effectively treating Joseph's claims of being a translator, we must provide a brief background on his history of becoming one. First, we will consider a brief introduction to Joseph's acquisition of the BOM and what exactly it was that he was translating.

The contemporary Book of Mormon is believed to be a translated copy of the writings of the ancient Israelites who came to America. God gave the command to these ancient Jews "that there should be an account engraven of the ministry of my people."[3] This engraved account was etched upon golden plates and contained the record of the people of Nephi. In 1 Nephi 1:1–2 it says, " . . . I make a record of my proceedings in my days. ²Yea, I make a record in the language of my father, which consists of the learning of the Jews and the language of the Egyptians." These plates were of great importance to the people of the ancient Americas as described in the BOM. They passed them down and continued their record from generation to generation ending with the final words of Moroni, the final Nephite Prophet, who sealed up the records.[4] These sacred golden plates, along with the Urim and Thummim, and the breastplate were buried by Moroni at the Hill Cumorah inside of a sort of stone box. Here they rested from around 421 AD until they were revealed to Joseph Smith in 1823. LDS Scholar H. Donl Peterson, in his article, *Moroni, the Last of the Nephite Prophets* provides a succinct history for how these plates were delivered to Joseph Smith.

> When the Prophet Joseph Smith first met the angel Moroni at the hill Cumorah about 1,400 years later [after Moroni had buried the items in 421 AD] on the evening of 22 September 1823, Moroni showed him the sacred contents and told Joseph that the sacred objects had been "sealed by the prayer of faith" (Cowdery 198). The plates remained there until 27 September 1827, when Moroni gave them to Joseph to allow him to translate them into English.[5]

That was a very brief description of how Joseph acquired the golden plates and it demonstrates their importance. These plates were defended and carried by the Prophet Moroni to the end when he buried them for their preservation until the right time. It should also be noted, that unlike the Old Testament of the Bible which can be corroborated

---

3. 1 Nephi 9:3
4. Moroni 10:2
5. "Moroni, the Last of the Nephite Prophets | Religious Studies Center,".

by many early copies of the manuscripts such as were found at Qumran, the golden plates are the *only* known record of this ancient American history with no known copies.

These golden plates were revealed to a young Joseph Smith who, after some time, was allowed to retrieve them and began his work of translating them. As briefly described above in 1 Nephi 1:2, the golden plates were engraved in a language now commonly referred to as Reformed Egyptian.[6] This was a very unique language that was thought to be a mixture of the original Hebraic language of the Jews and Egyptian hieroglyphs which were integrated during their enslavement in Egypt.

After Joseph Smith had taken these plates from their resting place at the Hill Cumorah, at the age of 21, in 1827 he began his translation. Although he began in 1827, the majority of this work was accomplished between April and June of 1829.[7]

As we have now traced the history of how the plates came to be and how Joseph acquired them, we may consider Joseph's particular method of translation.

How did Joseph Smith Translate the BOM?

Perhaps the most orthodox LDS answer to give in answer to this question is that Joseph Smith translated the plates "by the gift and power of God."[8] However, I will leave that conclusion for the reader to decide as we continue to elaborate upon the specific methodology used by Joseph in his translation. When one thinks of a person translating an ancient document, they might imagine a scholarly figure poring over some old parchment covered in ancient symbols and passionately scribbling down the proper contemporary meaning. Suffice it to say, Joseph's approach differs quite extraordinarily from this method or, indeed, any method one's mind would conjure when thinking of translation.

Before we describe his actual process, I want to lay out one of the barriers that made his translation so impressive. This point is commonly presented by LDS missionaries and apologists to demonstrate the miraculous nature of the coming about of the BOM.

---

6. "Golden Plates to Book of Mormon,".
7. Kimberly Richter, "The Book of Mormon: From Plates to Press,".
8. Church of Jesus Christ of Latter-day Saints, *The Holy Bible*.

First, Joseph was known to have little in the way of formal education. This is frequently cited to prove that there is no way that he could have taken on such a scholarly task of deciphering an ancient and unknown language into perfect King James English.[9]

Joseph's practice for translating the plates included himself and one other person acting as a scribe to write down the words that he was translating. Occasionally this was his wife, Emma Smith although, his right-hand man, Oliver Cowdery fulfilled this role the majority of the time. Joseph would call out words as they appeared to him and Cowdery would write them down as they were spoken. Thus far this is not entirely surprising or unorthodox. However, we must consider how Joseph did the actual *translating*. His preferred method has been very well documented within LDS history and has even been presented in Church essays.[10]

Joseph would utilize one of two instruments in his translation approach. One, would be the Urim and Thummim and the other would be his seer stone. Both of these tools were used similarly and accomplished the same goal. I will provide an excerpt from the LDS Church Essay *Book of Mormon Translation* to describe the translation instruments and procedure lest anyone assume I am creating a caricature of my own.

> One instrument, called in the Book of Mormon the "interpreters," is better known to Latter-day Saints today as the "Urim and Thummim." Joseph found the interpreters buried in the hill with the plates. Those who saw the interpreters described them as a clear pair of stones bound together with a metal rim. The Book of Mormon referred to this instrument, together with its breastplate, as a device "kept and preserved by the hand of the Lord" and "handed down from generation to generation, for the purpose of interpreting languages."
>
> The other instrument, which Joseph Smith discovered in the ground years before he retrieved the gold plates, was a small oval stone, or "seer stone." As a young man during the 1820s, Joseph Smith, like others in his day, used a seer stone to look for lost objects and buried treasure. As Joseph grew to understand his prophetic calling, he learned that he could use this stone for the higher purpose of translating scripture.[11]

---

9. "Book of Mormon Translation,".
10. "Book of Mormon Translation."
11. "Book of Mormon Translation."

CHAPTER 17: JOSEPH'S CLAIMS OF TRANSLATOR

As described, Joseph Smith would use both of these instruments in his translating, but it has been noted that frequently he would use the single seer stone rather than the Urim and Thummim for personal preference. How exactly would this method proceed? Another excerpt from the Church essay shines a little light on the details.

> According to these accounts, Joseph placed either the interpreters or the seer stone in a hat, pressed his face into the hat to block out extraneous light, and read aloud the English words that appeared on the instrument.[12]

Yes, as is described here, in his translating process, he would place his seer stone into a hat which he would then place his face into to block out any additional light and would read the words on the plates in their English form. An Institute Director for the Church Educational System of thirty-four years, Grant H. Palmer, further supports the basis for this translation practice. He lists a handful of Joseph's family and friends who corroborate that this was, in fact, his method. The list includes "Emma Hale Smith (Joseph's wife), Isaac Hale Joseph's father-in-law), Michael Morse (brother in law), Martin Harris [one of Joseph's early scribes and one of the three witnesses[13]], and Joseph Knight Sr[an employer and friend of Joseph Smith's]."[14][15] This description of Joseph's process is repeatedly mentioned by those who were witnesses to him working.

This was not a one-time event, rather, it was his primary approach. Joseph's wife, Emma Smith described the process herself from her time assisting as his scribe. "I frequently wrote day after day, often sitting at a table close by him, he sitting with his face buried in his hat, with the seer stone in it, and dictating hour after hour with nothing between us."[16] Additionally, Isaac Hale, Martin Harris, and Joseph Smith Sr. all confirmed that not only were the plates not in use during translation, but they were hidden in the woods.[17]

It is a well-documented fact of LDS history that Joseph Smith utilized a magic seer stone and placed his face into a hat to perform his translation of the BOM. This account is more than a little befuddling.

12. "Book of Mormon Translation."
13. Matthew McBride, "The Contributions of Martin Harris,".
14. Larry Porter, "The Joseph Knight Family,".
15. Palmer, *An Insider's View of Mormon Origins*.5.
16. *The Saints Herald Volume 26 1879.*
17. Palmer, *An Insider's View of Mormon Origins*.4.

After all, as I mentioned earlier, Joseph's approach to translation sounds vastly unlike what an ordinary person would expect. Aside from the somewhat strange appearance of this practice, it poses some real issues that ought to be sorted through. First, we will consider the use of a seer stone in his work of translation. Second, we will look at the implications this method has on ancient LDS history, and finally we will examine Joseph's other known attempts to act as a translator. Once this investigation is completed, a reader may be able to discern for oneself if "by the gift and power of God" is truly the most accurate depiction of the translation strategy of the BOM.

Joseph and the Seer Stone:

We have established that Joseph, similar to many others of his day, had a magical worldview. He believed (or at least claimed to believe) in the functionality of divining rods, seer stones, and spells protecting ancient, buried treasure. It was not uncommon for people in New England during the 19th century to believe in magic or that there may be buried treasure scattered throughout their lands. As such, many New England farmers would try their hand at digging for this buried treasure, perhaps in an effort to escape a life of backbreaking labor and poverty.

It should be further noted that this kind of practicing a spiritual sight or, second sight, as it is commonly referred to is not a unique product of the New England community. It has been practiced for much of history. One author describes "Egyptians stared into a pool of ink, the Greeks into a mirror, the Aztecs into a quartz crystal, and Europeans into a sword blade or glass of sherry- any translucent surface that made the eyes blur when long gazing. When Joseph Smith first began to use his seer or "peep" stone, he employed the folklore familiar to rural America."[18] It is important to note that, as many LDS apologists readily point out, the questionable method of Joseph Smith's translation (i.e. using a seer stone) is not necessarily condemning to his character as they were merely artifacts of his culture.

While it is true that the simple use of a seer stone for translation may not be deeply distressing (though perhaps a bit strange), Joseph's other purposes for his peep stone may spark a less favorable impression.

18. Fawn McKay Brodie, *No Man Knows My History: The Life of Joseph Smith, the Mormon Prophet*, 2nd ed., rev.enl.1st Vintage Books ed (New York: Vintage Books, 1995).21.

CHAPTER 17: JOSEPH'S CLAIMS OF TRANSLATOR

Like many in his day, Joseph Smith was a treasure hunter. Influenced by the culture around him, he began to practice using his seer stone in an attempt to lead others to find buried treasure. Treasure hunting, however, is not the only kind of work which Joseph applied himself to. He also engaged in laborious farm work. In fact, it was digging a well for a man named Mason Chase that Joseph discovered his favored seer stone. It may even be true that a majority of Joseph's work prior to organizing the church did not rely upon his magical gifts.

Despite this truth, it is indisputable that Joseph Smith was engaged in treasure hunting. One neighbor is recorded sharing that Joseph Smith advised that "there was buried money on his property, but that it could not be secured until a black sheep was taken to the spot, and "led around a circle" bleeding, with its throat cut."[19] Intrigued by this proposition, the neighbor offered up the sheep and allowed it to be used as was prescribed. However, apparently due to some failure to execute the process properly, the treasure was not apprehended.

Joseph acquired some notoriety for his ability to find "lost objects and buried treasure."[20] In fact, Joseph's mother described that Josiah Stoal "came all the way from Pennsylvania to see her son "on account of having heard that he possessed certain keys by which he could discern things invisible to the natural eye."[21] Joseph was then hired by Stoal to help him dig for an old Spaniard silver mine in Pennsylvania.[22] For his services, he was compensated with fourteen dollars per month[23] and free boarding. After "nearly a month" they were unable to locate this silver mine and gave up their search.[24]

While I feel that it has been well supported that Joseph was involved in treasure-hunting and use of magical objects, I want to provide two more resources that cement this part of Joseph's history. My redundancy in this study is warranted because there are some who attempt to provide a narrow view of LDS history which fails to account for the full extent of Joseph's participation in this activity.

First, it is documented that in 1826, during his employment with Josiah Stoal, Joseph Smith was arrested and taken to court on account

19. Brodie.20.
20. "Book of Mormon Translation."
21. Brodie, *No Man Knows My History*.28.
22. "Joseph Smith—History 1,".
23. "Volume 3 Chapter 3," *BYU Studies* (blog), 3.
24. "Joseph Smith—History 1."

of complaints of his being "a disorderly person and an impostor." His treasure hunting tendencies were corroborated by numerous witnesses including himself as he shared his testimony (this time lacking any religious content or a witness of the restored gospel) under oath. Below is what Joseph stated under oath.

> Prisoner Examined: says that he [. . .] had small part of time been employed in looking for mines, but the major part had been employed by said Stowel on his farm, and going to school. That he had a certain stone which he had occasionally looked at to determine where hidden treasures in the bowels of the earth were; that he professed to tell in this manner where gold mines were a distance underground, and had looked for Mr. Stowel several times, and had informed him where he could find these treasures, and Mr. Stowel had been engaged and digging for them. That at Palmyra he pretended to tell by looking at this stone where coined money was buried in Pennsylvania, and while at Palmyra had frequently ascertained in that way where lost property was of various kinds; that he had occasionally been in the habit of looking through this stone to find a lost property for three years, but of late had pretty much given it up on account of its injuring his health, especially his eyes, making them sore.[25]

Second, Joseph Smith further reports his activity in the third volume of *History of the Church* of which he was the editor.[26] In Chapter 3, there are a list of questions which are posed to Smith. One of these questions addresses his past as a "money digger". "Tenth—" Was not Joseph Smith a money digger?" Yes, but it was never a very profitable job for him, as he only got fourteen dollars a month for it."[27] Here it is confirmed that not only was he engaged in these activities, but he was also professionally involved (no matter how disappointing the compensation).

Here we have taken a brief excursion into Joseph Smith's history prior to founding the church. I hope that this study has added some context to Joseph's translating process and provided some insight into his personal background. This kind of an examination both illuminates the origins of some of Joseph's teachings and contextualizes his approach to translating using magical objects. As I asserted previously, Joseph's magical worldview was in no way anomalous to his time and culture. As such,

---

25. *Fraser's Magazine* (London : Longmans, Green, 1870).
26. "Elders' Journal, November 1837, Page 29,".
27. "Volume 3 Chapter 3," 3.

his belief in these things may not necessarily reflect poorly on his intellect or character. Although, it is true that if Joseph knowingly led people after treasure which he did not believe was there he would indeed be the fraud that many made him out to be.

As with many other things from the 19th century, the United States has all but completely moved past believing in myths of buried treasure, guardian spirits, enchantments, divining rods, and seer stones. I will leave it to the reader to decide for themselves if, in light of his magical worldview and his process of translation, Joseph Smith was truly carried along by the "gift and power of God" or if there was something other animating his work. Joseph's use of a seer stone as his primary tool in translation also encourages investigation into other aspects of his work on translating the golden plates as well as his claims of being a translator in general.

The Purpose of the Plates:

Another questionable item that Joseph's chosen method of translation presents is the purpose of the golden plates. Let us not forget that these plates were kept and carefully protected by the Nephite people. They were commanded by God to keep their record upon these plates and were committed to protecting them throughout the many wars that they fought. Finally, Moroni, in the last chapter of the BOM describes how he sealed up the records with the clear intention that they ought to be recovered and read in the future. The plates were sealed, hidden away, in a stone box for hundreds of years until they were ready to be revealed to Joseph Smith. These plates contain the only record of the Nephite people. If genuine, these plates are of inestimable value. It cannot be stressed enough how the history of the LDS church, indeed, of the entire foundation of the LDS belief structure is built upon these plates.

With this clearly being the case, we have to ask why they were not used in the translation. The Nephite peoples, Moroni, and even God Himself committed to the creation and preservation of the sacred golden plates and Joseph spent the majority of his time translating them with his face inside of his hat. This sounds nothing like *translation* how does one begin to translate an ancient document that they are not even looking at? Under this process, there might just as well have been *no writings* on the plates at all. Extending this reasoning further, there would be no need for *the plates* at all.

Is it truly tenable that the only apparent purpose for these allegedly invaluable plates is to inspire faith from witnesses in the truth of this story? It is not even the case that Joseph required anything that was found in the stone box prepared by Moroni. I could see some protestation that although the plates could, hypothetically, not be absolutely necessary, the Urim and Thummim were still needed for Joseph to look into to see the translation. However, as was already noted above, Joseph did not even need these. Rather, he exchanged them for his personal seer stone which he had been using long before.

These points that we have examined lead us to question whether or not what Joseph was doing truly looks like *translating*. He himself did not claim to be merely speaking inspired words as could have been the case. Instead, he insisted upon the authority and reality of these golden plates and the fact that he was translating them thus making them an essential element in his narrative. It is curious that, in his practice of translation, he would have no need of the very items Moroni provided.

Continuing our investigation of Joseph's role and ability as a translator, we will examine a couple other instances of Joseph practicing his skills.

Chapter 18: Book of Abraham

THERE ARE TWO OTHER well-known attempts of translation performed by Joseph Smith. One of these attempts has been included in the canon of LDS scripture and has been the cause of skepticism to many both in and outside of the church. The other is somewhat less well known but is worthy of careful examination in its own rite. The first of these is known as the Book of Abraham.

The Book of Abraham is one of the most important topics in LDS studies. I believe that it may be the single greatest threat to Joseph Smith's credibility. True, we have already compiled quite a list of items that ought to give an investigator pause. However, this topic is unique in the clarity of its conclusions. The LDS apologists have a response for almost every critique of the LDS Church. They say that the specificity of prophecy is miraculous and that anachronisms can be explained away by the fact that only 1% of the Americas has been surveyed.

However, on this topic the apologists have very little to say and what little they can say is replete with concessions. There are no "silver bullets" as far as Joseph's credibility is concerned, however, if there was one this would be it.

The Book of Abraham, as it is known in the LDS community is a 5-chapter book of doctrine held within the Pearl of Great Price. It "was first published in 1842 and was canonized as part of the Pearl of Great Price in 1880."[1]

The introduction to the book reads "A Translation of some ancient Records, that have fallen into our hands from the catacombs of Egypt- The

---

1. "Translation and Historicity of the Book of Abraham,".

writings of Abraham while he was in Egypt, called the Book of Abraham, written by his own hand, upon papyrus." This book contains, among other things, a narrative of Abraham nearly being sacrificed by a pagan priest, a brief account of Egyptian government, an early account of the creation of the earth, and a preliminary theology of a plurality of gods. As described by the introduction, it was translated by Joseph Smith from Papyri that came into his possession.

Around July, 3 1835, a man named Michael H. Chandler brought his touring Egyptian exhibit to Kirtland Ohio where Joseph Smith and the Saints were located. His exhibition contained "four Egyptian mummies and a selection of Egyptian papyrus documents."[2] As we recall that the BOM was translated from a reformed Egyptian language, it is no surprise that this exhibit was fascinating to Joseph Smith who "offered preliminary translations to the exhibitor."[3] Not long after Joseph's interest was piqued, the early LDS Church purchased the exhibit for $2,400. Esteemed Egyptologist Robert K. Ritner describes Joseph's discoveries as he sorted through the Egyptian documents.

> Smith quickly recognized several biblically themed compositions within the papyri, eventually including the Book of Abraham (P. Joseph Smith 1), the record of Joseph of Egypt (P. Joseph Smith 2 and 3) and a tale of an Egyptian Princess Katumin or Kah tou mun (P. Joseph Smith 4). Only the first of these translations was ever published.[4]

When displaying his collection of Egyptian artifacts to visitors he was recorded describing some of the hieroglyphs on the papyri saying: "That is the handwriting of Abraham, the Father of the Faithful; this is the autograph of Moses, and these lines were written by his brother Aaron."[5] This is a similar description to what was included in the introduction that the papyri were written by Abraham "by his own hand".

These papyri, allegedly written by Abraham himself, (although this view has been abandoned by many contemporary LDS apologists) were translated by Joseph Smith between the Summer of 1835 and the Spring of 1842 when all five chapters were published in the Church's newspaper

---

2. Robert Kriech Ritner, Marc Coenen, and Robert Kriech Ritner, *The Joseph Smith Egyptian Papyri: A Complete Edition ; P. JS 1 - 4 and the Hypocephalus of Sheshonq* (Salt Lake City, Utah: Signature Books, 2013).1.

3. Ritner, Coenen, and Ritner.1.

4. Ritner, Coenen, and Ritner. 2.

5. Brodie, *No Man Knows My History*. 293.

CHAPTER 18: BOOK OF ABRAHAM

alongside the printed copies of the papyri Joseph translated them from.[6] These copies of the papyri, however, contained only the drawings separated from the actual "hieroglyphs or hieratic characters that originally surrounded the vignettes."[7] The copies of these papyri are now referred to as facsimiles 1, 2, and 3.

A church essay describes what happened to the papyri after they were translated. "Joseph Smith's family sold the papyri and the mummies in 1856. The papyri were divided up and sold to various parties; historians believe that most were destroyed in the Great Chicago Fire of 1871." For quite some time it was believed that the Joseph Smith papyri were gone; never to be seen again. This presented a particularly difficult problem for scholars who wanted a way to check Joseph's claims of being a translator. In a way similar to the BOM, the Book of Abraham was now untestable. The papyri, just like the golden plates, had disappeared.

On November 27, of 1967 "eleven pieces of Egyptian papyri originally purchased by Joseph Smith were recovered from the Metropolitan Museum of Art in New York City. Among them were facsimile 1 and Papyrus 11, both important to Joseph Smith in his translation of Abraham 1 through 2:18 in the Pearl of great price."[8] These papyri were confirmed to be the very ones used in Joseph's translation as they were fixed to paper which had drawings of an LDS temple and maps of the Kirtland, Ohio area on the back. Further, they came with "an affidavit by Emma Smith verifying they had been in the possession of Joseph Smith."[9]

This was an invaluable discovery. At last, there was a concrete way to test the translating capabilities of Joseph Smith. Papyri containing hieroglyphs which Joseph translated had been discovered. To say that the following studies failed to support Joseph's credibility as a translator would be an understatement. Indeed, the result of the evaluation of Joseph's translation has become one of the most powerful and damaging blows to credibility of the LDS Church. Many, of those who have left the church provide this as a key reason that they lost their testimony. As we continue with this topic, we will explore the results of the critical examination of the translation and historicity of the Book of Abraham and why these results have been so destructive for the narrative of the LDS Church.

6. "Translation and Historicity of the Book of Abraham."
7. "Translation and Historicity of the Book of Abraham."
8. Palmer, *An Insider's View of Mormon Origins*. 12.
9. Jeremy T Runnells, *CES Letter: My Search for Answers to My Mormon Doubts* (United States: CES Letter Foundation, 2017). 42.

In brief, the studies have unanimously concluded that the translation of the Book of Abraham is completely inaccurate. The words that comprise the LDS book of doctrine *in no way* conform to the Egyptian hieroglyphs that composed the writing on the documents which Joseph claimed to have translated. For a more thorough examination of the critiques made of the Book of Abraham there are several points that I want to highlight. First, who is it, exactly, who disagrees with Joseph's translation? Was it merely a handful of uneducated anti-Mormons? Second, in what ways did Joseph's translation fall short? Third, we will look at some additional peculiar elements within the Book of Abraham.

First, who is claiming that Joseph's translation is inaccurate? The essay released by the LDS Church on this topic *Translation and Historicity of the Book of Abraham* offers the following answer to this question. "Mormon and non-Mormon Egyptologists agree that the characters on the fragments do not match the translation given in the book of Abraham."[10] That is, they concede that this is no small faction of individuals trying to seed doubt. No, on the contrary, even the LDS scholars in the field of Egyptology agree that the translation of the Book of Abraham does not match the Egyptian characters. This is striking. There is no way around it. Joseph's skills as translator have been put to the test and have been definitively denounced even by those who are sympathetic to his cause. Far from a handful of malicious skeptics gathering to discredit the LDS Church by falsifying translations, the LDS scholars themselves are forced to submit to this conclusion.

It has been concretely demonstrated that Joseph's translation was false in its entirety. The case for the Book of Abraham has been closed, as Ritner describes, "for well over a century,"[11] and it is not only LDS critics who understand this. Rather, this conclusion has been communicated by "Mormon and non-Mormon Egyptologists"[12] alike.

Secondly, in what ways was Joseph's translation inadequate? There are at least two significant errors that Joseph made in his translation attempt. Joseph failed to properly identify the Egyptian manuscripts and he utterly failed to properly translate the words on them.

Joseph described the papyri he used to translate the Book of Abraham to be a record written by the very hand of Abraham. However, those who have studied the texts have discovered that "these fragments

---

10. "Translation and Historicity of the Book of Abraham."
11. Ritner, Coenen, and Ritner. 7.
12. "Translation and Historicity of the Book of Abraham."

date to between the third century B.C.E. and the first century C.E., long after Abraham lived."[13] As such, the papyri were certainly not written "by the hand" of Abraham himself. This inaccuracy is not completely condemning however as many LDS apologists point out, the "in the hand of" may not have been literal.

Indeed, it would be no problem if the papyri that Joseph Smith possessed were the preserved copies of copies of the original record by Abraham. Thus, even if it were not the original record written by Abraham, as long as the record was reliably preserved it could be translated as holy doctrine of the church. This is the way the Bible has been preserved. When dealing with ancient documents, it is highly unlikely to find original manuscripts for a number of reasons. As a result, one response to this objection is to state that Joseph possessed, a record of Abraham's writing preserved by its copies.

Though the challenge presented by verbiage "the hand of Abraham" can be resolved it does not answer what the text actually was. In contradiction to what was claimed by Joseph Smith, "scholars have identified the papyrus fragments as parts of standard funerary texts that were deposited with mummified bodies."[14] That is, they contain no record of Abraham about to be sacrificed nor an account of creation. Rather, they were discovered to be part of the standard funerary texts that were buried with the deceased. Facsimile 1 from Joseph's papyri was evaluated by Egyptologists John A. Wilson and Richard A. Parker in 1968 and discovered to be "sections of a late mortuary text known as a "Book of Breathings," copied for a Theban priest named Hor."[15] This conclusion has been shared by virtually every informed scholar on the topic.

This discovery demonstrated that Joseph drastically failed to identify the documents that he was handling, much less translate them. Not only was this not the record *written* by Abraham, but it was not a record of Abraham at all. Rather, it was found to be generic, pagan funerary texts. With these preliminary errors, one can easily guess the level of accuracy in Joseph's "translation."

Regarding the translation itself, there are three documents, called facsimiles, included in in the Pearl of Great Price which are the materials from which the Book of Abraham was translated. Each of these facsimiles

---

13. "Translation and Historicity of the Book of Abraham."
14. "Translation and Historicity of the Book of Abraham."
15. Ritner, Coenen, and Ritner, *The Joseph Smith Egyptian Papyri*. 63.

will be provided below along with Joseph's translation compared to the current academic translation of the Egyptian imagery

Due to their age, some of the papyri were damaged when Joseph obtained them. Joseph took it into his own hands to complete the missing pieces. In these cases the accurate versions and translations of the facsimiles are supported by "egyptology and the same scene discovered elsewhere in Egypt."[16]

---

16. "Book of Abraham | CES Letter,". 43.

Facsimile 1

CHAPTER 18: BOOK OF ABRAHAM

Joseph's Version

1. The Angel of the Lord.
2. Abraham fastened upon an altar.
3. The idolatrous priest of Elkenah attempting to offer Abraham as a sacrifice.
4. The altar for sacrifice.
5. The idolatrous god of Elkenah.
6. The idolatrous god of Libnah.
7. The idolatrous god of Mahmackrah.
8. The idolatrous god of Korash.
9. The idolatrous god of Pharoah.
10. Abraham in Egypt.
11. Represents the pillars of Heaven.
12. Raukeeyang, expanse or firmament over our heads.

Egyptological Version

1. The *ba*-spirit of Osiris.
2. The prone image of Isis.
3. The god Anubis.
4. The lion couch.
5. The god Qebehsenuef.
6. The god Duamutef.
7. The god Hapi.
8. The god Imseti.
9. The god Horus-Sobek.
10. Offering stand.
11. Niched brick.
12. The Nile river

Facsimile 2

Joseph's Version

1. Kolob.
2. Oliblish, the next grand governing creation.
3. God sitting upon his throne.
4. Raukeeyang, expanse or firmament of the heavens.
5. Enish-go-on-dosh, a governing planet, the Sun.
6. The earth in its four quarters
7. God sitting upon his throne.
8. Numbers 8–21 are untranslated

Egyptological Version

1. The God Atum. (22 and 23 are worshipping apes crowned with lunar discs.)
2. Two-headed deity with the standard of Wepwawet.
3. A fictional interpolation by Joseph Smith.
4. The mummiform god Sokar.
5. Hathor the heavenly cow with a goddess whose head is a disc with the Wedjat-Eye, holding a water lily.
6. The mummiform four sons of Horus.
7. The god Min-Amon in half-bird half-human form with an erection.
8. Not providing translation for 8–21.

Facsimile 3

Joseph's Version

1. Abraham on Pharoah's throne.
2. King Pharoah.
3. Abraham in Egypt.
4. Prince of Pharoah.
5. Shulem, one of the king's principal waiters.
6. Olimlah, a slave of the prince

Egyptological Version

1. The god Osiris.
2. The goddess Isis.
3. A libation table with a Nile lily blossom on top.
4. The goddess Ma'at.
5. The deceased priest, Hor.
6. The god Anubis

CHAPTER 18: BOOK OF ABRAHAM

To provide a brief summary, Joseph got *none* of the names correct. He failed to correctly name any of the Egyptian gods. He utterly failed to identify what was happening in each vignette. He confused gods for servants and males for females. His mistranslation of figure 7 in facsimile 2 is particularly appalling.

The portions of the papyri that were not extant due to damage he filled in himself. More than half of the figures in facsimile 2 he did not even attempt to provide a translation for. Ritner points out that Joseph's numbering "indicates that he could not recognize the usual order of texts (right to left), nor could he distinguish texts written upside down."[17]

These errors are not minor. They represent a complete misunderstanding of virtually every detail of the images. Is it appropriate for the Book of Abraham to be called a translation? It deviates completely from what is written on the manuscripts.

If not from translation, from whence came the content in the Book of Abraham? Three-time director of LDS Institutes of Religion in CA and UT, Grant H. Palmer describes some curious similarities between the Book of Abraham and certain other sources. Palmer notes Joseph Smith's familiarity with the works of Jewish historian Josephus who "identified Abraham as a resident of Chaldea"[18] among other things. He advises that certain descriptions of this patriarch within the Book of Abraham seem to echo what was written of him by this early historian which Joseph is known to have studied.

Further, Palmer advises that 86 percent of the verses in Abraham chapters 2, 4, and 5 "are quotations or close paraphrases of KJV wording" of Genesis chapters 1, 2, and 11. Marquardt also describes the similarity between the content of the Book of Abraham and that found in the book of Genesis, especially the KJV.[19]

The Book of Abraham is one of the most important pieces of LDS history. Whether one chooses to believe that it is divine Scripture or not, the book as well as its implications must be contended with. Joseph claimed to have found the handwritten record of Abraham. He then translated this record into the same book that the LDS Church quotes as scripture. For a great time, the papyri were lost and, similar to the Book of Mormon, Joseph's translation was not able to be tested by scholars. Due to their rediscovery, those papyri have been placed under the spotlight of

17. Ritner, 265.
18. Palmer, *An Insider's View of Mormon Origins*.17.
19. Ritner, 11-52.

academic scrutiny and have yielded ruinous results. Joseph claims to be a translator, but his translation here is invariably false.

After reviewing his attempt to translate the Book of Abraham and finding it unreliable are we to trust his translation of the BOM which has remained, to this day, untestable? If he was unable to translate the Book of Abraham, why should we believe he had the ability to translate from the golden plates? Before we conclude our study on Joseph Smith's claims of being a translator, we will look to one more, somewhat less well known, instance of Joseph's exercise of this divine skill.

Chapter 19: **Kinderhook Plates**

IN ADDITION TO HIS work on the BOM and the Book of Abraham, Joseph Smith made at least one more known attempt at translating an ancient record. This record is now known as the Kinderhook plates. Unlike the other two attempts, this one never received a formal translation and was never published. The Kinderhook plates were allegedly found at an American Indian burial mound near the city of Kinderhook Illinois in 1843 by a man named Robert Wiley. The plates contained an ancient text which was unreadable to its discoverers.

In a letter to the editor of the LDS publication, *Times and Seasons* penned by a W. P. Harris, it was described that Wiley was digging in a "large mound" in the Kinderhook vicinity. After digging a hole about 10 feet deep, he struck rock, it began to rain, and he took a pause from his project. We will recall that money-digging was not an uncommon practice in that culture. For such a reason, Wiley's behavior was not likely deemed completely out of the ordinary.

Approximately a week later Wiley solicited some assistance and returned to his digging. After removing two feet of rock the prospectors discovered their treasure; charcoal, ashes, burnt human bones, and "a bundle [. . .] that consisted of six plates of brass of a bell shape, each having a hole near the small end, and a ring through them all, and clasped with two clasps. The rings and clasps appeared to be iron very much oxydated. The plates appeared first to be copper, and had the appearance of being covered with characters."[1] This description of

---

1. "Volume 5 Chapter 19," *BYU Studies* (blog).

the findings and the history of their discovery was attested to by at least nine citizens in an affidavit.

As one might expect, much like the papyri which Joseph reviewed in his translation of the Book of Abraham, the Kinderhook plates were a point of great curiosity to Joseph Smith and many others in his community. As described in one of the Church's essays on the topic, the Kinderhook plates were "six bell-shaped brass plates about three inches in height."[2] These plates were covered in symbols which appeared to be unknown ancient symbols.[3] As Joseph Smith had acquired a reputation for his ability to translate ancient documents, he found himself in a position to examine these plates.

As previously described, no formal translation of these plates was ever published. This is a point that the LDS apologists cling to. While it is true that no *formal* translation ever occurred, there is a report that Joseph encountered the plates and provided a preliminary examination and translation. In *History of the Church Volume 5* it even appears that Joseph himself claimed that he translated them. The text reads: "I have translated a portion of them, and find they contain the history of the person with whom they were found. He was a descendant of Ham, through the loins of Pharaoh, king of Egypt, and that he received his kingdom from the Ruler of heaven and earth."[4] Despite the first-person language, this quotation was appropriated from the journal of Joseph's clerk, William Clayton. In the 1930 publication of *History of the Church*, overseen by B.H. Roberts, the text was altered from Clayton's description of Joseph's translation to read as though it were described from Joseph's own first-person perspective. No doubt this alteration was endorsed to further emphasize the importance of the discovery.[5] Indeed, another ancient record had been discovered and Joseph, once again, committed himself to providing a translation.

The community was so certain of the value of this discovery and the results of its impending translation that they published the following in the May 1843 issue of *Times and Seasons* "We learn there was a Mormon present when the plates were found, who it is said, leaped for joy at the

2. "Kinderhook Plates," .
3. John Dehlin, "Kinderhook Plates," *Mormon Stories* (blog).
4. "Volume 5 Chapter 19."
5. Dehlin, "Kinderhook Plates."

discovery, and remarked that it would go to prove the authenticity of the Book of Mormon- which it undoubtedly will."[6]

Unfortunately, the exact location of the plates became unknown from around the year 1844.[7] This severely complicated further studies which were warranted by statements provided by the individuals who initially discovered the plates.

Contrary to Joseph's description that the plates were an ancient record containing the history of a descendant of Ham. Wilbur Fugate and Robert Wiley, both provided letters describing that the Kinderhook plates were not of ancient origin, rather, they were created and planted to appear ancient. Fugate, Wiley, and a local blacksmith conspired together to create the Kinderhook plates, or so they described. In his letter, Fugate even provides the methods used for the creation of the plates.

> Wiley and I made the hieroglyphics by making impressions on beeswax and filling them with acid and putting it on the plates. When they were finished we put them together with rust made of nitric acid, old iron and lead, and bound them with a piece of hoop iron, covering them completely with the rust.[8]

Despite the claims by the creators of these plates declaring that they were intentionally fabricated in order to test Joseph Smith, the LDS community continued to believe in the authenticity of the plates. Because they were lost and, as a result, unable to be tested, there was no reason to doubt Smith's credibility in asserting the legitimacy of the plates. Indeed, a couple of troublesome fellows who had only personal letters to demonstrate their alleged hoax held no weight whatsoever when compared to the word of the living prophet himself. Thus, once again, we have an example of a lost record partially translated by Joseph Smith.

Though apologists assert that Joseph never claimed to have translated them, his clerk claimed that he did, and it appears that the rest of the Church believed the same as is demonstrated by numerous early church documents. Having only the word of the men who found the plates versus that of Joseph Smith, there was no way to definitively vindicate either perspective regarding the authenticity of the Kinderhook plates.

---

6. "Times and Seasons Vol 4,".

7. Stanley B. Kimball, "Kinderhook Plates Brought to Joseph Smith Appear to Be a Nineteenth-Century Hoax,".

8. Kimball.

In 1920 one of the Kinderhook plates was discovered "and came into the possession of the Chicago Historical Society."[9] In a very similar circumstance to that of the Book of Abraham, the Kinderhook plates were now available for testing. Rigorous academic testing could help to determine whether these plates were genuinely of ancient origin.

In the decades that followed, numerous tests were performed by a variety of individuals. One of these tests was even conducted by a Dr. Paul Cheesman who was associated with Brigham Young University. Unfortunately, these tests were inconclusive. That is because they were using only "non-destructive" testing methods. This means that the process of testing would restrict researchers to examine using any given method so long as it did no damage to the plate. While the ethic of protecting the artifact can be admired, it impeded the investigation as the accuracy of these non-destructive tests failed to provide conclusive results. Because of the lack of a conclusive answer, "Church historians continued to insist on the authenticity of the Kinderhook plates until 1980."[10]

In 1980 permission was granted to begin destructive testing on the plate. Through a process of rigorous testing which, it appears, included both LDS and Non-LDS scholars the conclusion was reached that the plate was *not* of ancient origin. The scholars working on these tests also carefully considered the possibility that the plate owned by the Chicago Historical Society was not an original, but a copy of the Kinderhook plates. Through a process of careful examination, they determined with great certainty that this was not the case. The Church essay *Kinderhook Plates Brought to Joseph Smith Appear to Be a Nineteenth-Century Hoax* provides a succinct explanation of the conclusive discoveries. "The conclusion, therefore, is that the Chicago plate is indeed one of the original Kinderhook plates, which now fairly well evidences them to be faked antiquities."[11]

Here then, we have another example of Joseph's skills in translation. While it is true that no formal translation was provided, we have a piece of a preliminary translation that Joseph gave. In this translation, not only did he fail to translate accurately, he failed to recognize that the plates were fraudulent. This is not encouraging news for those who hold to the belief that Joseph possessed great god-given powers in translating

---

9. Kimball.

10. Richard L. Bushman, *Joseph Smith: Rough Stone Rolling*, 1. Vintage Books ed (New York: Vintage Books, 2007).490.

11. Kimball, "Kinderhook Plates Brought to Joseph Smith Appear to Be a Nineteenth-Century Hoax."

CHAPTER 19: KINDERHOOK PLATES

ancient documents. Indeed, the Kinderhook plates appear to be another testament against Joseph Smith and his claims of being a translator.

As we come to our conclusion concerning Joseph's role as a translator, it is worthwhile to take stock of what we have covered. We examined Joseph's preferred method of translation, which he used in his work on the BOM, placing his face inside of a hat with his seer stone. We then continued to evaluate two additional attempts that Joseph made at translation. In all three cases, the BOM the Book of Abraham, and the Kinderhook plates, the translation was initially thought untestable because the plates or papyri were lost. However, in two of these instances, the materials were rediscovered, and testing was completed. In both cases the testing revealed that Joseph catastrophically failed to provide accurate translations. Indeed, he failed to ascertain the identity of the documents that he was attempting to translate.

This leaves only the BOM. As we consider Joseph's three translations, the two which were testable proved to be thoroughly erroneous. Are we to believe that the one which is unable to be subjected to testing is true? Is a one out of three record probable or even believable? In careful consideration of these topics, along with everything else that has been described in the previous chapters, I ask: can one continue to believe with any confidence that Joseph Smith was a translator using the gift and power of God?

Chapter 20: Joseph Smith's Missing Works Cited Page

WITH ALL THE FLAWS and Joseph's questionable translation method, is the BOM truly to be seen as an inerrant and inspired work translated by Joseph Smith through the gift and power of God? I assert that the answer is an emphatic "no." If I am to dispense with the LDS theory for the production of the BOM, it is only proper that I attempt to establish my own. In the pages to follow I will provide an explanation for the creation of the BOM as a literary work authored by Joseph Smith.

As any LDS apologist will advise, I have my work cut out for me. After all, Joseph Smith was young, with little education and the BOM is a powerful 531-page witness of Christ. The accomplishment of writing the BOM is indeed very impressive and with the following study I do not pretend to know for certain *exactly* how it was accomplished. Rather, in the pages to follow, I endeavor to provide a speculative description of how the BOM *might* have been created. Though I recognize the potential inadequacy of this study, throughout its course I have made some discoveries that I find profoundly convincing. Indeed, I believe that the theory which I lay out is vastly more reasonable than the traditional LDS perspective.

How could the BOM have been written if it was not translated from an ancient record by the gift and power of God?

My answer will be comprised of two main elements. These are—a review of Joseph Smith's mental capacity and the influences around him; both literary and otherwise.

CHAPTER 20: JOSEPH SMITH'S MISSING WORKS CITED PAGE

It is worth noting that in the earliest translations of the BOM Joseph did not even call himself the translator. Whereas in modern editions the title page reads: "Translated by Joseph Smith, Jun." the original 1830 edition reads "By Joseph Smith, Junior, Author and Proprietor." While I am aware that this is not necessarily an admission of authorship, it is a curious artifact especially as this is exactly what I will be proposing as we proceed. Entertainingly, at least in the early print, it appears that Joseph and I do not disagree as to how the book was created.

Chapter 21: Joseph's Abilities

WE BEGIN BY EXAMINING Joseph's mind. Far from being the ignorant or simple-minded child that so many assert him to have been, Joseph Smith had quite an active mind and was eager to learn. There are numerous details in his background which help us understand how it is possible for him to have written the BOM. The three that we will focus on presently are his education, his active and imaginative mind, and his speaking ability and background.

First, as we have stated numerous times up to this point, one of the common claims that LDS apologists use to bolster their claims that Joseph could never have written the BOM, is that he had very little education. This characteristic is more than likely drawn from a quote that Lucy Smith (Joseph's Mother) made about him in a history concerning their family. She says: "he seemed much less inclined to the perusal of books than any of the rest of our children, but far more given to meditation and deep study."[1] In addition to this description that Joseph was not an avid reader, there are claims that Joseph had very "little formal education."[2] These claims paint the picture of Joseph as a simple pioneer boy who would not have had the mental talent for authoring such an impressive work, or indeed any work of literature at all. While it is true that Joseph Smith was no highly trained scholar, he did have some exposure to formal education.

---

1. "Biographical Sketches of Joseph Smith the Prophet, and His Progenitors for Many Generations, Page i,".

2. Elder Jay E. Jensen Of the Seventy Executive Director and Curriculum Department, "The Prophet Joseph Smith, an Extraordinary Teacher,".

In an essay exploring the topic of Joseph's education, scholar William Davis concludes that cumulatively, Joseph likely achieved about 7 years of formal academic training.³ While this does not indicate that he was a prestigious academic, it is certainly not the case that he was fundamentally without an education.

In addition, many are unaware of the fact that both of Joseph's parents had connections to formal education. Lucy Smith's mother, Lydia Mack, was a schoolteacher and, Joseph Smith Sr., in addition to farming, was also a professional schoolteacher for a portion of his life. Education was held in high esteem in the Smith house.⁴ Davis elaborates further in his essay that "after his training at the prestigious Moor's Charity School, Hyrum, Joseph's second oldest brother, would have been expected to share in the education of his younger siblings."⁵ With these details added to the narrative, one can see that Joseph was far from being isolated from academic learning. In many ways it was well within his grasp, and he seems to have partaken quite freely.

In addition to his described education, Joseph Smith appears to have had a powerful imagination and an active mind from a young age. His stories were captivating to others. I believe that Joseph's involvement in magical practices (even to the point of being hired as a professional treasure hunter) demonstrates the unique power of his creative mind. If, as is almost certainly the case, we assume that the modern reader does not believe that Joseph's stories or practices during his money-digging days were based in reality, we find a compelling illustration of the strength of his imagination. A similar conclusion regarding the character of Joseph's mind is presented by B.H Roberts who described him as possessing "a vivid, and strong, and creative imagination."⁶ Joseph's mother also gives an important description of Joseph's imaginative abilities. She describes:

> I presume our family presented an aspect as singular as any that ever lived upon the face of the earth- all seated in a circle, father, mother, sons, and daughters, and giving the most profound attention to a boy, eighteen years of age [. . .] He would describe the ancient inhabitants of this continent, their dress, mode of travelling, and the animals upon which they rode; their cities,

---

3. William Davis, "Reassessing Joseph Smith Jr.'s Formal Education," *Dialogue: A Journal of Mormon Thought* 49, no. 4 (December 1, 2016): 1–58.

4. Davis.30-31.

5. Davis.30-31.

6. Roberts and Madsen, *Studies of the Book of Mormon*.50.

their buildings, with every particular; their mode of warfare; and also their religious worship. This he would do with as much ease, seemingly, as if he had spent his whole life among them.[7]

This description is very telling. The whole family would sit before Joseph as he would describe to them the particulars of the practices of the ancient Americans. Lucy proceeds to state that Joseph's description was so lucid it was as if he had lived his whole life among them. This story further supports the perspective that Joseph had a strong and vivid imagination.

There are some who will assert that Joseph's stories, as described by his mother, had a different origin than his imagination. As LDS history states, Joseph met with the angel, Moroni, numerous times before his acquisition of the plates. In their meetings, Moroni taught Joseph about the ancient Americans, "who they were, and from whence they came; a brief sketch of their origin, progress, civilization, laws, governments, of their righteousness and iniquity, and the blessings of God being finally withdrawn from them as a people"[8]

For some, this will be a compelling explanation for the origin of Joseph's stories. However, I still find this difficult to believe. Poignantly, Lucy mentions that Joseph described "the animals upon which they rode" and other such details. This specific point is important because we know that the ancient Americans did not ride animals. This is an anachronism as we have discussed previously.

Further, as B.H. Roberts points out, "all this happened *before* even *the second interview with Moroni* had taken place."[9] Are we to believe that Joseph met with the angel Moroni a single time and acquired enough information to amuse his family as though "he had spent his whole life among them?" Beyond this, why did Moroni give him inaccurate information? Or is it more reasonable to assume that he conjured this information (or at least a portion of it) from his own mind?

One final point solidifies the fact of Joseph's creative mind. He himself admits this. In a letter to Oliver Cowdery who was arranging a "publication of a series of historical letters," he wrote:

---

7. "Biographical Sketches of Joseph Smith the Prophet, and His Progenitors for Many Generations, Page i."

8. Smith Joseph, *History of the Church: 1839-1842*. (Place of publication not identified: Deseret Book, 1991).439.

9. Roberts and Madsen, *Studies of the Book of Mormon*.244.

> As is common to most, or all youths, I fell into many vices and follies; but as my accusers are, and have been forward to accuse me of being guilty of gross and outrageous violations of the peace and good order of the Community, I take the occasion to remark that, though, as I have said above . . . I fell into many vices and follies, I have not, neither can it be sustained, in truth, been guilty of wronging or injuring any man or society of men; and those imperfections to which I allude, and for which I have often had occasion to lament, *were a light, and too often, a vain mind, exhibiting a foolish and trifling conversation.*

Roberts elaborates upon Joseph's statement, "and whence came these manifestations of human weakness . . . but from that fruitful source of both folly and strength, the over strong faculty of imagination?"[10]

Joseph not only displayed some education and an active mind, but he was a compelling speaker. Joseph's proven skill as an orator was likely essential for him as he was in the process of writing the BOM. His speaking is especially significant as the whole book was initially dictated to a scribe. William Davis describes that "the Book of Mormon stands as one of the longest recorded oral performances in the history of the United States."[11] Davis wrote an entire book on how Joseph's exposure to the extemporaneous preaching culture of Methodist ministers is to be recognized as an explanatory key for this accomplishment. Davis' work on the subject is technical, enlightening, and convincing.

Considering this, one sees that it is appropriate to view the authoring of the BOM as an oratory as well as a literary achievement. We will proceed by reviewing a couple of points that help to illustrate Joseph's skill in this discipline. First, as his mother detailed, he seems to have been able to provide exciting and detailed descriptions/stories. Per her description, he is shown to be at least exciting enough to capture the ears of his family members.

Second, according to an Orasmus Turner, Joseph was known to have participated in a "juvenile debating club," where he would "help us solve some portentous questions of moral or political ethics."[12] In the

---

10. Roberts and Madsen.245.

11. William L. Davis, *Visions in a Seer Stone: Joseph Smith and the Making of the Book of Mormon* (Chapel Hill: The University of North Carolina Press, 2020). 2.

12. Turner, O. (Orasmus), *History of the Pioneer Settlement of Phelps and Gorham's Purchase, and Morris' Reserve; Embracing the Counties of Monroe, Ontario, Livingston, Yates, Steuben, Most of Wayne and Allegany, and Parts of Orleans, Genesee and Wyoming. To Which Is Added, a Supplement, or Extension of the Pioneer History of Monroe*

same description it is noted that Joseph found himself involved (however briefly) in a role with the Methodist Church.

Joseph himself states that he was well acquainted with numerous Christian denominations, however, he found himself to be "somewhat partial to the Methodist sect," to the point that he "felt some desire to be united with them."[13] It is not surprising that Joseph found himself drawn to this denomination. The Methodists were active, at the time, near where Joseph lived in Palmyra New York. There was even a "Methodist camp meeting held one mile from Palmyra, New York on 7 June 1826- a pivotal time in Joseph Smith's life."[14] LDS Scholar Dan Vogel notes that:

> At one time he [Joseph Smith] joined the probationary class of the Methodist church in Palmyra, and made some active demonstrations of engagedness, though his assumed convictions were insufficiently grounded or abiding to carry him along to the saving point of conversion, and he soon withdrew from the class.[15]

At some point during these classes, it appears that Joseph even became a lay exhorter for the Methodist preachers. Even Orasmus Turner, who viewed Joseph rather critically, described Joseph's skill and involvement. "After catching a spark of Methodism in the camp meeting, away down in the woods, on the Vienna road, he was a very passable exhorter in evening meetings."[16] William Davis describes the attributes necessary for being a successful exhorter. "Exhortation skills thus involved active listening to and repetition of the minster's message, the performance and repetition of formulaic patterns, and improvisational techniques that could respond to immediate concerns of any given sermon or audience."[17] Davis goes on to say:

County ... (Rochester: W. Alling, 1851).

13. "Joseph Smith—History 1."48.

14. Palmer, *An Insider's View of Mormon Origins*. 96.

15. Dan Vogel, *Early Mormon Documents*. (Salt Lake City: Signature Books, 2000). 396.

16. Turner, O. (Orasmus), *History of the Pioneer Settlement of Phelps and Gorham's Purchase, and Morris' Reserve; Embracing the Counties of Monroe, Ontario, Livingston, Yates, Steuben, Most of Wayne and Allegany, and Parts of Orleans, Genesee and Wyoming. To Which Is Added, a Supplement, or Extension of the Pioneer History of Monroe County ...*

17. Davis, *Visions in a Seer Stone*. 37.

Smith's participation as an exhorter also suggests his religious aspirations. The engagement of unlicensed exhorters in repeated performances during class meetings inevitably indicated their growing desires to become fully licensed preachers. Apart from being an instrument in God's hands to awaken souls to their spiritual condition, exhortations functioned as entry-level sermons that revealed the speaker's talents, providing a way for aspiring preachers to develop their oratorical skills.[18]

Joseph likely never achieved the position of becoming a licensed exhorter as he failed to remain in the classes long enough to secure membership to the church.[19] However, it certainly appears that his exposure to this tradition gave him the opportunity to hone his rhetorical skills. "Methodist preaching valorized the dynamic, affective appeals to an audience over the less effective, pedantic styles."[20] Rather than appearing academic and scrutinous, these ministers were known to be exciting and emotionally stirring. They took special care to speak with passion and emotion, believing that by doing so their sermons would be filled with the power of the Spirit.[21] Palmer appropriately references the words of "Presbyterian Charles G. Finney [who] praised this preaching style:"[22] stating "Many of their ministers are unlearned, in the common sense of the term, [though w]herever the Methodists have gone, their plain, pointed and simple, but warm and animated mode of preaching has always gathered congregations."[23]

This mode of preaching may sound familiar to those who have read the BOM and are well acquainted with the ministry of Joseph Smith. There is a clear similarity between the preaching of the Methodists in the early 1800s and the speaking that is frequently seen from Joseph. He is passionate, even electric. He sticks primarily to the topics of the gospel and the importance of relying on Christ. It is no wonder that Joseph was such an effective speaker when one sees that he had exposure to great Methodist preachers and even worked alongside them as a "very passable exhorter" for a time.

18. Davis. 37.

19. *The Doctrines and Discipline of the Methodist Episcopal Church in America. With Explanatory Notes by Thomas Coke and Francis Asbury. The Tenth Edition*, n.d.

20. Davis, *Visions in a Seer Stone*. 37.

21. Davis.37.

22. Palmer, *An Insider's View of Mormon Origins*.109.

23. Palmer.109.

We could easily go on and list numerous other factors that likely played their part in the strengthening of Joseph Smith's mind. However, for this brief examination, I believe the point has been illustrated robustly enough. It is apparent that Joseph had some education, a uniquely powerful and imaginative mind, and was a compelling speaker. However, this is certainly not enough on its own to build a case for the creation of the BOM. Perhaps there are some investigators who are willing to concede that Joseph was uniquely well equipped intellectually. But it still seems unreasonable that even his level of intellectual skill could produce a book of almost 270,000 words in just 85 days! This critique is well taken. I wholeheartedly agree. Unaided, Joseph could never have been able to produce the BOM in 85 days even with his strength of mind.

As we continue to build a secular case for the creation of the BOM, we turn to ten sources which I believe help to piece together a little more of the puzzle.

Chapter 22: **10 Sources**

UP TO THIS POINT, we have established that Joseph Smith possessed a uniquely powerful mind. Now, we will look to potential influences and source materials for his writing of the BOM. I want to reiterate that I do not pretend to lay out the exact sources that Joseph used and how he used them. Rather, this study looks at the similarities between the BOM and other sources. Regarding these parallels, I encourage the reader to consider them in accord with all of the other information that we have addressed in this book.

While a single point of similarity may not be strong enough to change one's perspective, I am hoping that a preponderance of evidence will be sufficiently forceful. Thus, as we proceed, please examine these points with an open mind and consider the true force of them when viewed as one cumulative argument. Although there are *many* sources which scholars have presented that share a similarity with the BOM. That is, many may have furnished some peculiar element for its creation, here I will focus on just ten. I chose these as they appear to me to be both; the most pervasive throughout the BOM and the most compelling.

1. 1769 KJV BIBLE

The first source material that we will examine is the 1769 edition of the King James Version Bible. Anyone who has read both, the Bible and the BOM, will notice that they share a striking resemblance in many areas. Some elements that appear in common include, the general language, the books of the New Testament, the words of the prophet Isaiah, and many names. There are at least two reasons why this is surprising.

First, from our understanding of the translation process, it appears clear that Joseph did not utilize a Bible. As a result, if we hold to the orthodox LDS view, the similarities between the KJV Bible and the BOM are almost coincidental. While it may reasonably be assumed that there would be some overlap between the general teachings of the BOM (a record kept by ancient American Jews) a great degree of similarity may be suspect. I am of the perspective that the KJV Bible was a fundamental source text for the BOM. Indeed, I find that this conclusion is almost unquestionable. In the words to follow I rely heavily upon the studies of LDS Scholar Grant H. Palmer in his book *An Insider's View of Mormon Origins*. I recommend this book to all who desire to take their study on this topic to a deeper level.

The KJV Bible and the BOM share a similar language. That is, the BOM is written in an old English which is nearly indistinguishable from the King James Bible. It has been posited by some that this similarity is attributable to the fact that the King James language carried a sense of tradition and reverence during the time that the BOM was being written. It is then unsurprising to find that a book written in the early 1800s would reflect this language to bolster its religious appeal.[1] It makes sense that Joseph, would utilize this language in his great religious writing to make it more appealing and give it a tone of authenticity. There is an issue with this language being used, however. The English used in the writing of the KJV Bible was the product of a specific time and culture. When one evaluates the early Greek, Hebrew, or Aramaic texts or even their translations into Latin and Greek, one would not find the particulars of Old English in them. As such, why is it that the BOM, allegedly an ancient record written in reformed Egyptian, would have been translated into KJV English if there was not at least some influence of the KJV Bible on its authorship or translation?

The BOM contains a myriad of quotes from the New Testament, especially within the book of 3 Nephi when Jesus visits the Nephites. I will refrain from listing them all out with their text, but I will provide a couple that effectively demonstrate how virtually identical many of these passages are. Let us not forget as we review these examples that there is no way that the Nephites had the words of the New Testament. While the LDS position would hold that Jesus just said similar things to the Nephites as he did to his disciples, a critical scholar may see these quotes

---

1. "The King James Bible and the Book of Mormon | Religious Studies Center,".

as clearly borrowed and re-purposed from the New Testament of the King James Bible, which would, of course, be anachronistic.

3 Nephi 9:15–18	John 1:11–12, 14:11; Rev. 22:13
"I am in the Father, and the Father in me ... I came unto my own and my own received me not ... And as many as have received me, to them have I given to become the sons of God; and even so will I to as many as shall believe on my name .. I am Alpha and Omega, the beginning and the end ... "	"I am in the Father, and the Father in me ... He came unto his own, and his own received him not. But as many as received him, to them he gave power to become the sons of God, even to them that believe on his name ... I am Alpha and Omega, the beginning and the end ... "

3 Nephi 11:33–34	Mark 16:16
"And whoso believeth in me, and is baptized, the same shall be saved ... and whoso believeth not in me ... shall be damned ... "	"He that believeth and is baptized shall be saved; but he that believeth not shall be damned."

3 Nephi 15:17	John 10:16
"Other sheep I have which are not of this fold; them also I must bring, and they shall hear my voice; and there shall be one fold and one shepherd."	"And other sheep I have which are not of this fold: them also I must bring, and they shall hear my voice; and there shall be one fold, and one shepherd."

In addition to these that I have written out, please review the following passages which share a great deal of similarity:

3 Nephi 17:10, 14, 21.	Luke 7:38; John 11:33, 35; Mark 10:16
3 Nephi 18:12–13, 28–29	Matt. 7:24-27; 1 Cor. 11:27-29
3 Nephi 19: 20, 23, 29–30	John 17:1, 6, 20-21, 9-10; 18:1
Helaman 14:25; 3 Nephi 23:9	Matt. 27:52–53
3 Nephi 26:3–5	2 Peter 3:10; Rev. 20:12; John 5:29

While these verses do not comprise an exhaustive list, they suffice to demonstrate the point of the incredible (occasionally word for word) similitude of the BOM and the KJV Bible.

Another peculiar element within the book of 3 Nephi is found in the review of its miracles. In 3 Nephi there are miracles found very similar to those which occurred in the New Testament; however, they have been exaggerated in some way. For instance, at the time of the death of Christ the New Testament reports that the sun went dark for three hours and there was an earthquake. (Matt 27:45,51) However, in the BOM, the sun went dark for three days, and the earthquake is described with a terrible force. (3 Nephi 8) Another miracle which is replicated in the BOM is the feeding of the 5,000. 3 Nephi 20 describes Jesus multiplying food to feed a very large crowd. These are just two out of the numerous examples of biblical-style miracles which are presented within the BOM.

There are also similar wordings found between New Testament parables and BOM passages. For example, see how the language of the parable of the sower is used in the book of Alma.

Matthew 13:3–8	Alma 32:28–43
"[A] sower went forth to sow ... [S]ome seeds fell by the wayside ... [Some] sprung up ... [But] when the sun was up[, some] ... were scorched; and because they had no root, they withered away ... [But some] brought forth fruit ... "	"Now, we will compare the word of God unto a seed ... [I]f ye do not cast it out by your unbelief ... [it] sprouteth ... up ... [But] when the heat of the sun cometh[, it] ... scorcheth it, because it hath no root[, and] it withers away ... [But some seeds] bring forth fruit ... "

In this example, we find less of a word for word copy. In many ways, this is more typical of the way that the Bible has influenced Joseph's writing of the BOM. Rather than always utilizing exact quotations, Joseph frequently uses some amalgamation of verses or biblical concepts in a single BOM sermon. Frequently he paraphrases or elaborates on certain points to emphasize or modify their meaning.

Another point of interest is found in the many parallels between the lives of Paul and Alma. Palmer presents several which create a fascinating study.

Both men were wicked before their dramatic conversion, ... Both traveled about persecuting and trying to destroy the church of God, ... saw a heavenly vision, ... Their companions fell to the earth, ... Both were asked in vision why they persecuted the Lord, ... Both preached the gospel and performed the same miracle, ... they supported themselves by their own labors, ... They were put in prison. After they prayed, an earthquake resulted in their bands being loosed.[2]

In addition to the Pauline similarities, there are many similarities between the writings in Alma and those in the book of Hebrews. The text of Hebrews, particularly chapters 3 and 7, is found throughout the book of Alma.

Another striking use of the writings of Paul can be found in Moroni's great sermon concerning charity in Moroni 7.

1 Cor. 13:2, 4–6	Moroni 7:44–46
"[If I] have not charity, I am nothing ... Charity suffereth long, and is kind; charity envieth not; charity vaunteth not itself, is not puffed up. Doth not behave itself unseemly, seeketh not her own, is not easily provoked, thinketh no evil; Rejoiceth not in iniquity, but rejoiceth in the truth; Beareth all things, believeth all things, hopeth all things, endureth all things. Charity never faileth."	"[I]f he have not charity he is nothing ... [C]harity suffereth long, and is kind, and envieth not, and is not puffed up, seeketh not her own, is not easily provoked, thinketh no evil, and rejoiceth not in iniquity but rejoiceth in the truth, beareth all things, believeth all things, hopeth all things, endureth all things ... [C]harity never faileth ... "

This example appears to be particularly concerning as there is no reasonable way that Moroni would have had these words of Paul. Beyond this, it is highly unlikely that translating from an ancient record, the language would have been presented in such similar KJV English. This example alone appears to present a legitimate reason to believe that, at very least, a KJV Bible was present in the translation of the BOM.

In addition to the New Testament material which is clearly present in the BOM, there is a great portion of content from the Old Testament, especially from the Prophet Isaiah.

---

2. Palmer, *An Insider's View of Mormon Origins*. 50-51.

ISAIAH IN THE BOM:

The presence of the book of Isaiah within the BOM is of great importance and has encouraged controversy amongst scholars. As such, there are many conflicting studies providing accounts which differ slightly concerning exact details. In our treatment of this fraught topic, I will provide a general overview from what I find to be most accurate and relevant. However, as there is some variability in the precise details depending on which scholarly source is used, I encourage the reader to conduct a study of their own to pin down a personal perspective on the intricate details.

As I described earlier, my goal here is to create a secular case for the BOM. One of the means to achieving this is describing the sources used. We have already satisfactorily demonstrated the use of the KJV Bible in the BOM especially regarding the New Testament. As we continue, we cement that case by demonstrating that Isaiah was a substantial resource as well.

It is well documented that about one third of the book of Isaiah is quoted within the BOM. Nineteen chapters are quoted in their entirety and there are two other chapters which are quoted all except for two words. That accounts for almost 21 full chapters of Isaiah out of the total 66 chapters in the book.[3] Beyond this, the numbers start to get a bit murkier. At the level of quoted verses, one source asserts that 425 verses of Isaiah are present[4] while another source claims that 478 are quoted.[5] In either case, it is clear that a *substantial* portion of the book of Isaiah is represented in the BOM.

Rather than bore the reader with an exhaustive list of the verses and arguments for the exact number, I will look at a general overview of the way that Isaiah provided a source text for the BOM. One LDS church resource cites that: "Thirty-two percent of the book of Isaiah is quoted in the Book of Mormon; another three percent is paraphrased."[6] We will assume these estimates as we build our case below.

---

3. "Nephi Regarded Isaiah as Important Prophet of Own Time and of Future," *Church News* (blog), January 25, 1992.
4. "Nephi Regarded Isaiah as Important Prophet of Own Time and of Future."
5. "Isaiah Variants in the Book of Mormon | Religious Studies Center," accessed July 29, 2022.
6. "Who Was Isaiah?," 2022.

CHAPTER 22: 10 SOURCES

There are approximately 37,036 words in the book of Isaiah.[7] The 1830 edition of the BOM was calculated to be 269,318 words.[8] If you take one third (33%) of 37,036 that is 12,345. This number divided by 269,318 equals .0458. Thus, if one is willing to accept these basic calculations, the book of Isaiah makes up approximately 4.6% of the BOM. This is a stunning number.

Not including the New Testament sources discussed previously or any of the others which we will continue to list, we have ascertained nearly 5% of the content of the BOM. Joseph Smith could have gotten nearly 5% of his material from the book of Isaiah in the KJV Bible.

The LDS apologists are bound to respond, the witnesses to Joseph's translation unanimously report[9] that he had no "book or manuscript" with him during translation.[10] True as this may be, it is apparent that the BOM has KJV influences. Both the style of verbiage and the content match the BOM so closely that there is almost no question. While Joseph may not have had a KJV Bible in front of him to read from as he translated, it is most certainly a source material.

This is even further demonstrated by the work of BYU linguistics professor Royal Skousen in the essay *Textual Variants in the Isaiah Quotations in the Book of Mormon*.[11] As with all of the most effective evaluations of the authorship of the BOM Skousen utilizes the original 1830 edition of the BOM for his study. The contemporary BOM contains almost 4,000 changes compared to the original edition.[12] In order to obtain the clearest possible picture of Joseph's work exclusively, one must filter out as much of the later editing as possible.

It is important to understand a couple of things about the KJV translation in order for one to most fully benefit from Skousen's work. First, the KJV Bible contains words which are italicized. These are words which were not original to the biblical languages[13] but were added to make for

---

7. "How Many Words in Each Book of the Bible," *The Holy Word Church of God* (blog).

8. Brian C Hales, "Naturalistic Explanations of the Origin of the Book of Mormon" 58 (2019): 45.

9. "Question: Could Joseph Have Used a Bible during and Simply Dictated from It during Book of Mormon Translation? - FAIR,".

10. *The Saints Herald Volume 26 1879*.

11. "About Royal Skousen," *BYU Studies* (blog).

12. Jerald and Sandra Tanner, *3,913 Changes in the Book of Mormon*, 91.

13. "Why Are Some Words Italicized in the Bible?,".

improved readability in English.¹⁴ Beyond this, Skousen notes that "the King James Version of the Bible is not an independent translation from the original biblical languages, but instead is a revision based on early English Bibles published in the 1500s."

The reason that this is important is because if the BOM aligns closely with the KJV then it can be confidently asserted that the KJV was more likely the source material for the BOM than was some ancient document. Expected similarities, if this were the case, could take the form of sharing the KJV's unique phrasing or the utilization of its same italicized words. Of course, the traditional LDS view supports that the quotations from Isaiah are taken from the ancient record of the plates of Laban.¹⁵ In spite of this, Skousen came to a different conclusion. He argues: "The base text for the Isaiah quotations in the Book of Mormon is indeed the King James Version of the Bible." He supports this in part by sharing the work of one of his students.

> Andrew Stewart, a student in my 1991 course on textual criticism of the Book of Mormon, identified unique readings in the various early English Bibles (including the King James Version); he then compared those readings with the Book of Mormon text. Not surprisingly, in every case except one Stewart found that the Book of Mormon agreed with the unique readings in the King James Version.¹⁶

Stewart here describes how the BOM very clearly shares the phrasing of the KJV bible. In fact, the correlation is so strong that it occurs in all but one circumstance. This sole instance of disagreement is the one which LDS apologists latch on to because it reads very similarly to early Greek and Hebrew translations.

In addition to the similar phrasings, it is noted that although there are numerous alterations of the quotes from Isaiah in the BOM, the majority have nothing to do with the italicized words added by the KJV. Skousen articulates: "The majority of differences between the Book of Mormon text and the Isaiah text are not associated with italicized words in the King James Version."

---

14. Walter F Specht, "THE USE OF ITALICS I N ENGLISH VERSIONS OF THE NEW TESTAMENT," n.d., 22.

15. Victor Ludlow, "The Writings of Isaiah in the Book of Mormon," *Search Isaiah* (blog), January 4, 2018.

16. Andrew Stewart, "KJV as a Source for the Biblical Quotations in the Book of Mormon" (unpublished research paper for Royal Skousen' s course on textual criticism of the Book of Mormon, Brigham Young University, 1991),1.

CHAPTER 22: 10 SOURCES

This is significant because it would be expected that these added words would not have existed in Joseph's translation. Joseph was allegedly translating from an ancient record and the italicized words were late additions by KJV translators.[17] As a result, it is more than a little curious that the majority "(62 percent) of italicized words are unchanged in the Book of Mormon."[18]

We can see clearly the ways in which New and Old Testament passages are present throughout the BOM. But there are even more examples of similarities that may be drawn upon.

For a third point of agreement, we examine a potential source for many of the names in the BOM which were extant in the KJV Bible. The scholar Wesley P. Walters examines the names within the BOM.

In his study he found at least 365 unique names in the BOM. This includes places and people. From this study he excluded variations of names that were created from the addition of prefixes or suffixes etc. For example, he notes that it would not be of much value to qualify Zoram and Zoramites as unique names. He concluded that out of the approximate 365 names in the BOM, 141 of them were found in the Bible. Strikingly then, about 39% of the names in the BOM were acquired from the KJV Bible and are not unique to the BOM.

It is interesting to find that one of the most important names in the BOM does not occur in the standard Bible. The name Nephi, which occurs about 2,788 times in the BOM[19] (making up a surprising 1% of the entire BOM) is found in 2 Maccabees 1:36 which is an apocryphal book included in some versions of the KJV Bible. Thus, even the name Nephi has an apparent 'biblical' source which Joseph was likely privy to.

As if there is any remaining doubt of the role that the KJV played in the authorship of the BOM, let me remind you of one point that we touched upon previously. That is the presence of numerous translation errors in the KJV and the BOM.

For an example of one of these coincidental translation errors, the KJV incorrectly uses the words Cherubims and Seraphims. Both errors are also contained in the 1830 edition of the BOM. Is it likely that God, when providing Joseph Smith, the translation through his seer stone, made a mistake or intentionally caused Joseph to err in the exact same

17. Runnells, *CES Letter*.14.

18. Royal Skousen, "Textual Variants in the Isaiah Quotations in the Book of Mormon," n.d., 23.

19. David, "Gospel Cougar: Word Frequency in the Book of Mormon," *Gospel Cougar* (blog), December 23, 2007.8,2]]},"issued":{"date-parts":[["2007",12,23]]}}],"schema":"https://github.com/citation-style-language/schema/raw/master/csl-citation.json"}

way that Joseph's KJV Bible was mistaken? Is it not far more reasonable, in light of all of these points, to assent to the fact that the KJV played an essential role in Joseph's authorship?

This study may have proved a bit pedantic for some, but I believe that it provides a very compelling case that the KJV Bible was instrumental in the authorship of the BOM. Before we proceed, I will present one final point to consider on this subject. Daniel L. Belnap, a BYU professor of Ancient Scripture[20] has the following to say about the similarities between the BOM and the KJV Bible.

> The KJV influence is so extensive throughout the Book of Mormon. More than fifty thousand phrases of three or more words, excluding definite and indefinite articles, are common to the Bible and the Book of Mormon.[21]

It is important to note, that Belnap is not saying definitively that the BOM borrowed from the Bible. However, it is incredible that they share such similarity. If you will indulge me to utilize some calculations once again, we can see what a high degree of similarity this is. On the conservative end using, 50,000 phrases of three words we would have 150,000 words shared. This figure divided by 269,318 equals .5569 which indicates that using only these phrases, we could account for a 56% similarity between the BOM and the KJV Bible.

Is it reasonable to believe that it is a mere coincidence that Joseph's translation of an ancient record so perfectly matches the very Bible edition that he would have possessed and studied?

In consideration of the BOM's similarities to both, the Old and New Testament it appears indubitable that the KJV was one of Joseph's most utilized source texts. We will now proceed to examine nine other potential sources which leave notable footprints in the authorship of the BOM.

---

20. "Dan Belnap," Religious Education.
21. "The King James Bible and the Book of Mormon | Religious Studies Center."

Chapter 23: 2. The View of the Hebrews

THE NEXT SOURCE THAT we will examine, which appears to have played a major role in the authorship of the BOM, is a book called *View of the Hebrews* by Ethan Smith. This book is confidently purported to be a source text in the vast majority of the secular critiques written of the BOM. As we continue to regard the parallels, it will not be difficult to see why. Before we look at the similarities between these two books and how View of the Hebrews (hereafter VOH) may have influenced the BOM, it is important to understand a bit of context regarding the VOH and whether or not Joseph may have had access to a copy.

If the book were not published until long after the BOM, then we would have no reason to believe that it was a seminal text in its creation. Much in the same way that geologists study the earth, by noting that its deeper layers are older than those on top of them, a literary scholar reviews potential source texts by considering the publishing timeline. In the same way that deeper layers of rock form the foundation for those on top of them, earlier textual content may serve as the foundation for later literary works.

The VOH was written by the pastor, Ethan Smith, and was originally published in 1823.[1] A subsequent edition was published in 1825.[2] Both of these editions were published before the initial publication of the BOM

---

1. Runnells, *CES Letter*.

2. Ethan Smith, *View of the Hebrews: Or The Tribes of Israel in America*, [Repr. of the] 2. ed., improved and enlarged, 1825 (Colfax, Wis: Ancient American Archaeology Foundation, 2002).

in 1830. Ethan pastored a church and published his book in Poultney, Vermont which is in a county adjacent to the one where the BOM was originally published. In addition to the fact that VOH predates the BOM by more than five years, it can be connected to Joseph Smith through one of his witnesses and chief scribe, his cousin, Oliver Cowdery.[3] Cowdery "lived in the same small town as the author, Reverend Smith, who was the Cowdery family's Congregationalist pastor from 1821 to 1826."[4] B.H. Roberts speaks to the likelihood of Joseph's familiarity with VOH saying:

> The likelihood of Joseph Smith coming in contact with Ethan Smith's book is not only very great, but amounts to a very close certainty. For being published in an adjoining county to the one in which their home had been for so long, and the interest in the subject being very general, not only in New England but in New York also, it would be little short of miraculous if they did not know of Ethan Smith's book.[5]

Palmer elaborates on Roberts noting "that if the Smiths did not purchase a copy, it could easily have been supplied by Oliver Cowdery."[6] Thus, while we may not have proven that Joseph Smith personally owned or even read a copy of Ethan Smith's book, it is incredibly likely that he was aware of it and he would certainly have had access to it. It will be up to the reader to decide whether or not it appears to have been used in the authoring of the BOM.

Below I present a short list of the parallels that may be found between the BOM and VOH. I rely on the work of B.H. Roberts for the following study. Roberts shares the following concerning his survey of the similarities. "not a few things, merely, one or two, or a half dozen, but many; and it is this fact of many things of similarity and the cumulative force of them that makes them so serious a menace to Joseph Smith's story of the Book of Mormon's origin." The following descriptions refer to the VOH but are equally applicable to the BOM.

> It not only suggests, but pleads on every page for Israelitish origin of the American Indians.
>
> It deals with the destruction of Jerusalem and the scattering of Israel.

3. Runnells, *CES Letter*. 25.
4. Palmer, *An Insider's View of Mormon Origins*. 58-64.
5. Roberts and Madsen, *Studies of the Book of Mormon*. 235.
6. Palmer, *An Insider's View of Mormon Origins*. 58-64.

It deals with the future gathering of Israel, and the restoration of the 10 tribes.

It emphasizes and uses much of the material from the prophecies of Isaiah, including whole chapters.

It makes special appeal to the Gentiles of the New World—having in mind more especially the people of the United States.

It holds that the peopling of the New World was by migrations from the Old.

It takes its migrating people into a country where "never man dwelt," just as the Book of Mormon takes its Jaredite colony into "that quarter where they're never had man been."

In both cases the journey was to the northward; in both cases the colony entered into the valley of a great river; they both encountered "seas" of "many waters" in the course of their journey; in both cases the journey was a long one. The motive in both cases was the same—a religious one;

Ethan Smith's book supposes that his last tribes divided into two classes, the one fostering the arts that make for civilization, the other followed the wild hunting and indolent life that ultimately led to barbarism, which is just what happens to the Book of Mormon peoples.

"Long and dismal" wars break out between Ethan Smith's civilized division and his barbarous division. The same occurs between Nephite and Lamanite, divisions drawn on the same lines of civilized and barbarous in the Book of Mormon.

The savage division utterly exterminates the civilized in Ethan Smith's book; the Lamanites, the barbarous division of the Book of Mormon, utterly destroyed the civilized division—the Nephites.

Ethan Smith's book assumes for the ancient civilized people a culture of mechanic arts; of written language; of the knowledge and use of iron and other metals; and of navigation.

Ethan Smith's book assumes unity of race for the inhabitants of America—the Hebrew race, *and no other*.

It assumes the Indian tongue to have had one source—the Hebrew;

Ethan Smith's book describes an instrument among the mound finds comprising breast plate with two white buckhorn buttons attached, "in imitation of the precious stones of the Urim," says Ethan Smith. Joseph Smith used some such instrument in translating the Book of Mormon, called Urim and Thummim.

Ethan Smith's book admits the existence of idolatry and human sacrifice;

Ethan Smith's book extols generosity to the poor and denounces pride, as traits of the American Indian;

Ethan Smith book denounces polygamy, the Book of Mormon under certain conditions does the same.

Ethan Smith's book quotes Indian traditions of a "Lost Book of God" and the promise of its restoration to the Indians, with a return of their last favor with the Great Spirit. This is in keeping with the lost sacred records to the savage Lamanites of the Book of Mormon.

Ethan Smith's sacred book was buried with some "high priest," "keeper of the sacred tradition"; the Book of Mormon sacred records were hidden or buried by Moroni, a character that corresponds to this Indian tradition in the Hill Cumorah.

Ethan Smith's book describes extensive military fortifications linking cities together over wide areas of Ohio and Mississippi valleys, with military observatory or "watch towers" overlooking them; the Book of Mormon describes extensive fortifications erected throughout large areas with military "watch towers" here and there overlooking them.

Ethan Smith's book also describes sacred towers, or "high places" in some instances devoted to true worship, in other cases to idolatrous practices; the Book of Mormon also has its prayer or sacred towers.

Part of Ethan Smith's ancient inhabitants affect a change from monarchial governments to republican forms of government; Book of Mormon peoples do the same.

In Ethan Smith republics the civil and ecclesiastical power is united in the same person; this was a practice also with the Book of Mormon people.

Some of Ethan Smith's peoples believed in the constant struggle between good and the bad principle, by which the world is governed; Lehi, first of Nephite prophets, taught the existence of a necessary opposition in all things—righteousness opposed to wickedness—good to bad; life to death, and so following.

Ethan Smith's book speaks of the gospel having been preached in the ancient America; the Book of Mormon clearly portrays a knowledge of the gospel had among the Nephites.

Ethan Smith gives, in considerable detail, the story of the Mexican culture-hero Quetzalcoatl—who in so many things is reminiscent of the Christ; the Book of Mormon brings the risen Messiah to the New World, gives him a ministry, disciples and a church.

Can such numerous and startling points of resemblance and suggestive contacts be merely coincidence?[7]

I must apologize for such a lengthy quotation from Roberts. I will not blame the reader if they skimmed portions of it. I believe it was necessary to include because it so clearly and extensively parallels the BOM. For one who has not read the BOM in its entirety the impact of reading Roberts' analysis will be less severe. However, for those familiar with the BOM, the similarities are more than striking.

This book which Joseph Smith may have owned, and clearly had access to contains an unbelievable number of unique BOM teachings. The VOH provides not only a framework for the ten lost tribes and the implications thereof (which the BOM also heavily relied upon) but added narrative details! VOH describes a barbarous nation which annihilated a civilized nation. It also asserts many of the very same anachronistic details which are persistent in the BOM. As Roberts asks, is it possible that *so many* similarities are only by coincidence?

It is not even the case that both the BOM and VOH are accurate in all their depictions. If this were the case, one may understand and excuse the striking—verging on plagiaristic—similitude. After all, two different scientists may come to the same accurate conclusion independently. However, both books deviate *in detail* from what is now understood of ancient American history. For instance, the BOM and VOH both assert (at least traditionally) that the origin of the North American peoples was Hebraic. As we have already addressed, DNA studies have comprehensively disavowed this conclusion. Beyond this, there are numerous

---

7. Roberts and Madsen, *Studies of the Book of Mormon*.242.

markings of advanced civilization described in both books which have no representation in the archaeological record.

Will an honest investigator truly depart from this study concluding that these two books have no connection whatsoever? Need we remind the reader of the geographic proximity of VOH's publication or the years which it predated the translation of the BOM?

Chapter 24: 3. The Lost 116 Pages

THE NEXT ELEMENT FOR our examination is not so much a source material as an answer to one of the great challenges that Joseph Smith had in his writing of the BOM. As we have frequently repeated, the LDS missionaries and apologists are quick to mention the fact that there is no way Joseph could have written the book on his own because of, one, his lack of ability and, two, the amazing time he did it in.

The Church Essay, *How long did it take Joseph Smith to translate the Book of Mormon?* points out just how miraculous this feat was. "One of the most amazing facts about the Book of Mormon is that it took Joseph Smith only about sixty-five working days to translate a book that, in current edition, is 531 pages long."[1] This indeed is quite impressive. There is, however, reason to believe that there was far more time involved in the process than is readily noted by this statement.

It is true that the BOM that we have today was dictated and written down during this period of about 65 working days. However, reducing the authoring process to merely the time it takes to put the words on paper is deceptive.

For example, when a pastor preaches a sermon, he prepares beforehand. It would be out of the ordinary to gush about how impressive it is that he articulated such great truths in only 40 minutes. No, this would be to neglect the hours of preparation that he had weeks before. Great works of oratory are rarely also works of improvisation. We may apply a similar analysis to the BOM. One author asserts that the BOM is largely

---

1. "How Long Did It Take Joseph Smith to Translate the Book of Mormon?"

an impressive feat of oratory as Joseph dictated its entirety to a scribe.[2] This being the case, much like a pastor's sermon we ought to examine the time that went into his preparation. This is, in part, is what we are doing as we review potential source materials for the BOM. We are looking at the details in Joseph's life, be they cultural, literary, or otherwise which may have been useful in preparation for his magnum opus.

I contend that one piece of the BOM's history which was of exceptional benefit to its authorship was the loss of its first 116 pages. While the translation for the official BOM began "between 7 April and 30 June 1829, before that, from 12 April to 14 June 1828, Joseph had translated the 116 pages that Martin Harris lost when he borrowed them to show members of his family."[3]

Martin Harris is an important figure in LDS studies. He was one of the three witnesses of the plates, a scribe of Joseph Smith,[4] and was one of the chief financial backers for the publication of the BOM. He was one of the greatest supporters of Joseph Smith in the early church, but was also, on occasion, a troublemaker. This is rarely demonstrated so clearly as when he lost the 116 pages.

The lost 116 pages are a portion of Joseph's initial translation attempt in 1828. "Joseph wrote that the lost pages contained the book of Lehi."[5] It is unknown what exactly was contained in this record, but Nephi "explained that this record contained accounts of Lehi's dreams, visions, prophecies, and teachings to his children."[6] Martin Harris was Joseph's scribe during the translation of this record and desperately wanted to take the 116 pages to his family to prove to them the authenticity of the work that he was aiding in.

He asked Joseph twice for permission to borrow the pages. Joseph inquired of the Lord each time but the Lord said no. Martin continued pleading with Joseph for a chance to take the pages home and Joseph, worn down by Harris' persistent pleas, inquired of the Lord a third time. This time, "the Lord said Martin could take the pages if he agreed to show them only to his wife and certain other members of his family."[7] Thus, with the Lord's permission, Martin took the pages home and, despite his

---

2. Davis, *Visions in a Seer Stone*.
3. "How Long Did It Take Joseph Smith to Translate the Book of Mormon?"
4. "Chapter 4: Martin Harris and the Lost Pages: 1827–1828,".
5. "Lost Manuscript of the Book of Mormon,".
6. "Lost Manuscript of the Book of Mormon."
7. "Chapter 4," 4.

promise to show the pages only to his family, he presented them to others as well. This disobedience led to severe consequences.

The lost 116 pages, aptly named, were lost. It is unknown exactly how they disappeared or where to, but one leading theory opines that Martin Harris' wife, Lucy, stole them as she may have had the most to gain by their mysterious disappearance.[8] While this mystery may be of some intrigue, it is not the purpose of this study. What is incredibly interesting is Joseph's response to the loss of these pages.

Needless to say, he was devastated. His trusted scribe had caused him great distress by betraying his trust and, what was likely even more painful, Joseph felt that he had failed in his divine duty to translate and protect this record. He then halted from his work of translating for approximately nine months.[9]

Joseph later asked for a revelation concerning whether he should attempt to retranslate the portion that was lost. The response Joseph received was both brilliant and tactical. As you will read, whether this epiphany came by divine intervention or human cunning, it is strategic all the same. This revelation can be found now in Doctrine and Covenants 10.

> [9]Therefore, you have delivered them up, yea, that which was sacred, unto wickedness.
>
> [10]And, behold, Satan hath put it into their hearts to alter the words which you have caused to be written, or which you have translated, which have gone out of your hands. [11]And behold, I say unto you, that because they have altered the words, they read contrary from that which you translated and caused to be written; [12]And, on this wise, the devil has sought to lay a cunning plan, that he may destroy this work; [13]For he hath put into their hearts to do this, that by lying they may say they have caught you in the words which you have pretended to translate.

In this revelation, Joseph is encouraged not to re-translate the portion that was stolen because of the possibility for conspiracy against him. A critical scholar may read this from the opposite perspective. We have previously examined Joseph's method of translation. Is it possible that his unique practice of translation would render him incapable of providing the same reading twice? If that were the case, those who stole pages would merely have to bring them forth and demonstrate the disparity. This could discredit Joseph in a potent way.

8. "The Lost 116 Pages Story: What We Do Know, What We Don't Know, and What We Might Know | Religious Studies Center," 116.

9. "Lost Manuscript of the Book of Mormon."

Conveniently, in his revelation, Joseph was encouraged not to fall into this trap and refrained from providing the translation a second time. As is a common theme throughout Joseph's translating efforts, in this instance there would appear to be no clear way of testing his work as we have done with the Book of Abraham and the Kinderhook plates.

The lost 116 pages did not only provide an opportunity for scholarly skepticism. This loss significantly extends the timespan of translation. As previously addressed, the BOM was dictated in 65 days. However, this excludes the preparation time. Are we truly to doubt that the translation of the 116 pages and the nine-month pause following their theft had nothing to do with Joseph's future work? For 63 days between April 12 and June 14, Joseph practiced and prepared. In a sense, this could have been his rough draft for the BOM. Over 63 days he may have refined his dictation process and outlined content which he later expanded during his dictation of the BOM itself. Further, this expands the time from when Joseph began working on the BOM from the 84 days between April 7 and June 30. To a far less extraordinary 360 days between April 12, 1828 and April 7, 1829.

For illustration, I had a very similar experience in my authoring of this book. The framework came out of a letter that I wrote to some LDS missionaries. This letter was far more concise and contained many of the same points that I address here. A time later I decided to expand and rework those same topics in a more comprehensive treatment. Joseph may not have been writing for 360 days, but he had almost an entire year from the inception of his project to the end of translation during which he could devote himself to contemplation and organizing his thoughts. When one looks at this contextual history of the events surrounding the authoring of the BOM it all but dispels the issue created by a time constraint. Perhaps Joseph Smith would have been incapable of authoring his entire record in the short period of time so often touted by the LDS apologists. However, this task seems far less insurmountable given almost a complete year for the undertaking.

I will also add that this is only measuring his preparation that occurred following his first attempt at translating the 116 pages. As we look into additional sources which may have supplied some material for the BOM, this preparation process may extend even further. For instance, we know Joseph was telling his family stories about the American Indians far earlier than 1828. As we continue to examine potential sources for the BOM, it is valuable to keep in mind the time that Joseph spent in preparation.

Chapter 25: 4. Denominational Debates

THE NEXT POTENTIAL SOURCE material for Joseph Smith's creation of the BOM is the myriad of denominational issues contemporary to New England in the early mid 1800s. Of particular interest here are those topics which were most frequently discussed in Joseph's time, we may also describe this collection of Christian ideas as anachronistic to the BOM.

The pertinent fact is that the BOM contains and responds to denominational controversies that were prevalent during Joseph Smith's lifetime. Depending on one's presuppositions this may make perfect sense. A devout saint may point out that this was exactly the purpose of the BOM. The world fell into a great apostasy and Joseph was troubled because he did not know which was the true church. The churches in Joseph's environment all disagreed over their doctrines which made it a puzzle for a young seeker to find any specific denomination to place his full confidence in. The solution to Joseph's problem came when he prayed and received the revelation that he was to reinstitute the one true church and restore the fullness of the gospel to the earth.

Given this story, it makes perfect sense in terms of the narrative pattern of the BOM that this book would contain all the solutions to the issues which divide modern churches. How else could unity be acquired and maintained?

Compelling as this line of thinking may seem, one must contend with the fact that many problems solved by the BOM were not issues that the ancient Jews dealt with. Further, the issues are the *exact* issues that were being considered during the early-mid 1800s. By discussing these specific doctrinal questions, Joseph has left a 19th century fingerprint in ancient America.

In 1831, a minister named Alexander Campbell, became acquainted with the BOM and wrote a critique that clearly elaborates the discovery that we have just laid out. He supposes that the clarity brought about by the BOM is evidence against its antiquity. He says:

> This Prophet Smith, through his stone spectacles, wrote on the plates of Nephi, in his book of Mormon, every error and almost every truth discussed in N. York for the last ten years. He decides all the great controversies–infant baptism, ordination, the trinity, regeneration, repentance, justification, the fall of man, the atonement, transubstantiation, fasting, penance, church government!, religious experience, the call to ministry, the general resurrection, eternal punishment, who may baptize, and even the question of freemasonry, republican government, and the rights of man. All these topics are repeatedly alluded to.[1]

One clear example of this can be found when reviewing what the BOM has to say about baptism. The topics of how baptism should be performed, and whether infants should be baptized are settled. Moroni 8:11 says "And their little children need no repentance, neither baptism." 3 Nephi 11, gives clear instructions for how baptism is to be completed.

> And now behold, these are the words which ye shall say, calling them by name, saying: [25]Having authority given me of Jesus Christ, I baptize you in the name of the Father, and of the Son, and of the Holy Ghost. Amen. [26]And then shall ye immerse them in the water, and come forth again out of the water.

Here they are taught to baptize in the names of all three persons of the Trinity and are taught to practice baptism by immersion. The topics of paedobaptism and immersion were both active theological debates in the 1800s as they continue to be today in many circles. What are they doing in the BOM?

These topics are not those that the ancient Jews focused upon. Indeed, as we have discussed before, it is clearly anachronistic to see the preaching of the gospel hundreds of years before Christ was even born. This is especially the case when considering preaching the gospel unto

---

1. Alexander 1788-1866 Campbell, *Delusions an Analysis of the Book of Mormon; with an Examination of Its Internal and External Evidences, and a Refutation of Its Pretences to Divine Authority by Alexander Campbell ; with Prefatory Remarks by Joshua V. Himes* (Boston Benjamin H. Greene, 1832).

the gentiles. The notion that the sacrifice of Christ was for the gentile as well as the Jew was revolutionary.

Further, this is found unbelievably early in the BOM. The doctrine of the Trinity was not even firmly defined and established until the Council of Nicaea in 325 AD. There are clear passages of the BOM that discuss all these denominational issues which would have been completely foreign to the ancient Jews but fundamentally relevant to Joseph Smith's religious environment. Is it any coincidence that in the BOM we see a distinct lack of esoteric, ancient Jewish tradition, like that found in the Old Testament, but find such frequent elaboration on doctrines which were contemporary to the 1800s? Perhaps the ancient American Jews were ahead of their time. On the other hand, it may be that the distinct theological questions raised are telling of their author's setting in 1800s New England.

Chapter 26: 5. Joseph's Literary Style

THE NEXT POINT THAT I present as a unique source material for Joseph's writing is his particular writing style. Aside from his uneducated and folksy grammar one of the more prominent characteristics of Joseph's literary style is his affinity for repetition for repetition.

Joseph uses repetition frequently throughout his writing and while this does not constitute a whole new source material, it does minimize the amount of original material that needed to be created. We touched upon this very briefly above when discussing biblical names. That is, we pointed out how the name Nephi is used over 2,700 times in the BOM making it approximately 1% of the entire book. For more context on this detail, one study on the KJV Bible discerned that the most frequently used names were David (1064 occurrences), Jesus (983 occurrences), and Moses (847 occurrences).[1] Surprisingly, the name Nephi is used in the BOM almost as many times as the combined names of David, Jesus, and Moses occur in the entirety of the KJV Bible. I do not mean to say that there is no justification for the frequency of the use of this name, however it is very striking.

The name Alma receives similarly frequent use at an approximate 2295 times (0.85% of the entire BOM). However, these names are not nearly as significant as one of Joseph's other favorite literary devices.

The phrase "and it came to pass" appears a bewildering 1,404 times in the BOM.[2] That makes for 7,020 words which is 2.6% of the entire BOM. Over 2 and ½ percent of the entire BOM is just the phrase "and

---

1. *Frequency of Names in the Bible*, 2021.
2. "Why Is the Phrase 'and It Came to Pass' so Prevalent in the Book of Mormon?,".

it came pass." The frequency of this phrase has long been a point of amusement for many of Joseph's critics including Mark Twain who provided a statement in one of his biographies after reviewing the BOM. Twain shares:

> Whenever he found his speech growing to modern—which was about every sentence or two–he ladled in a few such scriptural phrases as "exceeding sore," "and it came to pass," etc., and made things satisfactory again. "And it came to pass" was his pet. If he had left that out, his Bible would have been only a pamphlet.[3]

In his characteristically facetious and exaggerated tone Twain highlights the startling frequency of this phrase throughout the BOM.

The LDS apologists are not silent on this issue and point out that there is a Hebrew word in the Bible, "Wayehi," which is frequently translated as "and it came to pass" as well. In fact, this word "is found about 1,204 times in the Hebrew Bible, [and] it was translated [. . .] 727 times as "and it came to pass" in the"[4] KJV. At other times wayehi is translated as ""and it happened," and . . . became," or "and . . . was.""[5] As such, the LDS scholars spin the presence of this phrase as evidence in support of the BOM.

A critical scholar views this similarity entirely differently. It is not at all surprising that the BOM is full of this phrase exactly *because* it appears with some frequency in the KJV Bible. As has been previously demonstrated, the BOM is loaded with phrases from the KJV Bible making it an undeniable primary source. I am not at all surprised to find more BOM content copied from its pages.

Aside from the question of the initial origin of this phrase, the frequency of its repetition is of some interest. As we did with the names earlier, I will provide some context for this pet phrase of Joseph's. The LDS apologists point out that wayehi (not even the phrase "and it came to pass") is found some 1,204 times in the Old Testament. The phrase, "and it came to pass" occurs far more frequently at 1,404 times in the BOM. In my standard format LDS scriptures, the BOM occupies 531 pages while the Old Testament occupies 1,184 pages.

---

3. Mark Twain and Elizabeth Frank, *Roughing It* (New York: Signet Classics, 2008).95
    4. "Why Is the Phrase 'and It Came to Pass' so Prevalent in the Book of Mormon?"
    5. "Why Is the Phrase 'and It Came to Pass' so Prevalent in the Book of Mormon?"

Thus, the BOM uses the phrase more times in less than half of the pages. It has been maintained that this could be partially explained by the fact that the BOM "contains much more narrative, chapter for chapter than the Bible."[6] I find that even if this were a compelling response it would not alter my bemusement at the incredible 2.6% of the book that the phrase makes up on its own.

Joseph's repetitious writing, while not a clear demonstration of plagiarism does lessen the amount of original material that he needed to author.

---

6. "Why Is the Phrase 'and It Came to Pass' so Prevalent in the Book of Mormon?"

Chapter 27: 6. The Late War of 1812

ANOTHER POTENTIAL SOURCE FOR the BOM is a book from the early 1800s called *The Late War Between The United States and Great Britain* by Gilbert J. Hunt. This book was published in 1816[1] in the New York region. This being the case, it was close to Joseph Smith in two important ways. First, it has an appropriately early timeline; and second it was near to him geographically. This book, a year or two later, was presented for use in schools to teach students the history of the War of 1812.

One of the most striking details about this book was the style of language it used. Earlier we described how the BOM shared similar style to the KJV Bible. The Late War also mimicked this "Scriptural"[2] or "Ancient Historical Style."[3] This was very likely an attempt to win the interest and reverence of its readers. For this reason and others, it is the opinion of many scholars that this book may have had a substantial influence on Joseph's unique literary style.

Until somewhat recently, however, these opinions have necessarily been speculative, relying on anecdotal evidence. Any similarities that were found between the books could only be pointed to by the committed scholars who tediously traced the similarities themselves. In October of 2013 brothers Chris and Duane Johnson devoted themselves to a technologically advanced study of BOM source material.

---

1. Gilbert Hunt, *The Late War Between the United States and Great Britain, From June 1812 to February 1815* (New York: David Longworth, 11 Park, 1816).

2. "The Book of Mormon and The Late War," accessed August 16, 2022.

3. Hunt, *The Late War Between the United States and Great Britain, From June 1812 to February 1815*.

The Johnsons' study utilized a computer program "comparing The Book of Mormon to over 100,000 books from the pre-1830's era."[4] This kind of study was unprecedented in the critical literature. As technology has improved, it has provided new capabilities that allow for more efficient studies with broader scopes than we could ever have dreamed of. Suppose a person read two books per week every year of their life for 100 years. Even at this pace, they would only reach a total of 10,400 books. To compare 100,000 books with the BOM is an incredible achievement of research that technology has allowed. The results of this study are equally exciting.

After removing the KJV Bible and Joseph's other projects such as the Book of Abraham or the Book of Moses, the Johnsons found that there was one book which was incredibly similar to the BOM, *The Late War*. This similarity was determined by finding "rare 4-grams" that the books had in common.

That is, they found phrases of 4 words that were highly unusual. Of course, it would not be significant to find that a book shares the words "and" or "the" with any other book as these words are very common. However, rare four-word phrases are far less likely to be found shared between numerous books. Further, the greater the number of rare 4-grams shared between books, the greater the significance of the correlation and, as a result, the discovery.

The computer testing found that "*The Late War* contained more rare 4-gram connections to *The Book of Mormon* than 99.999% of the other books published before 1830." This percentage represents unbelievable similitude. The discovered number of shared 4-grams was over 100.[5] In addition to these 4-word phrases, there is a great deal of shared vocabulary between the books.

For the reader to see firsthand how striking the similarities are I have compiled a brief list of some of the most prominent below.

First, unsurprisingly there is a smattering of "it came to pass;" "So it came to pass," "Now it came to pass," and "lo! it came to pass." There are over 80 occurrences of this phrase in the book which is almost 340 pages.

1. We find "Weapons of war" in both books.
   (TLW 19:13, BOM Ether 10:27)

---

4. "The Book of Mormon and The Late War."
5. "The Book of Mormon and The Late War."

2. There are items of "curious workmanship" in each. (TLW 12:12, BOM 1Nephi 18:1)

3. Both contain the term "fine workmanship." (TLW 54:7, BOM Jarom 1:8)

4. Both books utilize the word "stripling" to describe men ready for war. (TLW 19:32, BOM Alma 56:57)

5. Both books mention a band of robbers. There was a "band of sea robbers" in TLW 49:17 and the band of Gadianton robbers in the BOM Helaman 6:37.

6. The Late War contains "savages who had been instructed in the ways of God," (TLW 26:18) and the BOM describes the Lamanites (and other dissenters) as "having been instructed in the same knowledge of the Lord." (BOM Alma 47:36)

7. Both contain stories of two thousand men who fought for their country and were of "dauntless courage" (TLW 35:5-6) or were "exceeding valiant of courage." (BOM Alma 53:18-20)

Aside from these notable examples, there are some parallels which appear to be small variants of the same word especially when viewed in their contextual story structure. A few of the most prominent examples of this are:

8. The Late War describes an occurrence "near Moravian Town" (TLW 32:14) whereas the BOM discusses the "people of Morianton" (BOM Alma 50:32).

Both times these words are used to describe a location. While the borrowing here is not completely apparent, one can easily see how one would get "Morianton" from "Moravian Town." There is also a striking similarity between the names of military leaders between the books.

9. The Late War introduces a leader "and they [the army] were under the charge of a chief warrior, whom they called Tecumseh."(TLW 32:4) The BOM describes: "The army which was sent by Moroni, which was led by a man whose name was Teancum." (BOM Alma 50:35)

Once again, this is not obvious evidence of source material. However, in light of the contextual similarities, it does not appear to be an over-exertion of one's imagination to presume that there may be a bit more than a coincidental relationship between these two names.

In addition to the similar vocabulary used in both or the fact that there are similar 4-grams, there are some passages which share a noticeable structural resemblance. While these passages do not read identically, the sheer number of them makes it difficult to believe that there was not some relation between these two books.

Below I have provided three more examples demonstrating structural similarities between passages of these books.

The Late War 20:11–16	Ether 9:17–19
"… the land … most plentiful … yielding gold and silver, and … all manner of creatures which are used for food, And … the huge mammoth that once moved on the borders … It is more wonderful than the elephant;"	"… the land, … exceeding rich, … of gold, and of silver, and … all manner of … animals which were useful for the food of man. And … cureloms and cumoms; … and more especially the elephants …"

The Late War 29:20–23	Alma 49:20–25
"[men] were prepared … and they let loose their weapons of war … and smote … with great slaughter. And the deep ditch that surrounded the fort was strewed with their slain and their wounded."	"[men] were prepared, with their swords and their slings, to smite … with an immense slaughter … ditches … filled up in a measure with their dead and wounded."

The Late War 51:3–10	Mosiah 2–4
"it came to pass that the husbandmen … gathered together, and pitched their tents, [and] assembled together … And the people shouted with a loud voice, …"	"it came to pass that … the people gathered themselves together … And … pitched their tents … ye should assemble yourselves together … And they all cried with one voice, …"

The number of parallels between The Late War, a book which Joseph Smith almost certainly had access to, and the BOM create a real conundrum for LDS scholars. It seems to me that an objective investigator could not easily brush all these similarities aside. The statistical similarity between the two books is deeply convincing. If The Late War had been published in Europe or somewhere that Joseph could never have encountered it, the LDS apologist would have no problems. However, the book was published in Joseph's backyard. After a careful review of even just a fraction of the parallels, it appears that The Late War could easily have been a source material which, at very least, placed stories into Joseph's subconscious mind upon which he could draw during his dictation.

In his treatment of this issue, Rick Grunder, a "Former BYU Library Bibliographic Dept. Chairman and antique book specialist" states: "The presence of Hebraisms and other striking parallels in a popular children's textbook (Late War), on the other hand —so close to Joseph Smith in his youth —must sober our perspective."[6][7]

---

6. Runnells, *CES Letter*.28.

7. Grunder, R. *Mormon Parallels: A Bibliographic Source*. Rick Grunder Books, 2014.

Chapter 28: 7. Methodism

THE SECULAR CASE FOR the authorship of the BOM, would be incomplete without considering Joseph's exposure to the Methodist denomination. I want to highlight two specific elements from the Methodists that appear frequently throughout the BOM. The first is the evangelization style and the second is the practice of exhortation.

Grant Palmer addresses at least four traits which are characteristic of the Methodist preaching model which are also found throughout the BOM. These are: a camp setting, preaching style, the conversion formula, and denunciation of the apparent heresies of other denominations.

First, the camp setting was essentially a large campground where the preaching meetings would occur. Land would be prepared by erecting preaching stands, creating seating for meeting participants, and clearing land for tents of those who planned to attend the meetings for multiple days. The turnout for these meetings frequently numbered in the thousands.[1] Palmer describes one meeting where "families were drawn from all parts of the 100-mile conference district."[2] This broad draw was not unusual for revival meetings of this kind. The arrangement of the camp setting is described by one scholar as follows.

> A few weeks prior to the meetings, those planning to attend took teams and tools to clear and prepare the grounds, determining the sufficient size of ground for the tents, seats and preaching stand. The underbrush and fallen trees were removed.

---

1. Keith Dwayne Lyon, "God's Brush Arbor: Camp Meeting Culture during the Second Great Awakening, 1800-1860," n.d., 408.
2. Palmer, *An Insider's View of Mormon Origins*.97.

Other trees were cut down and laid to support planks for seats. Sleeping quarters were arranged for preachers. An altar rail was placed on four-foot high poles. The altar rail formed an enclosure of about twenty by forty feet, with entrances at the front corners. The enclosure was used for the penitents and mourners during the latter part of the service. [. . .] Each tenting family usually chose their own spot and erected their tent.[3]

This setting for preaching is evident in the BOM as can be seen from the account in Mosiah where "The people gathered themselves together throughout all the land, that they might go up to the temple to hear the words which king Benjamin should speak." (Mosiah 2:1) Further on in verse 5 we notice a familiar scene. "When they came up to the temple, they pitched their tents round about, every man according to his family [. . .] every family being separate one from another."

Second, the preaching style of the Methodists is used frequently by the BOM preachers. Previously we touched upon the lack of an academic approach by Methodist preachers of the 19th century. Palmer elaborates on their kind of preaching noting that it was "characterized by the extemporaneous interlacing of biblical passages with descriptive evangelical terminology that was designed to awake people emotionally to their sins."[4] Concurring with this description, scholar Debra Parcell notes that "each revival was an intense, emotional experience" these were even described by some as "barbarous emotional outbreaks."[5] An example of this emotionally charged preaching in the BOM is found in Jacob 6.

> [5]Wherefore, my beloved brethren, I beseech of you in words of soberness that ye would repent, and come with full purpose of heart, and cleave unto God as he cleaveth unto you. And while his arm of mercy is extended towards you in the light of the day, harden not your hearts.
>
> [6]Yea, today, if ye will hear his voice, harden not your hearts; for why will ye die?
>
> [7]For behold, after ye have been nourished by the good word of God all the day long, will ye bring forth evil fruit, that ye must be hewn down and cast into the fire?

3. Earl E Kerstetter, "THE GLORIOUS CAMP MEETINGS OF THE NINETEENTH CENTURY," n.d., 13.

4. Palmer, *An Insider's View of Mormon Origins*.130-133.

5. Debra Parcell, "Bound for the Promised Land: Camp Meetings and Their Impact on Antebellum Religion and Society," n.d., 25–41.

> ⁸Behold, will ye reject these words? Will ye reject the words of the prophets; and will ye reject all the words which have been spoken concerning Christ, after so many have spoken concerning him; and deny the good word of Christ, and the power of God, and the gift of the Holy Ghost, and quench the Holy Spirit, and make a mock of the great plan of redemption, which hath been laid for you?
>
> ⁹Know ye not that if ye will do these things, that the power of the redemption and the resurrection, which is in Christ, will bring you to stand with shame and awful guilt before the bar of God?
>
> ¹⁰And according to the power of justice, for justice cannot be denied, ye must go away into that lake of fire and brimstone, whose flames are unquenchable, and whose smoke ascendeth up forever and ever, which lake of fire and brimstone is endless torment.
>
> ¹¹O then, my beloved brethren, repent ye, and enter in at the strait gate, and continue in the way which is narrow, until ye shall obtain eternal life.

This passage is just one portion of the many sermons preached throughout the BOM that carry the same sort of emotional appeal. Other examples include Enos 1, Mosiah 2–5, Mosiah 15–16, and Alma 11–15, 18–19 among others. What is so incredible about this sermon from Jacob is the prevalence of New Testament-style evangelical language. This is especially astonishing when considering that this chapter was written between 544 and 421 B.C.

Here is a robustly emotional fire and brimstone sermon complete with appeals to repentance, the plan of redemption, the resurrection, and the gift of the Holy Ghost over 400 years before Jesus was even born. We have dealt with the anachronistic nature of the gospel being preached elsewhere but consider here the similarity this message bears to 19th century evangelical preaching. Below is a brief excerpt of a sermon preached by the immensely influential late-mid 1700s preacher,[6] George Whitefield for comparison.

> Those who [. . .] do not love God on earth, will be most deformed in hell, and their bodies will suffer proportionately there. There is no dressing in Hell, northing but fire and brimstone there, and the wrath of God always awaiting on thee, O

---

6. "The Great Awakening and George Whitefield —Mapping the Great Awakening," accessed August 20, 2022.

> sinner [. . .] O that God may bless you tonight with Godly sorrow [. . .] May the love of God make you cry! May you not go home tonight without an arrow steeped in the blood of Christ [. . .] O earth, earth, hear the word of the Lord! May every faithful soul be made to hear it; to awake, arise from their sleep in sin [. . .] Jesus stands ready with open arms to receive you whom he has first pricked to the heart, and made you cry out, What shall I do to be saved! He will then make you believe in his name, that you may be saved.[7]

As one reads through this sermon, the commonalities are absolutely apparent. Just as described by Palmer, there is paraphrased Scripture intertwined with Evangelical phrases articulated in such a way as to cue an emotional response. This is characteristically protestant, revival-style preaching. It should be a point of great inquiry for the LDS scholars—why does the BOM style of preaching match so extraordinarily with the kind Joseph would have been familiar with? We find in the BOM precisely the style of preaching, which was contemporary to Joseph Smith's day, often down to the exact vocabulary used.

We ask ourselves, is it likely that this preaching style was used by ancient American Jews some 2,000 years before the life of Joseph Smith? Or, on the other hand, is it more likely that the preaching style Joseph Smith was acutely familiar with was replicated in his authorship of the BOM?

Third, we look to the model of conversion which is common between the BOM and Methodist revival preaching. Brent Lee Metcalfe noted that "the congregation's response to Benjamin's homily [in Mosiah] follows an identical non-biblical form of spiritual regeneration developed in antebellum revivals."

After the people gather together for the revival meeting (as occurs in Mosiah 2:1) there are three steps that follow. First, a "Guilt-Ridden Falling Exercise," second, "Petition for Spiritual Emancipation," and finally "Absolution and emotional ecstasy."[8] All three of these steps are found in King Benjamin's sermon in Mosiah. The people first encounter an emotionally heightened experience of their guilt. This is seen in Mosiah 4:1–2 which states:

> When king Benjamin had made an end of speaking [. . .] he cast his eyes round about on the multitude, and behold they had fallen to the earth for the fear of the Lord had come upon them.

7. Roberts and Madsen, *Studies of the Book of Mormon*.310.
8. Palmer, *An Insider's View of Mormon Origins*.(p.99-100)

> ²And they had viewed themselves in their own carnal state, even less than the dust of the earth.

Second, the people petition the Lord for forgiveness. In Mosiah 4:2 "they all cried aloud with one voice, saying: O have mercy, and apply the atoning blood of Christ that we may receive forgiveness of our sins, and our hearts may be purified."

Thirdly, they experience some peace or Joy at the knowledge of their salvation which is frequently demonstrated in a vociferous emotional display as occurs in Mosiah 4:3. "After they had spoken these words the Spirit of the Lord came upon them, and they were filled with joy, having received a remission of their sins, and having peace of conscience."

This sermon in Mosiah is one of numerous occurrences of the 19th century revivalist conversion formula in the BOM. This formula is also found in other places throughout the BOM such as Alma 15:3–12, 18:40–19:35, chapter 22, and 36:12–21.

Fourth, the BOM contains some denunciation of the apparent heresies of other Christian denominations contemporary to the 19th century. We have briefly treated this topic elsewhere, where we considered denominational issues as a potential source material for Joseph. As such, I feel no need to lay it out a second time. We will briefly recall how, as Alexander Campbell detailed, Joseph "decides all the great controversies–infant baptism, ordination, the trinity, regeneration, repentance, justification, the fall of man, the atonement, transubstantiation, fasting, penance, church government"[9] and many others. The BOM upholds a 19th century theology including "a Trinitarian view of deity, a conservative Arminian position on a fallen man, and the evangelical position of individual salvation."[10] The BOM appears almost explicitly to condemn the theologies of Calvinism, Catholicism, Unitarianism, Universalism, and other denominational topics.

We have examined the striking similarities between Methodist revivalist preaching and that in the BOM. This is not all that the Methodists had to offer Joseph Smith to aid him in his great undertaking. Another valuable tool is the practice of exhortation. It has already been described that Joseph was a lay exhorter for the Methodists and it was noted how this may have helped him in the way of becoming an effective speaker. Here I

---

9. Campbell, *Delusions an Analysis of the Book of Mormon; with an Examination of Its Internal and External Evidences, and a Refutation of Its Pretences to Divine Authority by Alexander Campbell ; with Prefatory Remarks by Joshua V. Himes.*

10. Palmer, *An Insider's View of Mormon Origins.*(p. 23)

want to point out that the Methodist practice of exhorting was likely used to extend messages and created a great deal of BOM content.

The Methodist preachers kept to the topics that had to do with conversion and salvation. They utilized evangelical phrases as well as quotations and paraphrases of Scripture to create powerful emotional experiences for their congregations. One of the tools that they used in their sermonizing is known as "amplification." That is, a speaker had the ability to take a single point and extend it through elaboration to some greater length. For illustration, rather than quoting a single verse and ending there, a minister would quote the verse and divide it into sub-topics; each receiving an extempore commentary.

In addition to amplification which could take a sermon from a handful of points to an extended oratory performance, exhorters would follow the preacher and reiterate the message that was preached by rearticulating key phrases and encouraging repentance and contemplation of sins.

We repeatedly see this structure throughout the BOM. Rather than a single, clear articulation of a doctrinal truth, the discourses are followed by amplification and exhortation which adds significantly to the length of the religious discourse. Exhortation is something for which Joseph had experience and talent. This becomes a very important realization in our study for a secular authorship of the BOM when we consider the amount of the BOM which is comprised of religious discourses.

After a thorough review of every book in the BOM, William Davis has determined, with what he notes is a conservative estimate, that religious discourses make up at least 108,099 words or just over 40% of the entire BOM. He further describes "many of which contain variations on the same fundamental Christian principles that require little or no preparation [. . .] it would not be inaccurate to say that Smith *preached* the Book of Mormon as much as he composed it."

While it is not impossible that all these skills and similarities are merely coincidental, it appears to me manifestly clear that the Methodist tradition had a great impact on the authorship of the BOM. Even in our brief examination we have seen the impressive prevalence of Methodist influence on Joseph's work.

The BOM contains revivalist camp settings, preaching styles, and conversion formulas. Beyond this, Joseph's background in Methodist oratory could reliably be expected to have created exactly the kind of religious discourse and sermonizing contained in the BOM. It seems to me that Methodism can be applied to understand the development of a substantial portion of the content in the BOM.

It is necessary to consider one final point concerning the Methodist influence on the BOM. When investigators are trying to discern the truthfulness of the BOM they are encouraged to read it and pray about it. The intended result of this prayer is a spiritual experience in which the Holy Spirit will testify the truthfulness of the BOM to them. All too often *spiritual* experiences are equivocated with *emotional* experiences. As such, a powerful emotional experience would constitute very compelling evidence indeed under this epistemological approach.

This fact is important to note because an emotional response is exactly what Methodist preaching, at that time, was attempting to draw out of people. If the BOM is full of sermons modeled after the exhilarating style of the great Methodist preachers, then emotional experience is the very intent. It is of value to consider the Methodist impact on the emotionalism, and as a result, the epistemic strategy of the BOM.

For a more complete evaluation of the impact of Methodism on Joseph's writing, I highly recommend the books *Visions in a Seer Stone* by William L. Davis and *An Insider's View of Mormon Origins* by Grant H. Palmer.

Chapter 29: 8. Names and Geography

THE NAMES OF JOSEPH's geographical surroundings may have provided some assistance in the construction of the BOM narrative. As previously mentioned, the BOM contains many names both of places and people. Jeremy Runnells, in his *CES Letter* has thoroughly researched this topic and presented a very compelling list of parallels between BOM names and places and those found in the environment of Joseph Smith.

The initial research on this topic was supplied by an essay by Vernal Holley entitled *Book of Mormon Authorship: A Closer Look*.[1] Runnells' further research on this topic was likely fueled, in part, by the immense amount of academic critique presented by LDS apologists. Runnells admitted that his letter contained some errors in its first edition. These he rectified upon receiving feedback from the scholarly community. His current edition has omitted previous errors and presents a well-supported list of these parallels. The lists of names presented below have been sourced from his work on the topic.

It is true that no one knows where the events described in the BOM allegedly occurred. As such, unlike what is common in many Bibles, there are no maps in the backs of BOMs detailing locations and paths of travel for main characters. This has not stopped some individuals from tracing a speculative map based upon the travel narratives listed in the BOM. While the locations are speculative, what is interesting is the names of the locations. In many cases, the names are very similar to those of the locations surrounding Joseph Smith in his environment.

---

1. L Ara Norwood, "Vernal Holley, Book of Mormon Authorship: A Closer Look," n.d., 11.

Though the names are rarely shared identically, as occurs with Jerusalem, there are numerous examples of words that share similar phonetic pronunciations and/or spellings. These kinds of changes could easily be attributed to Joseph's intentional effort to obfuscate the origin of his material. We see a great number of similarities in the names listed below.

Modern Geographic Place	Book of Mormon Name
Antrim	Antum
Antioch	Ani-Anti
Boaz	Boaz
Hellam	Helam
Jacobsburg	Jacobugath
Jerusalem	Jerusalem
Jordan	Jordan
Kishkiminetas	Kishkumen
Lehigh	Lehi
Mantua	Manti
Moraviantown	Morianton
Noah Lakes	Noah, Land of
Oneida	Onidah
Oneida Castle	Onidah, Hill
Rama	Ramah
Ripple Lake	Ripliancum, Waters of
Sodom	Sidom
Shiloh	Shilom
Sherbrooke	Shurr

When faced with so many locations that bear such similar names to those found in the BOM, are we really to believe that the correlation is merely coincidental? What is the likelihood of this number of parallels occurring?

The BOM shares names (or at least a great similarity with names) found in 19th century New England. Previously we surveyed the great number of BOM names found in the Bible. We will continue by examining one other fascinating source which shares an intriguing connection with BOM names.

Chapter 30: 9. Captain Kidd

In his youth Joseph Smith, enjoyed reading select works of fiction. Among his favorite novels were those recounting the tales of the pirate, Captain Kidd. Joseph's love of these novels is well-supported by many who knew him. Grant Palmer notes:

> Joseph may have read Washington Irving's short story on the adventurous life of *Kidd The Pirate*, which was published in Philadelphia in 1824 and in New York in 1825. More likely, Joseph and his family had read several of the many exaggerated "dime novel" knock-offs about Kidd and other pirates which were based on the 1724 and 1728 popular two volumes, *A General History of Robberies and Murders of the Most Notorious Pyrates*, by Daniel Defoe.[1]

A number of individuals from Joseph's community were recorded sharing that Joseph had even spent time digging for treasure which he thought was buried by Captain Kidd, although unfortunately for Joseph it appears that these efforts came to no avail. Palmer goes on to quote a "William R. Hine of Windsor, New York, [who] heard from young Joseph that:"

> He [Joseph] saw Captain Kidd sailing on the Susquehanna River during a freshet, and that he buried two pots of gold and silver. He claimed he saw writing cut on the rocks in an unknown language telling where Kidd buried it, and he translated it through

---

1. Grant H. Palmer, "Joseph Smith, Captain Kidd, Cumorah, and Moroni," *The John Whitmer Historical Association Journal* 34, no. 1 (2014): 50–57.

his peepstone ... [and then] dug for Kidd's money, on the west bank of the Susquenhanna, half a mile from the river.[2]

The purpose for sharing these stories is not to reiterate the reality or even persistence of Joseph Smith's magical worldview, but to demonstrate that the Captain Kidd novels were quite clearly literature that Joseph was familiar with. I can't blame Joseph for being enthralled with this character.

Captain Kidd was a real pirate, the history of whom is riveting. What is most relevant to our study, however, is that between 1697 and 1698 he spent a substantial period of time "in the Comoros Islands and the Indian Ocean" committing crimes which he was later executed for.[3] The Comoro islands, located "off the coast of East Africa,"[4] were not always recognized by the spelling "Comoro." In fact, a map from 1808, before the spelling was standardized, uses the spelling "Camora."[5]

The significant parallel here is found in comparing the islands "Camora" and "the hill Cumorah" where Mormon hid the golden plates (Mormon 6:6). Eventually, this is also where Joseph was led by Moroni to acquire the ancient record. The similarity between the words Camora and Cumorah is substantial; all but two letters. What makes this comparison even more gripping is the fact that in the 1830 edition BOM the words are even *more* similar. The 1830 BOM uses the spelling "Camorah." The only difference between the early spelling of Captain Kidd's haunt, the islands "Camora," and the tremendously important BOM location, the hill "Camorah," is the 'h' placed on the end of the word. As though this parallel was not surprising enough in and of itself, there is another spectacular contextual similarity.

The capital city of the Camora islands is "Moroni." This means that it is highly likely that the Pirate who Joseph Smith loved reading about spent a great deal of his time around Moroni in Camora. Palmer cites a Professor Ronald Huggins saying, "The fact that the pirate [Kidd] was hanged for crimes allegedly committed in the vicinity of Moroni on Grand Comoro [Island] is significant."[6] Palmer points out that these

---

2. Palmer.
3. Palmer.
4. "Comoros | Culture, History, & People | Britannica,".
5. Runnells, *CES Letter*.20.
6. Palmer, "Joseph Smith, Captain Kidd, Cumorah, and Moroni."

names are extraordinarily rare by themselves but are found together very frequently in LDS scholarship.[7]

Aside from discussing a chain of Islands East of Africa or the LDS teaching on how Joseph acquired the golden plates, in what other contexts would the name "Moroni" be used in the same sentence as the name "Camorah?" The odds of these two words occurring together spontaneously are infinitesimally small. Here we see these words paired together with a clear connection, Captain Kidd the pirate hero of young Joseph Smith.

All of this is to point out that Joseph's familiarity with Captain Kidd almost ensures that he was aware of the locations of his exciting adventures. Whether consciously or subconsciously it appears well within the realm of possibility that Joseph acquired two very prominent BOM names from these stories.

Here is yet another source from which Joseph may have found names for his BOM. Undoubtedly there are many other sources which could similarly be examined as source material. While these parallels may not constitute clear proof that these names were the source of those found in the BOM an inquisitive mind will see that they are plausibly source material.

---

7. Palmer.

Chapter 31: 10. Joseph's Family

THERE IS ONE FINAL source that I want to present for evaluation as we construct a secular case for the authorship of the BOM. Up to this point we have looked at nine potential sources which either provided content to Joseph or assisted him by sharpening his abilities or removing some difficulty. As we conclude our review of potential influences for a young Joseph Smith it is profitable to turn toward his youth and family life with special focus on the supernatural and religious leanings of the Smith family.

Lucy:

The Smiths were certainly religious, although not committedly so. Joseph Jr.'s mother, Lucy Smith was a religious seeker of sorts. She had a deep interest in the destiny of her soul and experiencing manifestations from God, but she never found herself able to commit to a specific church or denomination. In her youth, she experienced what may be seen as depression. She is recorded having said: "I was pensive and melancholy, and often in my reflections I thought that life was not worth possessing."[1] In response to her troubled state she sought religious experience to heal her heart. As she pursued religion, she was concerned with how she could know what church was teaching the truth. She lamented of this challenge.

---

1. "Biographical Sketches of Joseph Smith the Prophet, and His Progenitors for Many Generations, Page i."

> No church will admit that I am right, except the one with which I am associated. This makes them witness against each other; and how can I decide in such a case as this, seeing they are all unlike the Church of Christ, as it existed in former days!²

Due to her indecisiveness, she remained mostly church-less but continued to devote herself to reading of the Bible and prayer using "Jesus and his disciples for [her] guide." After some time, she concluded that it was necessary for her to comply with the ordinance of baptism. In an attempt to embrace this call, she found a minister who would baptize her without requiring her to be a member of any church or denomination and "yielded obedience to this ordinance."³

Joe Sr.:

Joseph Smith's father, Joseph Smith Sr., had a similar experience with religion, although he was appearingly far less devout than Lucy. As Bushman puts it, "Lucy's only explicit reservation about her husband was his diffidence about religion. After his brief flirtation with Universalism in 1797, Joseph Sr. hovered on the margins of the churches."⁴ He was still somewhat given to prayer but remained largely unmoved by religious passion. This changed slightly between 1810 and 1811 when his father-in-law converted. He "became much excited upon the subject of religion." In spite of this, "what he could not embrace was the institutional religion of his time."⁵

While Joseph Sr. did not hold devout commitments to specific denominations or churches, he was a spiritual man who believed deeply in the supernatural. He had a series of dreams which he deemed to hold religious meaning. We will examine one of the most famous of these dreams in some detail a little further on. The first of these dreams illustrates the confusion that Joseph Sr. was contending with concerning the topic of religion.

> He was traveling in an open, barren field and could see nothing except dead and fallen timber[. . . there was a] death-like silence [. . .] Joseph had [a . . .] spirit by his side, who told him that

---

2. "Biographical Sketches of Joseph Smith the Prophet, and His Progenitors for Many Generations, Page i."

3. "Biographical Sketches of Joseph Smith the Prophet, and His Progenitors for Many Generations, Page i."

4. Bushman, *Joseph Smith*.25.

5. Bushman.25

this field was the world and it was lying dumb in regard to true religion and the plan of salvation. [. . . H]e found a box. A spirit told him that if he ate the contents they "would make you wise, and give you wisdom and understanding." [. . .] In Joseph Sr.'s, attempt to eat, threatening animals kept him away from the food.[6]

Bushman interprets this dream noting that Joseph saw the world as "empty and silent, or fiercely hostile to true wisdom and understanding."[7] This dream caused Joseph Sr. to doubt the truth of any church or denomination. Lucy recorded that after this dream her "husband seemed more confirmed than ever, in the opinion that there was no order or class of religionists that knew any more concerning the kingdom of God, than those of the world, or such as made no profession of religion whatever."[8]

I provide this brief religious background for both of Joseph's parents to point out that there was no denominational stability for him as a child. As we looked at the religious dispositions of both parents a reader may have found a real familiarity as these exact same perspectives were held by Joseph himself. One may be tempted to view Joseph's revelation in the first vision as a unique and isolated epiphany where he was told "that the churches of the day believed "in incorrect doctrines and that none of them was acknowledged of God as His Church and kingdom.""[9] However, far from being a belief unique to himself, the distrust of all churches was a very natural part of his family environment.

One wonders if the BOM would ever have been written if Joseph's family had become committed members of a church. With such a lack of religious stability in his life, it is no surprise that Joseph failed to find membership at any church. Joseph's marked denunciation of all organized denominations would have been far more surprising coming from a child who had been intimately involved in a church where he had a strong community and authoritative teaching from a trained pastor. As it occurred, however, it is far less remarkable that Joseph came to his conclusion. In many ways he was just following the religious example set by his parents.

---

6. C Jess Groesbeck, "THE SMITHS AND THEIR DREAMS AND VISIONS," 1988, 8.

7. Bushman, *Joseph Smith*.39.

8. "Biographical Sketches of Joseph Smith the Prophet, and His Progenitors for Many Generations, Page i."

9. "First Vision,".

Treasure:

The distrust of churches is not the only supernaturalistic worldview held by the Smith family. There was a clear magical worldview in the Smith household. Joseph's mother "was known to practice chiromancy, or palm reading [. . .]; Joseph Smith Sr. made use of a dowsing rod, which [. . .] could be used for telling fortunes, divining spiritual answers to yes-and-no questions, [or] locating hidden treasure."[10]

Joseph inherited this magical worldview from his family and the culture around him. He "became a user of divining rods by about age thirteen, and then, around age sixteen, began using a seer stone to seek buried treasure."[11] His apparent gifting in these forms of folk magic proved to be extraordinarily useful for him when it came to translating the BOM.

What is even more interesting is the fact that some principles from 19th century folk magic appear in the BOM. We recall that during Joseph's treasure digging one of the greatest obstacles to the zealous treasure diggers would be a "slippery" treasure sinking down into the earth to avoid acquisition. Allegedly, if an incantation or magical rite was not perfectly executed the treasure's guardian spirits would drag their treasure deep into the earth to evade the diggers.

This set of magical beliefs is characteristic of the early 19th century and is exactly what Joseph is well known to have participated in. While these descriptions are not out of the ordinary in the early 1800s, it is interesting to find BOM peoples experiencing the same problems as they do in Helaman 13 and Mormon 1.

> [31]And behold, the time cometh that he curseth your riches, that they become slippery, that ye cannot hold them; and in the days of your poverty ye cannot retain them. [. . .] [35]Yea, we have hid up our treasures and they have slipped away from us, because of the curse of the land. [36]O that we had repented in the day that the word of the Lord came unto us; for behold the land is cursed, and all things are become slippery, and we cannot hold them.
>
> (Helaman 13:31, 35-36)
>
> [18]And these Gadianton robbers, who were among the Lamanites, did infest the land, insomuch that the inhabitants thereof began to hide up their treasures in the earth; and they became

---

10. Davis, *Visions in a Seer Stone*.12.
11. "Inside the Mind of Joseph Smith —02 |.

slippery, because the Lord had cursed the land, that they could not hold them, nor retain them again.

(Mormon 1:18)

When viewed in conjunction with the beliefs of Joseph's family and the surrounding culture, it is somewhat predictable that we should find these traces of a 19th century magical worldview in the BOM. A reader must decide, is this a fingerprint of 19th century authorship or mere coincidence?

Joseph Sr.'s Dream:

We now proceed to the most famous dream of Joseph Smith Sr. In 1811, he had the second of his seven recorded dreams. The reason that this dream has drawn so much attention from the community of LDS scholarship is because it very closely resembles the vision had by Lehi in 1 Nephi 8.

Before we examine the dream itself, it is notable to see the similarities between the men Joseph Smith Sr. and Lehi. Both were fathers with families, and both had sons who became important prophets. As we will see here, both had spiritual dreams or visions—at least one of which bears a very great resemblance. Below I will supply only a list of the parallels between the two dreams. However, if the reader is interested in comparing the two themself, I will provide both accounts, in full, in an appendix.

Joseph Smith Sr. 1811	Book of Mormon 1830
"I was travelling in an open, *desolate field* . . ."	"I beheld a large and *spacious field* . . ."
"The *road was so broad* and barren . . ."	" . . . leadeth them away into *broad roads* . . ."
"I came to a *narrow path* . . ."	" . . . I also beheld a strait and *narrow path* . . ."
"I beheld a beautiful *stream of water* . . ."	"I beheld a *river of water* . . ."
"*I could see a rope,* running *along the bank of it* . . ."	"*I beheld a rod of iron,* and it extended along the *bank of the river* . . ."

Joseph Smith Sr. 1811	**Book of Mormon 1830**
"... in which stood a tree such as I, had never seen before. It was *exceedingly handsome* ..."	"And I looked and beheld a *tree* ... and the *beauty* thereof was far beyond, yea, exceeding of all *beauty*;"
"... it bore a kind of *fruit*, in shape much like a chestnut bur, and as *white as snow*, or, if possible, *whiter* ..."	"I beheld that the *fruit* thereof was *white, to exceed all the whiteness* that I had ever seen."
"I drew near, and *began to eat of it*, and I found it *delicious beyond description*."	"I did go forth and *partake of the fruit* thereof; and I beheld that *it was most sweet*, above all that I ever before tasted."
"As I was eating, I said in my heart, 'I cannot eat this alone, *I must bring my wife and children, that they may partake with me*."	"I began to be *desirous that my family should partake* of it also; for I knew that it was desirable above all other fruit."
"I beheld a *spacious building* standing opposite the valley which we were in, and it appeared to *reach to the very heavens*."	"... and *behold*, on the other side of the river of water, a great and *spacious building*; and *it stood as it were in the air, high above the earth*."
"... they were all *filled with people*, who were *very finely dressed*."	"And it was *filled with people* ... and their manner of *dress was exceedingly fine*;"
"... they *pointed the finger* of scorn at us, and treated us with all manner of disrespect and contempt."	"... they were in the attitude of mocking and *pointing their fingers* ..."
"... what was the meaning of the *spacious building* which I saw. He replied, '*It is Babylon, it is Babylon, and it must fall*."	"And the large and *spacious building*, which thy father saw, is *vain imaginations and the pride of the children of men*."

This collection of parallels was obtained from an infographic on the LDS studies website, *Stuff You Missed In Sunday School.[12] The commonalities between the two accounts are profound. It is important to keep in mind, that Joseph Smith Sr. had this dream in 1811, before Joseph had done any translation of the plates containing the vision of Lehi. The two accounts are, allegedly, completely unique events. However, the immense similarity has caused some to question whether the visions may have a dependent relationship.

The fact that these accounts are remarkably similar is undebatable. Even the LDS apologists do not try to argue that they bear no true resemblance. Instead, they are forced to address the conundrum in a different manner. There are three main approaches to this issue as detailed by an author at FAIRLatterDaySaints.com. These are as follows:

1. Joseph Smith plagiarized Joseph Sr.'s dream when he wrote the Book of Mormon.

2. Joseph Sr. had a dream that was similar to the dream experienced by Lehi, and this was a sign to the Prophet's family that he was translating a real record that came from God.

3. Lucy Mack Smith's account of the dream (which she recorded many years after the fact, when the Book of Mormon account was well-known and published) may have influenced how she remembered and/or recorded her account of Joseph Sr's dream.[13]

Of course, the typical view of critical scholars is that the dream which Joseph Sr. had in 1811 would have been familiar to Joseph Jr. and he likely used it, consciously or not, as a structure for the vision of Lehi in the BOM. This is not at all unreasonable. The timeline is believable as the dream was had in 1811; well before the translation of the BOM took place. However, as is stated above, this is not the only explanation.

It is also possible that Joseph Sr. and Lehi just happened to share a dream with many similarities. While this is not by any means logically impossible, it appears to be *very* unlikely. It is a far more reasonable position to assume a kind of dependent relation between the two.

Finally, the approach of the LDS scholars is that the BOM proved to be an influential source material for Lucy Smith's record of Joseph Sr's

---

12. "Tree of Life," Stuff You Missed in Sunday School, April 7, 2018.

13. "Book of Mormon/Plagiarism Accusations/Joseph Smith, Sr.'s Dream and Lehi's Vision - FAIR,".

dream. This perspective also holds some water. While it is true that Sr.'s dream occurred in 1811, the record of it was not produced until 1853, over 20 years after the publication of the BOM. Rather than assume that Joseph Jr. took inspiration from the dream of his father, there are some who believe that the BOM influenced Lucy Smith's memory and she happened to mix the dream that Joseph Sr. had with the vision of Lehi.

Hypothetically, both theories are *possible*. In both cases, an individual is influenced by the words of another and each craft a narrative that shares similar wording and structure. I am not of the opinion that we can definitively prove which was the primary source text with the present information. However, if we reflect on the great number of items which appear to have made their way into the BOM from outside sources, it would not be difficult to believe that this is a similar case.

Here then, we have completed our brief review of the final potential influence on Joseph Smith as he wrote the BOM. It appears more than feasible that his unique religious upbringing, family culture, magical worldview, and dreams of his father could have left their mark on Joseph Smith's authorship of the BOM.

In the preceding pages I have endeavored to present a case for the secular authorship of the BOM. The LDS community is intent to declare that the *only* way this record could have come to be is by the gift and power of God. I fundamentally disagree with this presupposition and believe that the BOM quite clearly demonstrates its modern authorship.

Furthermore, it almost requires Joseph Smith to be its author and not merely its translator. In our treatment of this topic, we considered the mental capacity of Smith as well as just 10 of the many potential sources which the BOM could have depended upon for its creation.

I freely admit that parallels, which have largely comprised this study, do not necessarily indicate that dependent relationships exist between texts. However, as I have asked the reader multiple times, if one is attempting to objectively evaluate this text, is it truly the more reasonable option to hold that the presence of so many parallels is mere coincidence? The odds of just one of our sources bearing the demonstrated resemblance is very unlikely. The likelihood of *all* of the similarities being coincidental is next to impossible.

In a speech addressing the vision of Lehi, Boyd K. Packer, a member of the Quorum of the Twelve Apostles at the time of his speech, inquires: "Who wrote this incredible vision? There is nothing like it in the Bible.

Did Joseph Smith compose it? Did he write the Book of Mormon? That is harder to believe than the account of angels and golden plates."[14]

While Packer finds a secular authorship of the BOM difficult to believe, in light of the evidence which we have explored here, I find it far more difficult to believe that the BOM was not written by Joseph utilizing secular means.

---

14. Boyd K. Packer, "Lehi's Dream and You," *BYU Speeches* (blog).

Chapter 32: **Polygamy and Polyandry**

IN THE PREVIOUS PAGES we have touched upon a selection of the most prominent and important topics in LDS critical research. As we approach the end of this investigation, I want to address two final topics which are of some great interest to those engaged in LDS studies: polygamy and witness credibility. One of the most notorious topics associated with the LDS church, is the infamous practice of Polygamy. This is for good reason.

Polygamy and polyandry are among the most frequently addressed topics by those critical of the LDS church. In fact, it may be one of the greatest associations that people have in their heads when they hear the word "Mormonism." Almost anyone who dips their toe into the field of LDS studies has fallen down the rabbit hole of plural marriage.

While polygamy creates some high-quality entertainment for those curious about the LDS church, it has little to no bearing on the church's truth claims. This topic is a "red herring" of sorts, a distraction from the truly important question of whether the BOM is true and if Joseph was truly a prophet. The practice of plural marriage further mars the already questionable appearance of the history of the LDS church. It must be understood, however, that it does not form an argument against veracity of LDS claims.

This being the case, there remains a place for studies on the LDS practice of polygamy as it effectively paints a picture of the character of Joseph Smith. Up to this point I have refrained from addressing the content of Joseph Smith's character as I find that ad hominem, arguments would detract from what I hope to accomplish in creating a

CHAPTER 32: POLYGAMY AND POLYANDRY

cogent argument which will serve as a guide for those committed to discerning the truth.

Even in my treatment of this topic I endeavor not to paint him in too negative a light. When one examines this part of his history it appears that he merely fell prey to the same vice that has ensnared so many other powerful men. As Lord Acton famously stated in his 1887 letter to Archbishop Mandell Creighton "Power tends to corrupt and absolute power corrupts absolutely."[1]

There can hardly be a greater power than that which Joseph held being the very mouthpiece of God. Joseph received a revelation in 1830 and, speaking of himself from the perspective of God, he said "For his word ye shall receive, as if from mine own mouth, in all patience and faith." (D&C 21:5) In another revelation, as is his custom, Joseph once again presumed to speak on behalf of God saying, "whether by mine own voice or by the voice of my servants, it is the same." (D&C 1:38) Thus, Joseph effectively acquires for himself the supreme authority of God. As this kind of power has the tendency to do, it corrupted and unsurprisingly, Joseph, on occasion, exercised his authority to appease his sometimes narcissistic and domineering personality.

Evidence of these flaws in his character can be seen in many occurrences throughout his history. For instance, when Joseph received a revelation concerning Martin Harris that he should mortgage his farm to finance the publication of the BOM. For some context, Joseph Smith asked Martin Harris, who had already contributed a great deal to the cause, to sell his family's farm to acquire the finances necessary to publish the BOM. Harris said that he would not comply unless he received a revelation from the Lord commanding him to do so. Conveniently, Joseph received a revelation from the Lord mandating just that. D&C 19 records this revelation.

> [13]Wherefore, I command you to repent, and keep the commandments which you have received by the hand of my servant Joseph Smith, Jun., in my name; [. . .] [15] Therefore I command you to repent—repent, lest I smite you by the rod of my mouth, and by my wrath, and by my anger, and your sufferings be sore—how sore you know not, how exquisite you know not, yea, how hard to bear you know not. [. . .] [26]And again, I command thee that thou shalt not covet thine own property, but impart it freely to

---

1. "Acton, Letter on Historical Integrity, 1887,".

the printing of the Book of Mormon, which contains the truth and the word of God–

(D&C 19:13,15,26)

A critical reading of this interaction may cause one to question the motives of Joseph Smith. The tone of this revelation uses some powerful language to coerce Harris into selling his livelihood and its timing is highly suspect. Perhaps it was not the heart of Joseph to pressure his friend into supplying the money for the publishing of his great work. Maybe Joseph was even more upset about the prospect than Harris was. The Lord works in mysterious ways.

There are many examples that follow a similar pattern to the one I have just shared. None of the examples, however, illustrate this tendency in Joseph so clearly as his practice of polygamy and polyandry.

While most people are familiar with polygamy, fewer know what polyandry is. An Elder Marlin K. Jensen summarizes both succinctly. "Polygamy is when a man has multiple wives. Polyandry is when a man marries another man's wife. Joseph did both."[2] Polygamy is the practice of one man having multiple wives and Polyandry is the practice of one wife having multiple husbands. Jensen summarizes that Joseph Smith practiced both. He had multiple wives, some of whom were already married to other men.

Before we dive into the particulars of Joseph's plural marriages, we will look at the basis for his adoption of this holy command.

Joseph's revelation on eternal and plural marriage is found in D&C 132. The justification used draws primarily from the Genesis 15–16 account of Abraham and Hagar.

> [32]Go ye, therefore, and do the works of Abraham; enter ye into my law and ye shall be saved. [...] [34]God commanded Abraham, and Sarah gave Hagar to Abraham to wife. And why did she do it? Because this was the law; [...] [35]Was Abraham, therefore, under condemnation? Verily I say unto you, Nay; for I, the Lord, commanded it.

(D&C 132:32, 34–35)

Curiously, the salient point of this revelation, namely that Abraham and Sarah were commanded by God to give Hagar to Abraham to wife, is missing from the passage as provided in the Bible. In fact, Sarah laments

---

2. Runnells, *CES Letter*.57.

"My wrong be upon thee: I have given my maid into thy bosom;" (Gen. 16:5). This does not sound like the way one would describe following the commands of God. The passage in D&C 132 goes on to discuss the wives of David and Solomon as further confirmation of this principle.

A little further on, the revelation is addressed to Emma Smith directly with poignant and amusing directness.

> [52]And let mine handmaid, Emma Smith, receive all those [wives] that have been given unto my servant Joseph, [. . .] [54]And I command mine handmaid, Emma Smith, to abide and cleave unto my servant Joseph, and to none else. But if she will not abide this commandment she shall be destroyed, [. . .] [56]And again, verily I say, let mine handmaid forgive my servant Joseph his trespasses; and then shall she be forgiven her trespasses. (D&C 132: 52,54,56)

This is a stunning revelation. The Lord spoke directly to Emma and encouraged her to forgive Joseph of his trespasses. If this were not a revelation from God Himself one could easily believe that these are the attempts of a husband desperately trying to escape, what Congreve describes in his play *The Mourning Bride*, as possessing greater fury than Hell itself.[3] Needless to say, Emma was not at all pleased with the fact that Joseph had taken multiple wives.[4] In this revelation she is told to accept them. In essence, Joseph is justified in his spiritually condoned affairs, however, if Emma behaved similarly "she shall be destroyed."

A reading of Joseph's history makes it appear that Joseph held a deep love for his first wife, Emma. Though this was not always demonstrated by his actions, he maintained a unique affection for her which is attested to throughout his life. In a way not so uncommon for powerful men, he did not remain faithful to his first wife. Whether this was because of a command of the Lord or a result his own vices luring him I will let the reader decide.

The estimates have varied over time as to how many wives Joseph had. At this time, the generally accepted figure is thirty-four.[5] This number is compiled as a collection of both polygamous and polyandrous

---

3. Congreve, William. The Mourning Bride: A Tragedy. United Kingdom: J. Bell, 1797. As the phrase has become, "Hell hath no fury like a woman scorned."

4. Brittany Chapman Nash, *Let's Talk about Polygamy*, Let's Talk About (Salt Lake City, Utah: Deseret Book, 2021).11-12.

5. Nash.13.

marriages. Of Joseph's 34 wives, 11 of them of were already married, 8 were biological sister wives, and one was a mother-daughter pair.[6]

LDS Scholar Brittany Chapman Nash describes the age range of the women he married. "The majority of the women to whom Joseph Smith was sealed were between the ages of twenty and forty. The oldest woman he married was fifty-eight-year-old Rhoda Richards, [. . .] The youngest was fourteen-year-old Helen Mar Kimball."[7] We will look more closely at this relationship presently. This practice became an influential and defining aspect of Joseph's life. How did his religiously sanctioned philandering begin?

Joseph's first plural wife, Fanny Alger was likely around the age of 19 when they married. This is based upon her birth year of 1816[8] and the more speculative year of the marriage in 1835. Richard Bushman adds that "in 1836, after a time as a serving girl in the Smith household, she left Kirtland and soon remarried."[9] Nash describes the beginnings of this relationship.

> Fragmentary sources suggest that in the mid-1830s Joseph introduced the principle of plural marriage to Latter-Day Saint relatives of Fanny Alger, a church member who worked in the Smith home in Kirtland, Ohio. Joseph received permission from Fanny's parents to marry their daughter.[10]

Another source relates:

> There lived then with this family (the Prophet's) a neighbor's daughter, Fannie Alger, a very nice and comely young woman about my own age [Johnson was then seventeen], toward whom not only myself, but everyone, seemed partial, for the amiability of her character; and it was whispered even then that Joseph loved her. . . . Without a doubt in my mind, Fannie Alger was, at Kirtland, the Prophet's first plural wife.[11]

As these two sources relate, Fanny was a "comely" girl between the ages of 17 and 19 loved my many. She lived and worked in the Smith house and Joseph took a liking to her. Sometime before she departed in

---

6. Runnells, *CES Letter*.53-66.
7. Nash, *Let's Talk about Polygamy*.13.
8. "Fanny Alger,".
9. Bushman, *Joseph Smith*.323.
10. Nash, *Let's Talk about Polygamy*.9.
11. Brodie, *No Man Knows My History*.458.

1836, she became the first plural wife of Joseph Smith. Later on, in a letter to his brother, Oliver Cowdery described that Joseph was engaged in "a dirty, nasty, filthy affair" with Fanny Alger.[12] Perhaps we ought to extend some grace to Cowdery, however, because the revelation allowing plural marriage had not yet been recorded.

About 24 wives later, Joseph married Helen Mar Kimball. Helen was "the daughter of Joseph's close friends Heber C. and Vilate Murray Kimball." The Church essay *Plural Marriage in Kirtland and Nauvoo* admits that Helen was only 14 years old at the time of her marriage to Joseph who was, at the time, 38 years old.[13] Helen relates the experience of her marriage to the prophet in her own words in her autobiography, *A Woman's View*.

> Just previous to my father's starting upon his last mission but one, to the Easter states, he taught me the principle of Celestial marriage, and having a great desire to be connected with the Prophet Joseph, he offered me to him; [. . .] I will pass over the temptations which I had during the twenty four hours after my father had introduced to me the principle and asked me if I would be sealed to Joseph, who came next morning and with my parents I heard him teach and explain the principle of Celestial marriage- after which he said to me, 'If you will take this step, it will ensure your eternal salvation and exaltation and that of your father's household and all of your kindred.' [. . .] This promise was so great that I will-ingly gave myself to purchase so glorious a reward. None but God & his angels could see my mother's bleeding heart–[14]

The choice that this fourteen-year-old child was tasked with making is incomprehensibly heavy. She was offered by her father to the prophet Joseph Smith to be his wife. One can only imagine what she means by "the temptations which I had during the twenty-four hours after" her father had told her of their plans. What kind of weight must she have carried in those hours? In her noble naivete she consented to marry the prophet with the expected prize of an assurance of eternal life for herself and her family.

In addition to his polygamous relationships such as those just described, Joseph also engaged in polyandrous relations. In a couple of

---

12. Brodie.459.
13. "Plural Marriage in Kirtland and Nauvoo".
14. "Whitney, Helen Mar, 1828-1896,".

these marriages, Joseph married the men's wives after their husbands had been sent out on their mission to serve the Church. Two of these cases are found in the lives of Zina Jacobs Young and Nancy Marinda Johnson Hyde.

Zina was Joseph's fifth wife.[15] She was born in 1821 and joined the LDS church in 1835. "In 1840 Joseph Smith privately taught her about plural marriage and proposed to her. Uncertain about this practice, Zina declined."[16] On March 7, 1841 she was married to her first husband Henry Jacobs. Only "seven and one half months later, on October 27, 1841, she was married to Joseph Smith," at twenty years old. As is so often the case when studying obscure texts from history, we do not have many sources reporting how Zina's husband, Henry Jacobs, responded to her re-marriage. The few that we do possess, however, evoke strong feeling.

A John D. Lee relates that he embarked on a trip with Henry Jacobs and he "was bragging about his wife, what a true, virtuous, lovely woman she was. He almost worshipped her. Little did he think in his absence she was sealed to the prophet Joseph." A second source elaborates upon what absence Lee was recounting. William Hall writes: "A Mr. Henry Jacobs had his wife seduced by Joe Smith, in his time, during a mission to England. She was a very beautiful woman, but when Jacobs returned, he found her pregnant by Smith."[17] While we do not know for certain if Zina ever had a child with Joseph Smith (as the record is unclear) it does seem supported that Joseph sealed himself to Zina while her husband was away serving his mission for the church.

Nancy Marinda Johnson Hyde is a second instance of Joseph's polyandry. She was his eleventh wife.[18] Nancy was born in June of 1815 and joined the church in 1832. On September 4, 1834, she married Orson Hyde. Some years later around 1842, she was married to Joseph Smith.[19] Around this time also, Nancy's husband, Orson Hyde, a devout church member who was removed and restored to a position in the Quorum of the Twelve numerous times, was serving his mission in Palestine.[20] Here again the dates are a bit unclear and there is some debate over the exact time when Nancy was sealed to Joseph. In spite of the lack of clarity, the

15. Runnells, *CES Letter*.66.
16. "Zina D. H. Jacobs Young,".
17. Brodie, *No Man Knows My History*.466.
18. Runnells, *CES Letter*.66.
19. "Marinda Nancy Johnson Hyde —Biography,".
20. "Orson Hyde —Biography,".

CHAPTER 32: POLYGAMY AND POLYANDRY

evidence available leads to the conclusion that the relationship between Joseph and Nancy was built while Orson was away. This is based, in large part, off of a revelation that Joseph had for Nancy in December of 1841.

Joseph received a message from the Lord advising that "concerning my handmaid Nancy Marinda Hyde" she and her children should be given a better place to live and that they should be taken "care of faithfully and kindly until my servant Orson Hyde returns from his mission, or until some other provision can be made for her welfare and safety."

The revelation goes on to say, somewhat suspiciously, "let my handmaid Nancy Marinda Hyde hearken to the counsel of my servant Joseph in all things whatsoever he shall teach unto her, and it shall be a blessing upon her and upon her children after her, unto her justification, saith the Lord."[21] As we saw with Helen Mar Kimball, Joseph is known to teach of plural marriage and then leverage assurance of blessing and justification to seal the deal. It appears very reasonable to assume that Nancy hearkening unto "whatsoever he shall teach" "unto her justification" may suggest more than mere discussions of LDS doctrine.

If this timeline is accurate, here is a second example of Joseph sending missionaries and seducing their wives while they are away. There is at least one other case of a similar story that is worth sharing to investigate the way in which Joseph exercised his leadership in the early LDS community. We recall that just before Heber C. Kimball left for his final mission, Joseph requested his fourteen-year-old daughter's hand in marriage. After this, Heber responsibly served his mission only to find a devastating burden upon his return. *Heber C. Kimball: Mormon Patriarch and Pioneer* powerfully recounts his trial as follows:

> ... shortly after Heber's return from England, he was introduced to the doctrine of plural marriage directly through a startling test— a sacrifice that shook his very being and challenged his faith to the ultimate. He had already sacrificed homes, possessions, friends, relatives, all worldly rewards, peace, and tranquility for the Restoration. Nothing was left to place on the altar save his life, his children, and his wife. Then came the Abrahamic test. Joseph demanded for himself what to Heber was the unthinkable, his [wife] Vilate. Totally crushed spiritually and emotionally, Heber touched neither food nor water for three days and three nights and continually sought confirmation and

---

21. Smith, Joseph. *History of the Church of Jesus Christ of Latter-day Saints.* Vol. 4. Salt Lake City: Deseret Book, 1978, p.467.

comfort from God. On the evening of the third day, some kind of assurance came, and Heber took Vilate to the upper room of Joseph's store on Water Street. The Prophet wept at this act of faith, devotion, and obedience. Joseph had never intended to take Vilate. It was all a test.[22]

There are a couple of ways of viewing this 'test.' Is it possible that Joseph actually had planned to take Vilate for himself? In light of the previous two examples, this does not seem to be a stretch too great for one's imagination. Perhaps upon seeing the incredible grief he caused Heber, Joseph decided to relent at the last moment and shrug it all off as a test. Of course, this is just speculation. It could be that Joseph had planned this crucible for his friend from the very beginning. Although, one must ask, does this solve the clear character issue? True, such a test is far better than the actual intention of taking one's wife, but is it justified? Is it not still cruel and narcissistic at the very least?

After reviewing these examples of Joseph's philandering, the story of David in 2 Samuel 11 comes to mind. After King David had sent his army out to fight for him, he saw the beautiful wife of the soldier Uriah bathing, had her brought to his chamber, and had an affair with her. How similar is this story with the what the Prophet Joseph did in at least two cases; sending out his missionaries and sealing their wives to himself while they were away. In some ways, Joseph's conduct is even worse than David's. David attempted to cover up his misdeed, Joseph was shameless.[23]

One of the common responses which LDS apologists are quick to cite is that many of the marriages of Joseph were for "eternity only" meaning that they would be sealed for eternity, but not necessarily for the time here on earth. These marriages, the apologists assert, most likely excluded sexual intimacy. Marriages for "*time and* eternity," on the other hand, were those which also contained temporal marital relations and not only spiritual significance. It is manifestly clear as has been confirmed by the LDS church that Joseph had both kinds of relationships. In light of this fact, any argument that his plural marriages were strictly non-sexual is blatantly untrue.[24]

---

22. Kimball, Stanley B., "Heber C. Kimball: Mormon Patriarch and Pioneer." *Urbana: University of Illinois Press*, 1981, 93.

23. To his credit, Smith did not kill any of the husbands to cover his affairs as far as we know.

24. "Plural Marriage in Kirtland and Nauvoo."

For those who still want to deny the implicitly sexual nature of plural marriage, D&C 132:63 explicitly lays out one of the primary purposes of plural marriage: "for they [additional wives] are given unto him to multiply and replenish the earth." If there were no intention of sexual relations, the God-ordained purpose of multiplying and replenishing the earth would remain unfulfilled.

The influential ex-LDS author Jeremy Runnells provides a compelling argument to the same conclusion.

> If Joseph's polygamous/polyandrous marriages are innocuous "dynastic sealings" meant for the afterlife, as the church and apologists are now theorizing, [. . .] why was Heber C. Kimball so troubled by Joseph's command for his wife that he "touched neither food nor water for three days and nights?

There is one final point worth addressing in regard to the polygamy/polyandry of Joseph Smith. That is the eyebrow-raising timeline in which it occurred and was revealed to the church. While this revelation was first recorded in D&C 132 in 1843, there are sources which assert that the groundwork for this teaching was developed as early as 1831 when Joseph was studying the Old Testament.[25] Of course, this is important because if Joseph had not learned of this before 1843, none of his marriages up to that point would have been condoned by the Lord. The next important date on the timeline is April 1836. This is when Joseph received from, "the Old Testament prophet Elijah[, . . .] the priesthood keys necessary to perform ordinances" such as those required for eternal marriage. Without these keys, and this authority, all plural marriages would be merely earthly and, without the eternal component, adulterous.

This brings us back to Joseph's relation with Fanny Alger. The church holds that Fanny was married to Joseph sometime during the mid 1830s. As she and her family left in 1836, the marriage must have been prior to this. We refer to Cowdery's accusation of this being a "dirty, nasty, filthy affair." This alongside the fact that the marriage more than likely occurred in 1835 draws the conclusion that Joseph may have engaged in behavior which "was illegal under both the laws of the land and under any theory of divine authority; it was adultery."[26] Bushman, considering this situation eloquently poses the question: "Was he [Joseph] a blackguard

---

25. "Plural Marriage in Kirtland and Nauvoo."
26. Runnells, *CES Letter*.62-63

covering his lusts with religious pretentions, or a prophet doggedly adhering to instructions from heaven, or something in between?"[27]

The final concerning element of Joseph's actions is that they were engaged in deceitfully. Even if it were true (although it is doubtful) that there was overlap between the time which he was married to Fanny Alger and when he was awarded the keys by Elijah, Joseph still openly taught against polygamy.

First, polygamy is condemned in the BOM far more vehemently than it even is in the Bible. For instance, Jacob 2:24 addresses the issue very harshly. "Behold, David and Solomon truly had many wives and concubines, which thing was abominable before me, saith the Lord." Puzzlingly, in Jacob, God uses the same examples to condemn polygamy as he does to encourage it in D&C 132.

In addition, in the 1835 edition of the Doctrine and Covenants, polygamy is also condemned. 1835 D&C 13:7 commands: "Thou shalt love thy wife with all thy heart, and shall cleave unto her and none else."[28] D&C 65:3 of the same edition asserts: "Wherefore it is lawful that he should have one wife, and they twain shall be one flesh, and all this that the earth might answer the end of its creation."[29] The statement on marriage in 1835 D&C 101:4 articulates this position most strongly.

> Inasmuch as this church of Christ has been reproached with the crime of formication, and polygamy: we declare that we believe, that one man should have one wife; and one woman, but one husband, except in the case of death, when either is at liberty to marry again.[30]

This last revelation (101:4) was likely given around August of 1835[31] and, as such, was distributed for teaching after this date. That is, from the time of August 1835 until 1843, when the revelation on plural Marriage was recorded, Joseph was actively engaged in polygamy and polyandry while, at the same time, publicly condemning it. In fact, a number of

---

27. Bushman, *Joseph Smith*.323
28. "Doctrine and Covenants, 1835, Page 120,".
29. "Doctrine and Covenants, 1835, Page 191,".
30. "Doctrine and Covenants, 1835, Page 251,".
31. "Doctrine and Covenants, 1835, Page 251."

sources suggest that Joseph had 16 wives (not including Emma) before 1843, at least eight or nine of which were polyandrous.[32][33]

Joseph actively practiced polygamy and polyandry, before it was officially revealed to the church and all the while, preached against it as 1835 D&C demonstrates. Further, one of his marriages likely occurred even before he was given the sealing authority. This has placed Joseph in a veritable web of his own making and has made him and his church the subjects of an immense amount of well-deserved scrutiny.

As I conclude my treatment of this important topic, I want to reiterate the points I made at the outset. While I do believe that this topic is significant, I do not believe that it justifies or disqualifies the majority of the truth claims made by the contemporary LDS church. The fact that Joseph Smith practiced polygamy has nothing to do with whether Lehi and his family left Jerusalem and sailed to the Americas. Polygamy, in this day and age is widely condemned by the saints and is not practiced except for in very fringe groups. It has long since been removed from orthodoxy in the Church of Jesus Christ of Latter Day Saints. Rather than latching onto such legitimate moral failures and using them as evidence against the truth of all LDS beliefs, investigators should engage with the content of their belief structure thoroughly and critically as we have done throughout this book.

Though it has little bearing on the BOM's truth claims, the topic of Joseph's plural marriages effectively leads to at least three important conclusions. First, it may encourage particularly zealous LDS believers to remove Joseph from the pedestal of moral perfection which he has oft been placed upon.

Second, this study demonstrates that Joseph is not averse to operating in deceit or, at least in the shadows where certain beliefs or practices are concerned. As we unveil his character and find traits such as these it may lead us to consider more carefully his other teachings.

The third conclusion likely appeals only to those who hold a critical bias. That is, Joseph, like so many other men who have attained great power, appears to have been carried away by his vanity. He had a wandering eye which caused him to stumble—or rather dive headlong—into a ruling vice, lusting after women. Unfortunately, this practice and teaching came at an immense cost to Joseph and has plagued his church, as it likely

---

32. Brian C Hales, "The Joseph Smith-Sylvia Sessions Plural Sealing: Polyandry or Polygyny?," n.d., 17.

33. Nash, *Let's Talk about Polygamy*.

will continue to do, for as long as his church endures. Deplorably, Joseph Smith's teaching on and support of polygamy and polyandry has been the cause of great distress to many women even beyond his lifetime.

Was the teaching of plural marriage a revelation from God or the product of a young man with too much power who used religion to justify his lusts? If it was the work of God, the circumstances surrounding its origin and practice are certainly suspect.

Chapter 33: **The Eleven Witnesses**

To BOLSTER ITS CREDIBILITY the BOM does not *only* insist on the witness of the Holy Spirit to each individual and the words of Joseph Smith. The BOM includes two additional statements attesting to its veracity. One of these was signed by three witnesses, Oliver Cowdery, David Whitmer, and Martin Harris. The other was signed by eight witnesses, Christian Whitmer, Jacob Whitmer Peter Whitmer Jr., John Whitmer, Hiram Page, Joseph Smith Sr., Hyrum Smith, and Samuel Smith. These two records act as documents of authenticity and were originally placed at the end of the BOM (as can be seen in the 1830 edition). One scholar points out that "ancient documents often needed the signatures of witnesses in order to be considered authentic or legally binding." As such, the placement of these witnesses' testimonies at the end of the BOM acted "as a final seal of its veracity."[1]

These two documents are now known as The Testimony of the Three Witnesses and The Testimony of the Eight Witnesses. In each, the witnesses describe their encounter with the golden plates. Below I will provide an excerpt from each containing the most relevant parts of their statements.

> We know of a surety, that the work is true. And we also testify that we have seen the engravings which are upon the plates; and they have been shewn unto us by the power of God, and not of man. And we declare with words of soberness, that an Angel of God came down from heaven, and he brought and laid before our eyes, that we beheld and saw the plates, and the engravings

---

1. John Welch et al., "Testimony of the Three Witnesses" (Provo, UT: Foundation for Ancient Research and Mormon Studies, 1999).

thereon; [...] Nevertheless, the voice of the Lord commanded us that we should bear record of it; wherefore to be obedient unto the commandments of God, we bear testimony of these.

(The Testimony of the Three Witnesses)

Be it known [...] That Joseph Smith, Jun., [...] has shown unto us the plates of which hath been spoken, which have the appearance of gold; [...] we did handle with our hands; and we also saw the engravings thereon, [...] And this we bear record with words of soberness, that Smith has shown unto us, for we have seen and hefted, and know of a surety.

(The Testimony of the Eight Witnesses)

The LDS church holds that the testimony of these eleven men is convincing and ought to inspire a stronger testimony of the truth of the BOM. Though the golden plates were removed from the earth, which has inspired a great deal of skepticism, we have the statements from these men saying that they saw them and, in the case of the eight witnesses, even handled and hefted them. LDS Scholar Steven Harper describes the value of these statements. "The testimonies of the Three and Eight Witnesses printed in each copy of the Book of Mormon are some of the most compelling evidence in favor of its miraculous revelation and translation."[2]

The scholarly discussion surrounding the eleven witnesses focuses primarily on their reliability and how they saw what they claimed to see. As we proceed through our study, I will briefly address both topics.

First, what is it that the eleven witnesses saw? This is the easiest part of our investigation as it is so clearly stated in the testimonies which bear their names. The three witnesses saw an angel descend from heaven who laid the plates before their eyes. As they examined the plates, they noted the ancient engravings on them. The eight witnesses had a slightly different experience. Joseph himself showed them the plates and allowed them to "handle" them. This satisfied the curiosity of the witnesses who were afterwards able to say, "with words of soberness" that "Smith has got the plates of which we have spoken."[3] These are the alleged experiences of the witnesses.

---

2. "The Eleven Witnesses | Religious Studies Center,".
3. "Testimony of Eight Witnesses,".

CHAPTER 33: THE ELEVEN WITNESSES

There are a handful of responses that critical scholars propose regarding the statements of these witnesses. The theory that has gained the most traction is that the witnesses never actually saw the plates with their physical eyes. Understanding this position requires a bit of background on the witnesses.

As we have so frequently mentioned, the culture in New England during the 19th century had a casual acceptance of folk magic. All of the witnesses to the plates, were ensconced in this worldview. One of the notable expressions of this worldview was the wide acceptance of "second sight." "Traditionally," explains Palmer, "this included the ability to see spirits and their dwelling places within the local hills and elsewhere." This was a vitally important piece of the treasure hunting culture. "Seers," men who had the gift of second sight, would be able to see deep into the hills to find the location of buried treasures and the spirits guarding them. We recall that Joseph claimed to have this ability as, for a time, he even made use of it professionally.

This magical worldview was also prevalent amongst the witnesses. There is evidence supporting that "after meeting Joseph Smith, [Martin] Harris participated in his own treasure adventures."[4] Oliver Cowdery was known to be a "rodsman" meaning that he utilized a divining rod.[5] Hiram Page was reported to be a treasure hunter.[6] Aside from these men, we are left with only the Whitmers and the Smiths. The Smiths are well-known to have been raised with a magical worldview which they actively practiced; and there is plenty of support to show that the Whitmer family were also involved in the use of seer stones and the like.[7]

As the witnesses were all believers in this second sight, many scholars are of the opinion that they never truly saw the plates with their physical eyes. Rather, they perceived a manifestation of the plates in a vision which they saw through their "spiritual eyes." This perspective is not solely based on this conjecture. In fact, there are numerous records of interviews with these men in which they confirm that they saw the plates only with their spiritual eyes and not their physical ones. On the other hand, there are also a number of sources recanting those statements and doubling down that they truly saw the plates.

---

4. Palmer, *An Insider's View of Mormon Origins*.178.
5. Runnells, *CES Letter*.94.
6. Palmer, *An Insider's View of Mormon Origins*.179.
7. Palmer.180-185.

As can be expected, the LDS apologists stand firmly on top of the sources which state that the witnesses physically saw the plates and do their best to refute or deny the legitimacy of any document which disagrees with this conclusion. Equally predictably, the critical scholars discount the places where the witnesses affirm the physical nature of their encounter and champion the sources where the witnesses express that their visions were only spiritual.

Candidly, I do not believe that there is a definitive answer which constitutes proof for either position. While I hold to the critical perspective, I will note that this topic is challenging on account of the scant data and frequent contradictions. Did the witnesses believe that they saw the plates physically or spiritually? The answer to this is not manifestly clear.

To illustrate the difficulty of this subject and the conflict between the sources I will present just a couple of examples and let the reader come to their own conclusion.

David Whitmer gave multiple interviews in which he was asked about his encounter with the plates. In his conversation with LDS attorney James H. Moyle, it was described that he "was somewhat spiritual in his explanations." And that "he was not as materialistic in his descriptions as I wished." Further, in his own writing on the topic in *An Address to All Believers in Christ,* he described 'this experience as a "vision."'[8] In another conversation with and recorded by an excommunicated apostle, Thomas B. Marsh, Whitmer appears to contradict himself.

> I enquired seriously at David if it was true that he had seen the angel, according to his testimony as one of the witnesses of the Book of Mormon. He replied, as sure as there is a God in heaven, he saw the angel, according to his testimony in that book.[9]

The critical response to this quote is that in statements such as these Whitmer, and the other witnesses when speaking in like manner, never fully exclude second sight as a possibility. If to them second sight is legitimate, then they would be speaking truthfully when providing statements of this kind.

One of the most troubling quotations to those who sustain that the witnesses truly saw the plates with their physical eyes is by Martin Harris in 1838. He made a public statement which seriously threatens the

---

8. Palmer.196.

9. "Question: Did the Witnesses Who Left the Church Continue to Maintain Their Witness of the Book of Mormon? - FAIR,".

CHAPTER 33: THE ELEVEN WITNESSES

credibility of the testimony of the eleven. In a letter to Lyman Johnson three weeks after Martin's speech, Stephen Burnett states the following.

> When I came to hear Martin Harris state in public that he never saw the plates with his natural eyes only in a vison or imagination, neither Oliver nor David & also that the eight witnesses never saw them & hesitated to sign that instrument for that reason, but were persuaded to do it, the last pedestal gave way, in my view our foundations was sapped & the entire superstructure fell in a heap of ruins, . . . [later] M Harris arose & said he was sorry for any man who rejected the Book of Mormon for he knew it was true, he said he had hefted the plates repeatedly in a box with only a tablecloth or handkerchief over them, but never saw them only as he saw a city through a mountain. And said that he never should have told that the testimony of the eight was false, if it had not been picked out of [h]im but should have let it passed as it was.

Here Harris is recorded as saying that none of the witnesses actually saw the plates with their physical eyes and that their signatures were coerced. Further, at the end of this statement, he expresses regret at having shared these details.

LDS scholars, when addressing quotations reporting that the vision was spiritual and not physical, claim this as an act of piety. They propose that the experiences were so powerful that the witnesses may not have known themselves whether to articulate them as physical or spiritual. One scholar relates this to what Paul describes in 2 Corinthians 12:3. "And I know that this man was caught up into paradise—whether in the body or out of the body I do not know, God knows–"[10]

There are dozens more quotations which can be drawn from individuals supporting one perspective or the other of what the witnesses believed they saw. While I do hold to the perspective that the witnesses likely only saw using their "spiritual eyes" this is only because it coheres with my other biases on the topic. The LDS apologists appear to adopt a similar view, choosing to champion the sources which more closely support their previously held worldview.

Aside from what the witnesses believed or reportedly saw, we must also examine their reliability as individuals. This is where I find more compelling evidence which serves to caution investigators from readily accepting their accounts.

10. "The Eleven Witnesses | Religious Studies Center."

In a lecture concerning the historicity of the resurrection, Dr. Gary Habermas lists some of the most valuable traits for reliable witnesses. People who are either enemies or those who have changed their view make excellent witnesses because their biases are less likely to implicate them in whatever is being witnessed of.[11] Their skepticism forces them to require a higher quality of evidence. For this reason, if an enemy concludes that truth of a claim it is far more reliable than if a family member or partner does.

The eleven witnesses do not appear to possess either of these traits. Rather than appearing as skeptical outsiders, as Jeremy Runnells rightly points out, "all of the Book of Mormon witnesses, except Martin Harris, were related by blood or marriage to the Smiths or the Whitmers." These are hardly critical witnesses. Oliver Cowdery and Martin Harris had both served as Joseph's scribe, Hyrum, Samuel, and Joseph Sr. were all immediate family members of Joseph Smith Jr., and the rest of the witnesses were the Whitmer brothers with the exception of Hiram Page who along with Oliver Cowdery married into the Whitmer family. These early supporters were close friends and family members.[12] Considering the closeness of these relations alone, one has a right to be very skeptical of them as witnesses.

As we proceed to consider their credibility, we will look at their reputations, as well as their commitment to the Church. Though there is not an incredible amount of information regarding the eight witnesses, the three witnesses have many sources describing their character.

Martin Harris:

Martin Harris was a man who appeared to have a greater curiosity to religion than a commitment to it. Prior to joining Joseph's church, he "had been a Quaker, Universalist, Restorationist, Baptist, Presbyterian, and perhaps a Methodist. A Lorenzo Saunders wrote of Harris "Martin was a good citizen . . . a man that would do just as he agreed with you. But, he was a great man for seeing spooks."[13] Another account elaborates that "He told a man in Palmyra [. . . that he] met the Lord Jesus Christ, who walked

11. *Gary Habermas: The Resurrection Evidence That Changed Current Scholarship*, 2013.

12. "Why Was David Whitmer Excommunicated from the Church?," Book of Mormon Central, June 8, 2021.

13. Palmer, *An Insider's View of Mormon Origins*.177.

along by the side of him in the shape of a deer for two or three miles, talking with him as familiarly as one man talks with another."

Brigham Young said of Harris "as for Martin Harris, he had not much to apostatize from; he possessed a wild, speculative brain. I have heard Joseph correct him and exhort him to repentance for teaching false doctrines."[14] Harris was well known to have been superstitious and flighty. These and other descriptions of him make one question whether he could be relied upon to provide a trustworthy witness.

Most LDS apologists do not even deny Harris' superstitious and eccentric nature. Rather, they ask investigators to focus on his religiosity, virtue, and the fact that he made a few attempts to test the truth of the BOM naturalistically.[15] While it is true that he appears to have been a relatively virtuous man, this does not dispel the fact that, "he was a great man for seeing spooks" and this is not the mark of an excellent witness.

Oliver Cowdery:

Oliver Cowdery was less superstitious than the other two of the three witnesses, but nonetheless came from a background of treasure hunting where he used a divining rod. Aside from this, he was a schoolteacher, a lawyer,[16] and appears to have been quite a reasonable and intelligent man. In terms of his credibility as a witness, however, Cowdery was a relative of Joseph Smith and was the chief scribe for the translation of the BOM. While he may be the most objective of the three witnesses in terms of his clarity of mind, his proximity to Joseph makes him a questionable witness.

An LDS apologetics article addressing this topic notes that disqualifying Cowdery on account of his relationship with Joseph Smith is an occurrence of an ad hominem fallacy.[17] While this may be true in a sense, (as we are evaluating him based upon his involvement with Joseph) it is not exactly accurate that we are accusing his credibility solely on the basis of this trait. Rather, in many ways Cowdery is "on trial" alongside Joseph. As we are testing the truth claims of Joseph Smith, we cannot also use him as a key witness. He necessarily has an invested interest in proving his

---

14. Runnells, *CES Letter*.97.
15. "Martin Harris/Was He Unstable, Gullible and Superstitious - FAIR,".
16. "The Witnesses of the Book of Mormon Plates" Infographic.
17. "Oliver Cowdery/Related to Joseph Smith - FAIR,".

own credibility. This lessens his probability of remaining objective and, as a result, decreases his credibility. The same rule applies to Cowdery. It is not a specific characteristic that we find incredible, but his close association with Joseph in the creation of the BOM which removes him from the "witness" category and places him into the "on trial" category.

David Whitmer:

David Whitmer, as has been previously discussed, was also known to have been a treasure hunter and owned a seer stone. In addition to this description, there are a handful of depictions of him from members of his community. "A German Reformed Church minister for Page and the Whitmer family since 1822," Diedrich Willers, "characterized the Whitmers as good citizens but "gullible to the highest degree and even believe in witches." This accusation of their belief was also confirmed by a neighbor of theirs.[18] One of the more striking details regarding David Whitmer is that he believed that God spoke to him telling him to leave the LDS church.

> If you believe my testimony to the Book of Mormon; if you believe that God spake to us three witnesses by his own voice, then I tell you that in June, 1838, God spake to me again by his own voice from the heavens, and told me to "separate myself from among the Latter Day Saints, for as they sought to do unto me, so should it be done unto them ."

Whitmer went on to describe that he disagreed with church leadership and tried to correct the "error and blindness."

> In the spring of 1838, the heads of the church and many of the members had gone deep into error and blindness. I had been striving with them for a long time to show them the errors into which they were drifting, and for my labors I received only persecutions.

Why would God first give David Whitmer a revelation which would be used by so many to confirm a testimony of the truth of the LDS Church and then give him a subsequent revelation commanding him to depart from the one true church? If the LDS apologists believe that the witnesses are so reliable, will they continue to sustain David Whitmer's credibility

---

18. Palmer, *An Insider's View of Mormon Origins*.180.

when he reports that God commanded him to leave the church? If not, why believe his first revelation rather than his second? If the second is inaccurate or untruthful, why should the first be affirmed?

As time would show David Whitmer and his family did depart from the LDS Church. Between 1837 and 1838, David Whitmer, was excommunicated. From that point on, he never rejoined. In fact, David eventually became convinced that he was the rightful successor of Joseph Smith. In the 1870s he organized a church which followed his divine leadership. This was known as the "Whitmerite" church. Does this sound like a reliable witness?

In this review, I have only scratched the surface of what can and has been written concerning the credibility of these witnesses. In my attempt to remain brief, I have only individually addressed the three witnesses. If so desired, I encourage the reader to engage in further research on this topic to examine the other witnesses. Grant Palmer's *An Insider's View On Mormon Origins* is a phenomenal place to start.

One of the most convincing claims that the LDS Church can make on this subject is that none of the eleven witnesses ever denied their testimony. One may argue over whether the plates were seen physically or spiritually, but it does appear that all eleven witnesses sustained that they had some encounter with the golden plates. To their credit, this is a compelling argument. As it appears to me though, the eleven may or may not have believed and testified that they saw the plates with their physical eyes. Regardless of their beliefs about the plates, I am very leery of the witnesses themselves.

They all possessed a magical worldview, and they were all closely linked with Joseph Smith. Beside these common traits, there is one final point regarding the reliability of the eleven witnesses that I find exceptionally persuasive.

That is, of the three witnesses, *all three* were excommunicated within eight years of their testimony. In a letter he wrote from Liberty Jail in December of 1838, Joseph Smith addresses these men saying, "Such characters as McLellin, John Whitmer, David Whitmer, Oliver Cowdery, and Martin Harris, are too mean to mention; and we had liked to have forgotten them."[19] These are the same men who assisted him as he translated the BOM. Not even a decade later they are men he excommunicated wished he had forgotten.

19. Smith, Joseph. *History of the Church of Jesus Christ of Latter-day Saints*. Vol. 3. Salt Lake City: Deseret Book, 1978, p. 232

Of the eight witnesses, one was excommunicated (John Whitmer), two apostatized (Jacob Whitmer and Hiram Page), and the other five remained faithful church members for the duration of their lives (Christian and Peter Whitmer Jr. and Samuel, Hyrum, and Joseph Smith Sr.). It is likely however that this number would have changed had the Whitmers lived a little longer. Christian Whitmer died in 1835 and Peter Jr. in 1836. David, Jacob, and John all either apostatized or were excommunicated in 1838. As such, if Christian and Peter had survived that long it is likely that they would have followed suit.

Thus, six out of the nine witnesses who lived past 1838 left the church. The three that remained were Joseph's father and two of his brothers.

Martin Harris, indecisive as ever, returned to the Church after his excommunication and was baptized in 1842. Two years later he left the LDS church again and joined a few others. He was briefly involved with the Shakers, an offshoot of the LDS church run by a James Strang, and a Church of Christ which he helped to establish. In 1870 Harris returned to the LDS Church and returned to Utah at eighty-eight years old.[20]

Oliver Cowdery also returned to the church. Ten years after his excommunication, in 1848 Cowdery rejoined the Church where he remained for the rest of his life.

What I find so surprising is that these men, who I will grant never denied their testimony, evidently thought so little of it as to easily be led to other religions. Of the nine living witnesses, six left the church for a period of time. If Christian and Peter had been spared, the number would almost certainly be eight out of the eleven who left. Joseph's family remained constant, but this is not surprising.

Cowdery spent ten years before deciding to return and Harris spent over thirty years in other churches before returning. These are not at all models of unbridled devotion, but demonstrations religiously-curious men who appear to be "tossed to and fro and carried about by every wind of doctrine." (Ephesians 4:14) Is the record boasted by the LDS Church concerning the stability of their witnesses really an argument in their favor? I will leave that conclusion to the reader.

Runnells, in concluding this topic makes a point which I find to be deeply relevant as we end our study of the witnesses. In a very real sense, it does not matter whether the witnesses saw the golden plates.

---

20. "Was Martin Harris Ever Excommunicated from the Church?,".

CHAPTER 33: THE ELEVEN WITNESSES

That is because "Joseph did not use the gold plates for translating the Book of Mormon."[21]

Mark Twain, in his typical humorous and sarcastic style, left comments concerning how convinced he was of the truth of the BOM based upon the testimony of the witnesses and I will end this study by leaving his perspective for the reader to consider.

> Some people have to have a world of evidence before they can come anywhere in the neighborhood of believing anything; but for me, when a man tells me that he has "seen the engravings which are upon the plates," and not only that, but an angel was there at the time, and saw him see them, and probably took his receipt for it, I am very far on the road to conviction, [...] And when I am far on the road to conviction, and eight men, be they grammatical or otherwise, come forward and tell me that they have seen the plates too; and not only seen those plates but "hefted" them, I am convinced. I could not feel more satisfied and at rest if the entire Whitmer family had testified.[22]

---

21. Runnells, *CES Letter*.113.
22. Twain and Frank, *Roughing It*.96-97.

Chapter 34: **Conclusion**

WE HAVE REACHED THE end of our investigation. My purpose in these pages has been to provide a responsible belief forming/testing method and apply it to the LDS Church. We cannot rely only upon our feelings. It is *essential* that we select an approach that effectively guides us to the truth.

While it is true that the Spirit bears witness of the truth to our hearts, this does not excuse us from ensuring that what we believe aligns with reality. We are so easily fooled by our emotions. As Scripture tells us, "The heart is deceitful above all things and desperately sick; who can understand it?" (Jeremiah 17:9) It is often difficult to tell whether what we are experiencing is a product of our emotions or the prompting of the Holy Spirit.

In His great mercy, God gave us minds to contemplate His glory and seek His truth. More, He gave us Scripture which is "profitable for teaching, for reproof, for correction, and for training in righteousness," (2 Timothy 3:16). We must test our hearts and our minds lest they lead us astray. If something does not correspond with reality, it is not true regardless of how strongly we feel about it. How do we determine if what we read or believe corresponds with reality? We perform critical testing. These tests are historical, archaeological, textual, theological, geographical etc.

All these forms of testing we have applied to Joseph Smith's BOM to determine its truth. I ask, after all that we have examined, does the BOM stand up to scrutiny? The LDS tradition does not align with orthodox Christian teaching. The BOM is riddled with errors and fingerprints that betray its 19th century authorship. Is this truly "The most correct of any book on earth?" Does this book reflect divine inspiration? I echo the exhortations of Paul in 2 Thessalonians 5:21 to "test everything; hold fast what is good" and of Alma in Alma 32:17 to "awake and arouse your faculties, even to experiment upon my words, and exercise a particle of faith." Consider Joseph Smith, his book, and his religion. Is it true?

I also plead with you to apply the same studies that we have performed here to the Bible. On his mission, LDS missionary Micah Wilder was encouraged to read the New Testament as a child. This simple act changed his life.

Enraptured, he ended up reading the New Testament twelve times over the course of his mission. He discovered the true gospel of Christ and learned for the first time what the grace and love of God truly look like.[1] I ask you to do the same (though not necessarily twelve times). However, do not stop at reading as a child! Paul says in 1 Corinthians 13:11 "When I was a child, I spoke like a child, I thought like a child, I reasoned like a child. When I became a man, I gave up childish ways." He goes on in verse 14:20 "Brothers do not be children in your thinking. Be infants in evil, but in your thinking be mature."

Test the Bible! Test Christianity as we have examined Joseph's religion. You will find mountains of evidence that demonstrate its truth. Test it historically, philosophically, geographically, and archaeologically. Test the accuracy of its translation, and the reliability of our manuscripts. It is astonishing what even the most critical scholars must grant. This is how we go about forming beliefs responsibly. The BOM does not pass many of these tests. I pray that you apply them to the Bible to find the robustness of its truth. As Christ says Himself, "Sanctify them in the truth; your word is truth." (John 17:17)

I hope that this study has been of value to you. I have endeavored to present objective evidence and clarify my biases as they occur in my writing. I am not an "Anti-Mormon." The goal of this work has never been to denigrate the LDS people or their beliefs. I hold a deep love for the LDS church and pray that God would open the eyes of LDS church members to His word so they may "know the truth, and the truth will set you free." (John 8:32) In being freed from the man-made religion of Joseph Smith, I pray that you would encounter the One True God, come to understand His grace to you, and experience deeply His love for you.

In his service,

SDG

---

1. Micah Wilder, *Passport to Heaven* (Eugene, Oregon: Harvest House Publishers, 2021).

Exhortation:

For LDS Readers

IF YOU ARE READING this book, you have already taken a brave step. I commend you for your courage to critically evaluate your beliefs. I urge you to continue your studies and refrain from putting your doubts on the shelf. Thinking deeply about your faith is of eternal significance. Finding a relationship with the one true God is of incomparable value. Consider the words of Jesus in Matthew 16. "For what will it profit a man if he gains the whole world and forfeits his soul?" Given the whole world as a prize, it is still of greater value to be in communion with Christ.

I encourage you to pray that the Lord would reveal His truth to you. Take up the Bible and read it as a child. Pray that the Holy Spirit would enlighten your mind and guide you into His truth as you read.

I hope that this book has made some impact on you. If it has and you are ready to continue on this path, I encourage you to find a Christian pastor with whom you can speak. Try to find a strong Christian community with whom you can pray and worship. Stepping away from the LDS Church will likely be very challenging. I pray that the Lord would strengthen you and give you boldness. I pray that He would extend to you His incomprehensible peace.

For Christian Readers

I hope that this book has been of value to you in better understanding the LDS Church. The LDS Church is prominent, and it is very possible that you have some friends who are LDS. My exhortation to you is that you would use the information in this book to engage the Saints with love.

I confess that this is something I failed to do early on. In some of my early meetings with missionaries took pride in my ability to win a debate. I did my research and had my key verses on a note card. I was proud when I could quote obscure passages from the BOM or trap the missionaries with my clever rhetoric. Looking back on those meetings I am now deeply ashamed. It does not matter how much you know. It does not matter if you have pages of research to rattle off or if you can crush a debate opponent with your sharpness of mind.

The Saints are not opponents. They are people made in the image of God who need to hear of Christ and His saving love. I entreat you, do not jeopardize an opportunity to share the true gospel with someone by starting an argument about polygamy. Do not poison your witness to those whom Christ loves by using a demeaning or combative tone.

Engage the Saints with love. I am not saying not to disagree with them. I am not saying not to reason with them. Of course, those are the reasons that I have written this book. I just want to emphasize that we must speak the truth *in love*. As Paul teaches in 1 Corinthians 13, if what we do is not done in love it is worthless. Peter tells us to be ready to provide a defense for what we believe, but this must be tempered with gentleness and respect. When you witness to the Saints know that your love for them is as important as your words to them.

For those who love the Saints and want them to know the love of Christ I have a few exhortations. First, pray for your LDS friends and family members. Pray that God would open their eyes and lead them into His truth.

Second, engage them in conversation. When a couple of missionaries come up to your door do you point at your 'no-soliciting' sign and slam the door? Let them in! If your house is a mess, you can be sure they have seen worse. How often do people walk up to your front door asking to talk about Christ? I encourage you to take these opportunities as the blessings they are. Invite the missionaries in, treat them with kindness, and make them know that they are loved by God.

Third, understand your faith. By studying and deeply understanding your own faith you will more effectively be able to share with others. One of the challenges when engaging the LDS community is how similar the words they use sound to common Christian terms. If you understand your faith more thoroughly the distinctions will become apparent, and you will be more effective and confident sharing your beliefs with others.

Appendix A: **King Follett Discourse**[1]

BELOVED SAINTS: I WILL call [for] the attention of this congregation while I address you on the subject of the dead. The decease of our beloved brother, Elder King Follett, who was crushed in a well by the falling of a tub of rock has more immediately led me to this subject. I have been requested to speak by his friends and relatives, but inasmuch as there are a great many in this congregation who live in this city as well as elsewhere, who have lost friends, I feel disposed to speak on the subject in general, and offer you my ideas, so far as I have ability, and so far as I shall be inspired by the Holy Spirit to dwell on this subject.

I want your prayers and faith that I may have the instruction of Almighty God and the gift of the Holy Ghost, so that I may set forth things that are true and which can be easily comprehended by you, and that the testimony may carry conviction to your hearts and minds of the truth of what I shall say. Pray that the Lord may strengthen my lungs, stay the winds, and let the prayers of the Saints to heaven appear, that they may enter into the ears of the Lord of Sabaoth, for the effectual prayers of the righteous avail much. There is strength here, and I verily believe that your prayers will be heard. Before I enter fully into the investigation of the subject which is lying before me, I wish to pave the way and bring up the subject from the beginning, that you may understand it. I will make a few preliminaries, in order that you may understand the subject when I come to it. I do not calculate or intend to please your ears with superfluity of

---

1. Joseph Smith, Jr First President, and The Church of Jesus Christ of Latter-day Saints, "King Follett Discourse," accessed September 3, 2024.

words or oratory, or with much learning; but I calculate [intend] to edify you with the simple truths from heaven.

The Character of God

In the first place, I wish to go back to the beginning—to the morn of creation. There is the starting point for us to look to, in order to understand and be fully acquainted with the mind, purposes and decrees of the Great Eloheim, who sits in yonder heavens as he did at the creation of the world. It is necessary for us to have an under- standing of God himself in the beginning. If we start right, it is easy to go right all the time; but if we start wrong we may go wrong, and it will be a hard matter to get right.

There are but a very few beings in the world who understand rightly the character of God. The great majority of mankind do not comprehend anything, either that which is past, or that which is to come, as it respects their relationship to God. They do not know, neither do they understand the nature of that relationship; and consequently they know but little above the brute beast, or more than to eat, drink and sleep. This is all man knows about God and His existence, unless it is given by the inspiration of the Almighty.

If a man learns nothing more than to eat, drink and sleep, and does not comprehend any of the designs of God, the beast comprehends the same things. It eats, drinks, sleeps, and knows nothing more about God; yet it knows as much as we, unless we are able to comprehend by the inspiration of Almighty God. If men do not comprehend the character of God, they do not comprehend themselves. I want to go back to the beginning, and so lift your minds into more lofty spheres and a more exalted understanding than what the human mind generally aspires to.

I want to ask this congregation, every man, woman and child, to answer the question in their own hearts, what kind of a being God is? Ask yourselves; turn your thoughts into your hearts, and say if any of you have seen, heard, or communed with Him? This is a question that may occupy your attention for a long time. I again repeat the question—What kind of being is God? Does any man or woman know? Have any of you seen Him, heard Him, or communed with Him? Here is the question that will, peradventure, from this time henceforth occupy your attention. The scriptures inform us that "this is life eternal, that they might know thee the only true God, and Jesus Christ, whom thou hast sent." (John 17:3.)

If any man does not know God, and inquires what kind of a being He is—if he will search diligently his own heart—if the declaration of Jesus and the apostles be true, he will realize that he has not eternal life; for there can be eternal life on no other principle.

My first object is to find out the character of the only wise and true God, and what kind of a being He is; and if I am so fortunate as to be the man to comprehend God, and explain or convey the principles to your hearts, so that the Spirit seals them upon you, then let every man and woman henceforth sit in silence, put their hands on their mouths, and never lift their hands or voices, or say anything against the man of God or the servants of God again. But if I fail to do it, it becomes my duty to renounce all further pretensions to revelations and inspirations, or to be a prophet; and I should be like the rest of the world—a false teacher, be hailed as a friend, and no man would seek my life. But if all religious teachers were honest enough to renounce their pretensions to godliness when their ignorance of the knowledge of God is made manifest, they will all be as badly off as I am, at any rate; and you might just as well take the lives of other false teachers as that of mine. If any man is authorized to take away my life because he thinks and says I am a false teacher, then, upon the same principle, we should be justified in taking away the life of every false teacher, and where would be the end of blood? And who would not be the sufferer?

The Privilege of Religious Freedom

But meddle not with any man for his religion: all governments ought to permit every man to enjoy his religion unmolested. No man is authorized to take away life in consequence of difference of religion, which all laws and governments ought to tolerate and protect, right or wrong. Every man has a natural, and, in our country, a constitutional right to be a false prophet, as well as a true prophet. If I show, verily, that I have the truth of God, and show that ninety-nine out of every hundred professing religious ministers are false teachers, having no authority, while they pretend to hold the keys of God's kingdom on earth, and was to kill them because they are false teachers, it would deluge the whole world with blood.

I will prove that the world is wrong, by showing what God is. I am going to inquire after God; for I want you all to know Him, and to be familiar with Him; and if I am bringing you to a knowledge of Him, all persecutions against me ought to cease. You will then know that I am His servant; for I speak as one having authority.

God an Exalted Man

I will go back to the beginning before the world was, to show what kind of a being God is. What sort of a being was God in the beginning? Open your ears and hear, all ye ends of the earth, for I am going to prove it to you by the Bible, and to tell you the designs of God in relation to the human race, and why He interferes with the affairs of man.

God himself was once as we are now, and is an exalted man, and sits enthroned in yonder heavens! That is the great secret. If the veil were rent today, and the great God who holds this world in its orbit, and who upholds all worlds and all things by His power, was to make himself visible—I say, if you were to see him today, you would see him like a man in form—like yourselves in all the person, image, and very form as a man; for Adam was created in the very fashion, image and likeness of God, and received instruction from, and walked, talked and conversed with Him, as one man talks and communes with another.

In order to understand the subject of the dead, for consolation of those who mourn for the loss of their friends, it is necessary we should understand the character and being of God and how He came to be so; for I am going to tell you how God came to be God. We have imagined and supposed that God was God from all eternity. I will refute that idea, and take away the veil, so that you may see.

These ideas are incomprehensible to some, but they are simple. It is the first principle of the gospel to know for a certainty the character of God, and to know that we may converse with Him as one man converses with another, and that He was once a man like us; yea, that God himself, the Father of us all, dwelt on an earth, the same as Jesus Christ Himself did; and I will show it from the Bible.

Eternal Life to Know God and Jesus Christ

I wish I was in a suitable place to tell it, and that I had the trump of an archangel, so that I could tell the story in such a manner that persecution would cease forever. What did Jesus say? (Mark it, Elder Rigdon!) The scriptures inform us that Jesus said, as the Father hath power in himself, even so hath the Son power—to do what? Why, what the Father did. The answer is obvious—in a manner to lay down his body and take it up again. Jesus, what are you going to do? To lay down my life as my Father did, and take it up again. Do you believe it? If you do not believe it you do not believe the Bible. The scriptures say it, and I defy all the learning and wisdom and all the combined powers of earth and hell together to refute it. Here, then, is eternal life—to know the only wise and true God; and you have got to learn how to be gods yourselves, and to be kings and priests to God, the same as all gods have done before you, namely, by going from one small degree to another, and from a small capacity to a great one; from grace to grace, from exaltation to exaltation, until you attain to the resurrection of the dead, and are able to dwell in ever- lasting burnings, and to sit in glory, as do those who sit enthroned in everlasting power. And I want you to know that God, in the last days, while certain individuals are proclaiming His name, is not trifling with you or me.

The Righteous to Dwell in Everlasting Burnings

These are the first principles of consolation. How consoling to the mourners when they are called to part with a husband, wife, father, mother, child, or dear relative, to know that, although the earthly tabernacle is laid down and dissolved, they shall rise again to dwell in everlasting burnings in immortal glory, not to sorrow, suffer, or die any more, but they shall be heirs of God and joint heirs with Jesus Christ. What is it? To inherit the same power, the same glory and the same exaltation, until you arrive at the station of a god, and ascend the throne of eternal power, the same as those who have gone before. What did Jesus do? Why, I do the things I saw my Father do when worlds came rolling into existence. My Father worked out His kingdom with fear and trembling, and I must do the same; and when I get my kingdom, I shall present it to My Father, so that He may obtain kingdom upon kingdom, and it will exalt Him in glory. He will then take a higher exaltation, and I will take His place, and thereby be- come exalted myself. So that Jesus treads in the tracks of His Father, and inherits what God did before; and God is thus glorified and exalted in the salvation and exaltation of all His children. It is plain beyond disputation, and you thus learn some of the first principles of the gospel, about which so much hath been said.

When you climb up a ladder, you must begin at the bottom, and ascend step by step, until you arrive at the top; and so it is with the principles of the gospel—you must begin with the first, and go on until you learn all the principles of exaltation. But it will be a great while after you have passed through the veil before you will have learned them. It is not all to be comprehended in this world; it will be a great work to learn our salvation and exaltation even beyond the grave. I suppose I am not allowed to go into an investigation of anything that is not contained in the Bible. If I do, I think there are so many over-wise men here that they would cry "treason" and put me to death. So I will go to the old Bible and turn commentator today.

I shall comment on the very first Hebrew word in the Bible; I will make a comment on the very first sentence of the history of creation in the Bible—Berosheit. I want to analyze the word. Baith—in, by, through, and everything else. Rosh—the head, Sheit—grammatical termination. When the inspired man wrote it, he did not put the baith there. An old Jew without any authority added the word; he thought it too bad to begin to talk about the head! It read first, "The head one of the Gods brought forth the Gods." That is the true meaning of the words. Baurau signifies to bring forth. If you do not believe it, you do not believe the learned man of God. Learned men can teach you no more than what I have told you. Thus the head God brought forth the Gods in the grand council.

I will transpose and simplify it in the English language. Oh, ye lawyers, ye doctors, and ye priests, who have persecuted me, I want to let you know that the Holy Ghost knows something as well as you do. The head God called together the Gods and sat in grand council to bring forth the world. The grand councilors sat at the head in yonder heavens and contemplated the creation of the worlds which were created at the time. When I say doctors and lawyers, I mean the doctors and lawyers of the scriptures. I have done so hitherto without explanation, to let the lawyers flutter and everybody laugh at them. Some learned doctors might take a notion to say the scriptures say thus and so; and we must believe the scriptures; they are not to be altered. But I am going to show you an error in them.

I have an old edition of the New Testament in the Latin, Hebrew, German and Greek languages. I have been reading the German, and find it to be the most [nearly] correct translation, and to correspond near- est to the revelations which God has given to me for the last fourteen years. It tells about Jacobus, the son of Zebedee. It means Jacob. In the English

New Testament it is translated James. Now, if Jacob had the keys, you might talk about James through all eternity and never get the keys. In the 21st [verse] of the fourth chapter of Matthew, my old German edition gives the word Jacob instead of James. The doctors (I mean doctors of law, not physic) say, "If you preach anything not according to the Bible, we will cry treason." How can we escape the damnation of hell, except God be with us and reveal to us? Men bind us with chains. The Latin says Jacobus, which means Jacob; the Hebrew says Jacob, the Greek says Jacob and the German says Jacob, here we have the testimony of four against one. I thank God that I have got this old book; but I thank him more for the gift of the Holy Ghost. I have got the oldest book in the world; but I have got the oldest book in my heart, even the gift of the Holy Ghost. I have all the four Testaments. Come here, ye learned men, and read, if you can. I should not have introduced this testimony, were it not to back up the word rosh—the head, the Father of the Gods. I should not have brought it up, only to show that I am right.

A Council of the Gods

In the beginning, the head of the Gods called a council of the Gods; and they came together and concocted [prepared] a plan to create the world and people it. When we begin to learn this way, we begin to learn the only true God, and what kind of a being we have got to wor-ship. Having a knowledge of God, we begin to know how to approach Him, and how to ask so as to receive an answer.

When we understand the character of God, and know how to come to Him, he begins to unfold the heavens to us, and to tell us all about it. When we are ready to come to him, he is ready to come to us.

Now, I ask all who hear me, why the learned men who are preaching salvation, say that God created the heavens and the earth out of nothing? The reason is, that they are unlearned in the things of God, and have not the gift of the Holy Ghost; they account it blasphemy in any one to contradict their idea. If you tell them that God made the world out of something, they will call you a fool. But I am learned, and know more than all the world put together. The Holy Ghost does, anyhow, and he is within me, and comprehends more than all the world; and I will associate myself with him.

Meaning of the Word Create

You ask the learned doctors why they say the world was made out of nothing, and they will answer, "Doesn't the Bible say he created the world?" And they infer, from the word create, that it must have been made out of nothing. Now, the word create came from the word baurau, which does not mean to create out of nothing; it means to organize; the same as a man would organize materials and build a ship. Hence we infer that God had materials to organize the world out of chaos—chaotic matter, which is element, and in which dwells all the glory. Element had an existence from the time He had. The pure principles of element are principles which can never be destroyed; they may be organized and re-organized, but not destroyed. They had no beginning and can have no end.

Appendix B: Joseph Smith Sr.'s Second Dream:[1]

"I THOUGHT," SAID HE, "I was travelling in an open, desolate field, which appeared to be very barren. As I was thus travelling, the thought suddenly came into my mind that I had better stop and reflect upon what I was doing, before I went any further. So I asked myself, 'What motive can I have in travelling here, and what place can this be?'

My guide, who was by my side, as before, said, "This is the desolate world; but travel on.' The road was so broad and barren, that I wondered why I should travel in it; for, said I to myself, 'Broad is the road, and wide is the gate that leads to death, and many there be that walk therein; but narrow is the way, and straight is the gate that leads to everlasting life, and few there be that go in thereat.

Travelling a short distance further, I came to a narrow path. This path I entered, and, when I had travelled a little way in it, I beheld a beautiful stream of water, which ran from the east to the west. Of this stream I could see neither the source nor yet the termination; but as far as my eyes could extend I could see a rope, running along the bank of it, about as high as a man could reach, and beyond me, was a low, but very pleasant, valley, in which stood a tree, such as I, had never seen before. It was exceedingly handsome, insomuch that I looked upon it with wonder and admiration. Its beautiful branches spread themselves some. what like an umbrella, and it bore a kind of fruit, in shape much like a chestnut bur, and as white as snow, or, if possible, whiter.

---

1. "Lucy Mack Smith, History, 1845, Page 53," accessed December 11, 2024,60.

I gazed upon the same with considerable interest, and as I was doing so, the burs or shells commenced opening and shedding their particles, or the fruit which they contained, which was of dazzling whiteness. I drew near, and began to eat of it, and I found it delicious beyond description. As I was eating, I said in my heart, ' I cannot eat this alone, I must bring my wife and children, that they may partake with me.' Accordingly, I went and brought my family, which consisted of a wife and seven children, and we all commenced eating, and praising God for this blessing.

We were exceedingly happy, insomuch that our joy could not easily be expressed. While thus engaged, I beheld a spacious building standing opposite the valley which we were in, and it appeared to reach to the very heavens. It was full of doors and windows, and they were all filled with people, who were very finely dressed. When these people observed us in the low valley, under the tree, they pointed the finger of scorn at us, and treated us with all manner of disrespect and contempt. But their contumely we utterly disregarded.

I presently turned to my guide, and inquired of him the meaning of the fruit that was so delicious. He told me it was the pure love of God, shed abroad in the hearts of all those who love him, and keep his commandments. He then commanded me to go and bring the rest of my children. I told him that we were all there. "No,' he replied, 'look yonder, you have two more, and you must bring them also.

Upon raising my eyes, I saw two small children, standing some distance off. I immediately went to them, and brought them to the tree; upon which they commenced eating with the rest, and we all rejoiced together. The more we eat, the more we seemed to desire, until we even got down upon our knees, and scooped it up, eating it by double handfulls. After feasting in this manner a short time, I asked my guide what was the meaning of the spacious building which

He replied, 'It is Babylon, it is Babylon, and it must fall. The people in the doors and windows are the inhabitants thereof, who scorn and despise the Saints of God, because of their humility.' I soon awoke, clapping my hands together for joy."

1 Nephi 8:5–35

[5]And it came to pass that I saw a [a]man, and he was dressed in a white [b]robe; and he came and stood before me.

APPENDIX B: JOSEPH SMITH SR.'S SECOND DREAM: 291

⁶And it came to pass that he spake unto me, and bade me follow him.

⁷And it came to pass that as I followed him I beheld myself that I was in a dark and dreary waste.

⁸And after I had traveled for the space of many hours in darkness, I began to pray unto the Lord that he would have ᵃmercy on me, according to the multitude of his tender mercies.

⁹And it came to pass after I had prayed unto the Lord I beheld a large and spacious ᵃfield.

¹⁰And it came to pass that I beheld a ᵃtree, whose ᵇfruit was desirable to make one ᶜhappy.

¹¹And it came to pass that I did go forth and partake of the ᵃfruit thereof; and I beheld that it was most sweet, above all that I ever before tasted. Yea, and I beheld that the fruit thereof was white, to exceed all the ᵇwhiteness that I had ever seen.

¹²And as I partook of the fruit thereof it filled my soul with exceedingly great ᵃjoy; wherefore, I began to be ᵇdesirous that my family should partake of it also; for I knew that it was ᶜdesirable above all other fruit.

¹³And as I cast my eyes round about, that perhaps I might discover my family also, I beheld a ᵃriver of water; and it ran along, and it was near the tree of which I was partaking the fruit.

¹⁴And I looked to behold from whence it came; and I saw the head thereof a little way off; and at the head thereof I beheld your mother Sariah, and Sam, and ᵃNephi; and they stood as if they knew not whither they should go.

¹⁵And it came to pass that I beckoned unto them; and I also did say unto them with a loud voice that they should come unto me, and partake of the fruit, which was desirable above all other fruit.

¹⁶And it came to pass that they did come unto me and partake of the fruit also.

¹⁷And it came to pass that I was desirous that Laman and Lemuel should come and partake of the fruit also; wherefore, I cast mine eyes towards the head of the river, that perhaps I might see them.

¹⁸And it came to pass that I saw them, but they would ᵃnot come unto me and partake of the fruit.

¹⁹And I beheld a ᵃrod of iron, and it extended along the bank of the river, and led to the tree by which I stood.

²⁰And I also beheld a ᵃstrait and narrow path, which came along by the rod of iron, even to the tree by which I stood; and it also led by the head of the fountain, unto a large and spacious field, as if it had been a ᵇworld.

²¹And I saw numberless concourses of people, many of whom were ᵃpressing forward, that they might obtain the ᵇpath which led unto the tree by which I stood.

²²And it came to pass that they did come forth, and commence in the path which led to the tree.

²³And it came to pass that there arose a ᵃmist of darkness; yea, even an exceedingly great mist of darkness, insomuch that they who had commenced in the path did lose their way, that they wandered off and were ᵇlost.

²⁴And it came to pass that I beheld others pressing forward, and they came forth and caught hold of the end of the rod of iron; and they did press forward through the mist of darkness, ᵃclinging to the rod of iron, even until they did come forth and partake of the ᵇfruit of the tree.

²⁵And after they had partaken of the fruit of the tree they did cast their eyes about as if they were ᵃashamed.

²⁶And I also cast my eyes round about, and beheld, on the ᵃother side of the river of water, a great and ᵇspacious building; and it stood as it were in the ᶜair, high above the earth.

²⁷And it was filled with people, both old and young, both male and female; and their manner of dress was exceedingly fine; and they were in the ᵃattitude of ᵇmocking and pointing their fingers towards those who had come at and were partaking of the fruit.

²⁸And after they had ᵃtasted of the fruit they were ᵇashamed, because of those that were ᶜscoffing at them; and they ᵈfell away into forbidden paths and were lost.

²⁹And now I, Nephi, do not speak ᵃall the words of my father.

³⁰But, to be short in writing, behold, he saw other multitudes pressing forward; and they came and caught hold of the end of the ᵃrod of iron; and they did press their way forward, continually holding fast to the rod of iron, until they came forth and fell down and partook of the fruit of the tree.

³¹And he also saw other ᵃmultitudes feeling their way towards that great and spacious building.

³²And it came to pass that many were drowned in the ᵃdepths of the ᵇfountain; and many were lost from his view, wandering in strange roads.

³³And great was the multitude that did enter into that strange building. And after they did enter into that building they did point the finger of ᵃscorn at me and those that were partaking of the fruit also; but we heeded them not.

³⁴These are the words of my father: For as many as ᵃheeded them, had fallen away.

³⁵And ᵃLaman and Lemuel partook not of the fruit, said my father.

Bibliography

"About The Temple Endowment." Accessed May 14, 2024. https://www.churchofjesuschrist.org/temples/what-is-temple-endowment?lang=eng.

Achilli, Alessandro, Ugo A. Perego, Hovirag Lancioni, Anna Olivieri, Francesca Gandini, Baharak Hooshiar Kashani, Vincenza Battaglia, et al. "Reconciling Migration Models to the Americas with the Variation of North American Native Mitogenomes." Proceedings of the National Academy of Sciences 110, no. 35 (August 27, 2013): 14308–13. https://doi.org/10.1073/pnas.1306290110.

"Acton, Letter on Historical Integrity, 1887." Accessed August 27, 2022. https://history.hanover.edu/courses/excerpts/165acton.html.

Amesbury, Richard. "Fideism." In The Stanford Encyclopedia of Philosophy, edited by Edward N. Zalta, Summer 2022. Metaphysics Research Lab, Stanford University, 2022. https://plato.stanford.edu/archives/sum2022/entries/fideism/.

"AncestryDNA® Test Accuracy | AncestryDNA® Learning Hub." Accessed May 20, 2022. https://www.ancestry.com/c/dna-learning-hub/ancestrydna-test-accuracy.

Anselm, Thomas Williams, Gaunilo, and Anselm. Monologion and Proslogion: With the Replies of Gaunilo and Anselm. Indianapolis, Ind: Hackett, 1996.

"Are 'Mormons' Christian?" Accessed March 13, 2024. https://www.churchofjesuschrist.org/study/eng/manual/gospel-topics-essays/christians.

Bastow, David. "Otto and Numinous Experience." Religious Studies 12, no. 2 (1976): 159–76. https://doi.org/10.1017/S0034412500009148.

Battaglia, Vincenza, Viola Grugni, Ugo Alessandro Perego, Norman Angerhofer, J. Edgar Gomez-Palmieri, Scott Ray Woodward, Alessandro Achilli, Natalie Myres, Antonio Torroni, and Ornella Semino. "The First Peopling of South America: New Evidence from Y-Chromosome Haplogroup Q." PLoS ONE 8, no. 8 (August 21, 2013): e71390. https://doi.org/10.1371/journal.pone.0071390.

Bélanger, Claude. "Quebec History." Accessed May 19, 2024. http://faculty.marianopolis.edu/c.belanger/quebechistory/encyclopedia/DomesticationofanimalsbyIndians.htm.

Benson, Ezra Taft. The Teachings of Ezra Taft Benson. Salt Lake City, Utah : Bookcraft, 1988. http://archive.org/details/teachingsofezratoooobens.

Beukens, R. P., L. A. Pavlish, R. G. V. Hancock, R. M. Farquhar, G. C. Wilson, P. J. Julig, and William Ross. "Radiocarbon Dating of Copper-Preserved Organics." Radiocarbon 34, no. 3 (1992): 890–97. https://doi.org/10.1017/S0033822200064213.

"Biographical Sketches of Joseph Smith the Prophet, and His Progenitors for Many Generations, Page i." Accessed July 19, 2022. https://contentdm.lib.byu.edu/digital/collection/NCMP1820-1846/id/17401/.

Bondar, Maria. "Prehistoric Innovations: Wheels and Wheeled Vehicles." Acta Archaeologica Academiae Scientiarum Hungaricae 69 (December 1, 2018): 271–97. https://doi.org/10.1556/072.2018.69.2.3.

"Book of Abraham | CES Letter." Accessed June 19, 2022. https://read.cesletter.org/boa/#common-pagan-funerary-text.

"Book of Mormon and DNA Studies." Accessed May 18, 2022. https://www.churchofjesuschrist.org/study/eng/manual/gospel-topics-essays/book-of-mormon-and-dna-studies.

"Book of Mormon Animals." Accessed May 19, 2024. https://www.churchofjesuschrist.org/study/eng/friend/2008/08/for-little-friends/book-of-mormon-animals.

Book of Mormon Central. "How Could Laban Have Possessed a Sword of 'Most Precious Steel'?," January 29, 2018. https://bookofmormoncentral.org/qa/how-could-laban-have-possessed-a-sword-of-%E2%80%9Cmost-precious-steel%E2%80%9D.

Book of Mormon Central. "Why Are There So Many War Chapters in the Book of Mormon?," August 3, 2016. https://knowhy.bookofmormoncentral.org/knowhy/why-are-there-so-many-war-chapters-in-the-book-of-mormon.

Book of Mormon Central. "Why Was David Whitmer Excommunicated from the Church?," June 8, 2021. https://knowhy.bookofmormoncentral.org/knowhy/why-was-david-whitmer-excommunicated-from-the-church.

"Book of Mormon First Edition (1830)." Accessed June 1, 2022. //history.churchofjesuschrist.org/content/library/book-of-mormon.

"Book of Mormon Time Line." Accessed May 14, 2024. https://www.churchofjesuschrist.org/study/eng/ensign/2011/10/book-of-mormon-time-line.

"Book of Mormon Translation." Accessed May 25, 2022. https://www.churchofjesuschrist.org/study/eng/manual/gospel-topics-essays/book-of-mormon-translation.

"Book of Mormon/Plagiarism Accusations/Joseph Smith, Sr.'s Dream and Lehi's Vision - FAIR." Accessed August 26, 2022. https://www.fairlatterdaysaints.org/answers/Book_of_Mormon/Plagiarism_accusations/Joseph_Smith,_Sr.%27s_dream_and_Lehi%27s_vision.

Brannan, Rick, ed. The Apostolic Fathers: A New Translation. Lexham Classics. Washington: Lexham Press, 2017.

"Brass | Definition, Properties, & Facts | Britannica." Accessed May 19, 2024. https://www.britannica.com/technology/brass-alloy.

Bray, Warwick. "Gold-Working in Ancient America." Gold Bulletin 11, no. 4 (December 1978): 136–43. https://doi.org/10.1007/BF03216538.

Brodie, Fawn McKay. No Man Knows My History: The Life of Joseph Smith, the Mormon Prophet. 2nd ed., rev.enl.1st Vintage Books ed. New York: Vintage Books, 1995.

Bruce R. McConkie. Mormon Doctrine. 2d ed. Salt Lake City, Utah: Bookraft, 1979.

Bushman, Richard L. Joseph Smith: Rough Stone Rolling. 1. Vintage Books ed. New York: Vintage Books, 2007.bwv549.

"Who Is Doing the Loan Shifting?" A Careful Examination. Accessed May 19, 2024. https://faenrandir.github.io/a_careful_examination/excerpt-who-is-doing-the-loan-shifting/.

"BYU Religious Scholar Analyzes Book of Mormon Swords at FairMormon Conference – Deseret News." Accessed May 19, 2024. https://www.deseret.com/2016/8/12/20593859/byu-religious-scholar-analyzes-book-of-mormon-swords-at-fairmormon-conference/#matthew-rop-er-a-research-associate-at-the-neal-a-maxwell-institute-for-religious-scholarship-at-byu-spoke-about-mesoamerican-swords-and-cimeters-in-the-book-of-mormon-at-the-fairmormon-conference-last-week.

BYU Studies. "About Royal Skousen." Accessed July 29, 2022. https://byustudies.byu.edu/about-royal-skousen/.

BYU Studies. "Volume 3 Chapter 3." Accessed May 28, 2022. https://byustudies.byu.edu/further-study-lesson/volume-3-chapter-3/.

BYU Studies. "Volume 4 Chapter 27." Accessed June 1, 2022. https://byustudies.byu.edu/further-study-lesson/volume-4-chapter-27/.

BYU Studies. "Volume 5 Chapter 19." Accessed June 26, 2022. https://byustudies.byu.edu/further-study-lesson/volume-5-chapter-19/.

"C. H. Spurgeon: Spurgeon's Sermons Volume 60: 1914 – Christian Classics Ethereal Library." Accessed August 12, 2024. https://ccel.org/ccel/spurgeon/sermons60/sermons60.vi.html.

Callister, Tad R. A Case for The Book of Mormon. Salt Lake City, Utah: Deseret Book, 2019.

Campbell, Alexander 1788-1866. Delusions an Analysis of the Book of Mormon; with an Examination of Its Internal and External Evidences, and a Refutation of Its Pretences to Divine Authority by Alexander Campbell ; with Prefatory Remarks by Joshua V. Himes. Boston Benjamin H. Greene, 1832. http://archive.org/details/delusionsanalysio1camp.

Carden, Allen. Puritan Christianity in America: Religion and Life in Seventeenth-Century Massachusetts. Grand Rapids, Mich: Baker Book House, 1990.

Cassaniti, Julia L., and Tanya Marie Luhrmann. "The Cultural Kindling of Spiritual Experiences." Current Anthropology 55, no. S10 (December 2014): S333–43. https://doi.org/10.1086/677881. Chadwick, Jeffrey R. "Dating the Departure of Lehi from Jerusalem" 57 (2018): 47.

Chalcedon. "Athanasius, Champion of the Trinity," November 1, 2008. https://chalcedon.edu/resources/articles/athanasius-champion-of-the-trinity.

"Chapter 4: Martin Harris and the Lost Pages: 1827–1828." Accessed July 31, 2022. https://www.churchofjesuschrist.org/study/eng/manual/doctrine-and-covenants-stories/chapter-4-martin-harris-and-the-lost-pages-1827-1828.

"Chapter 4: The Book of Mormon: Keystone of Our Religion." Accessed June 1, 2022. https://www.churchofjesuschrist.org/study/eng/manual/teachings-joseph-smith/chapter-4.

"Chapter 11: The Life of Christ." Accessed March 18, 2024. https://www.churchofjesuschrist.org/study/eng/manual/gospel-principles/chapter-11-the-life-of-christ.

Cheesman, Paul R. "The Wheel in Ancient America." Brigham Young University Studies 9, no. 2 (1969): 185–97.

Church News. "Nephi Regarded Isaiah as Important Prophet of Own Time and of Future," January 25, 1992. https://www.thechurch-news.com/archives/1992-01-25/nephi-regarded-isaiah-as-important-prophet-of-own-time-and-of-future-145401.

Church of Jesus Christ of Latter-day Saints. Ensign of the Church of Jesus Christ of Latter-Day Saints. [Salt Lake City] Church of Jesus Christ of Latter-day Saints, 1971. http://archive.org/details/ensignofchurchofoochur.

———. Gospel Principles. 2009th ed. Salt Lake City, Utah: Church of Jesus Christ of Latter-Day Saints, 2009.

———. The Holy Bible: Containing the Old and New Testaments, Translated out of the Original Tongues: And with the Former Translations Diligently Compared and Revised ; by His Majesty's Special Command. The Book of Mormon : Another Testament of Jesus Christ. The Doctrine and Covenants of the Church of Jesus Christ of Latter-Day Saints. The Pearl of Great Price., 2015.

"Comoros | Culture, History, & People | Britannica." Accessed August 22, 2022. https://www.britannica.com/place/Comoros.

Crossway. "10 Things You Should Know about Athanasius," January 7, 2018. https://www.crossway.org/articles/10-things-you-should-know-about-athanasius/.

Dame, Marketing Communications: Web | University of Notre. "Alvin Plantinga | Features | University of Notre Dame." Alvin Plantinga. Accessed March 13, 2024. https://www.nd.edu/stories/plantinga/.

David. "Gospel Cougar: Word Frequency in the Book of Mormon." Gospel Cougar (blog), December 23, 2007. https://gospelcougar.blogspot.com/2007/12/word-frequency-in-book-of-mormon.html.

Davis, William. "Reassessing Joseph Smith Jr.'s Formal Education." Dialogue: A Journal of Mormon Thought 49, no. 4 (December 1, 2016): 1–58. https://doi.org/10.5406/dialjmormthou.49.4.0001.

Davis, William L. Visions in a Seer Stone: Joseph Smith and the Making of the Book of Mormon. Chapel Hill: The University of North Carolina Press, 2020.

Debra Parcell. "Bound for the Promised Land: Camp Meetings and Their Impact on Antebellum Religion and Society," n.d., 25–41.

Dehlin, John. "Kinderhook Plates." Mormon Stories (blog). Accessed June 26, 2022. https://mormonstories.org/truth-claims/the-books/kinderhook-plates/.

Deseret News. "LDS Church Buys Printer's Manuscript of Book of Mormon for Record $35 Million," September 21, 2017. https://www.deseret.com/2017/9/20/20619977/lds-church-buys-printers-manuscript-of-book-of-mormon-for-record-35-million.

Director, Elder Jay E. Jensen Of the Seventy Executive, and Curriculum Department. "The Prophet Joseph Smith, an Extraordinary Teacher." Accessed July 19, 2022. https://www.churchofjesuschrist.org/study/eng/ensign/2008/01/the-prophet-joseph-smith-an-extraordinary-teacher.

"Doctrine and Covenants, 1835, Page 120." Accessed August 27, 2022. https://www.josephsmithpapers.org/paper-summary/doctrine-and-covenants-1835/129.

"Doctrine and Covenants, 1835, Page 191." Accessed August 27, 2022. https://www.josephsmithpapers.org/paper-summary/doctrine-and-covenants-1835/200.

"Doctrine and Covenants, 1835, Page 251." Accessed August 27, 2022. https://www.josephsmithpapers.org/paper-summary/doctrine-and-covenants-1835/259.

"Elders' Journal, November 1837, Page 29." Accessed May 28, 2022. https://www.josephsmithpapers.org/paper-summary/elders-journal-november-1837/13.

"Facsimile 1." Accessed August 20, 2024. https://www.churchofjesuschrist.org/study/eng/scriptures/pgp/abr/fac-1.

"Facsimile 2." Accessed August 20, 2024. https://www.churchofjesuschrist.org/study/eng/scriptures/pgp/abr/fac-2.

"Facsimile 3." Accessed August 20, 2024. https://www.churchofjesuschrist.org/study/eng/scriptures/pgp/abr/fac-3.

FAIR. "Did God Have Sex with Mary?" Accessed March 18, 2024. https://www.fairlatterdaysaints.org/archive/publications/did-god-have-sex-with-mary.

FAIR. "'What Has Athens to Do with Jerusalem?': Apostasy and Restoration in the Big Picture." Accessed June 28, 2023. https://www.fairlatterdaysaints.org/conference/august-1999/what-has-athens-to-do-with-jerusalem-apostasy-and-restoration-in-the-big-picture.

"Faith." Accessed May 14, 2024. https://www.churchofjesuschrist.org/study/manual/true-to-the-faith/faith?lang=eng.

"Fanny Alger." Accessed August 27, 2022. https://www.churchofjesuschrist.org/study/eng/history/topics/fanny-alger.

Fazio, Lisa K., Nadia M. Brashier, B. Keith Payne, and Elizabeth J. Marsh. "Knowledge Does Not Protect against Illusory Truth." Journal of Experimental Psychology: General 144, no. 5 (October 2015): 993–1002. https://doi.org/10.1037/xge0000098.

"First Vision." Accessed August 26, 2022. https://www.churchofjesuschrist.org/study/eng/manual/gospel-topics/first-vision.

Ford, Coleman. "Trinitarianism in the Early Church." The Gospel Coalition. Accessed May 8, 2024. https://www.thegospelcoali-tion.org/essay/trinitarianism-in-the-early-church/.

Fraser's Magazine. London : Longmans, Green, 1870. http://archive.org/details/frasersmagazineo8unkngoog.

Frequency of Names in the Bible, 2021. https://www.youtube.com/watch?v=VUnEjU8n_QY.

Gary Habermas: The Resurrection Evidence That Changed Current Scholarship, 2013. https://www.youtube.com/watch?v=5znVUFHqO4Q.

Geraty, Lawrence T. "ARCHAEOLOGY AND THE BIBLE AT HEZEKIAH'S LACHISH," n.d., 11.

"Golden Plates to Book of Mormon." Accessed May 24, 2022. https://www.churchofjesuschrist.org/study/eng/friend/2017/02/golden-plates-to-book-of-mormon.

Grace Communion International. "Weapons and Warfare in Ancient Israel." Accessed May 19, 2024. https://www.gci.org/articles/weapons-and-warfare-in-ancient-israel/.

Groesbeck, C Jess. "THE SMITHS AND THEIR DREAMS AND VISIONS," 1988, 8.

Hales, Brian C. "Naturalistic Explanations of the Origin of the Book of Mormon" 58 (2019): 45.

———. "The Joseph Smith-Sylvia Sessions Plural Sealing: Polyandry or Polygyny?," n.d., 17.

Hassig, Ross. Mexico and the Spanish Conquest. Modern Wars in Perspective. London ; New York: Longman, 1994.

"Hell." Accessed November 6, 2023. https://www.churchofjesuschrist.org/study/eng/scriptures/gs/hell.

HISTORY. "6 Things You May Not Know About the Dead Sea Scrolls," May 12, 2023. https://www.history.com/news/6-things-you-may-not-know-about-the-dead-sea-scrolls.

"Homoousios | Definition, History, & Importance | Britannica." Accessed May 8, 2024. https://www.britannica.com/topic/homoousios.

Hosler, Dorothy. "Ancient West Mexican Metallurgy: South and Central American Origins and West Mexican Transformations." American Anthropologist 90, no. 4 (1988): 832–55. https://doi.org/10.1525/aa.1988.90.4.02a00040.

"How Can Jesus and Lucifer Be Spirit Brothers When Their Characters and Purposes Are so Utterly Opposed?" Accessed March 18, 2024. https://www.churchofjesuschrist.org/study/eng/ensign/1986/06/i-have-a-question/how-can-jesus-and-lucifer-be-spirit-brothers-when-their-characters-and-purposes-are-so-utterly-opposed.

"How Long Did It Take Joseph Smith to Translate the Book of Mormon?" Accessed May 22, 2022. https://www.churchofjesuschrist.org/study/eng/ensign/1988/01/i-have-a-question/how-long-did-it-take-joseph-smith-to-translate-the-book-of-mormon.

Howard, Dan. Bronze Age Military Equipment. Casemate Publishers, 2011.

Hunt, Gilbert. The Late War Between the United States and Great Britain, From June 1812 to February 1815. New York: David Longworth, 11 Park, 1816.

"Inside the Mind of Joseph Smith – 02 |." Accessed August 26, 2022. http://signaturebookslibrary.org/02-inside-the-mind-of-joseph-smith/.

Institute for Religious Research. "Changes to Latter-Day Scripture," July 1, 2011. https://mit.irr.org/changes-latter-day-scripture.

"Introduction to the Book of Deuteronomy." Accessed March 13, 2024. https://www.churchofjesuschrist.org/study/eng/manual/old-testament-seminary-teacher-manual/introduction-to-the-book-of-deuteronomy.

"Irenaeus | Theopedia." Accessed March 18, 2024. https://www.theopedia.com/irenaeus.

"Is Mormonism Christian?" Accessed March 13, 2024. https://www.luthercollege.edu/university/academics/impetus/winter-2013-impetus/is-mormonism-christian.

"Isaiah Variants in the Book of Mormon | Religious Studies Center." Accessed July 29, 2022. https://rsc.byu.edu/isaiah-prophets/isaiah-variants-book-mormon.

Jerald and Sandra Tanner. 3,913 Changes in the Book of Mormon, n.d.

"Jesus Wasn't the Only Man to Be Crucified. Here's the History behind This Brutal Practice. | Live Science." Accessed May 19, 2024. https://www.livescience.com/65283-crucifixion-history.html.

"John Wesley | Biography, Methodism, Beliefs, & Facts | Britannica," February 27, 2024. https://www.britannica.com/biography/John-Wesley.

Joseph Fielding Smith. Doctrines of Salvation Volume 2 - Joseph Fielding Smith, 1954. http://archive.org/details/Doctrines-of-Salvation-volume-2-joseph-fielding-smith.

"Joseph Smith." Accessed May 22, 2022. //history.churchofjesuschrist.org/landing/prophets-of-the-restoration/joseph-smith.

Joseph Smith. Lectures On Faith: Restoration Edition. 2020th ed. United States: Restoration Scriptures Foundation, 2020.

BIBLIOGRAPHY

"Joseph Smith—History 1." Accessed May 28, 2022. https://www.churchofjesuschrist.org/study/eng/scriptures/pgp/js-h/1.Journal of Discourses Volume 13. Accessed November 11, 2023. http://archive.org/details/JoDV13.

Jr, Joseph Smith. "The Wentworth Letter." Accessed May 20, 2022. https://www.churchofjesuschrist.org/study/eng/ensign/2002/07/the-wentworth-letter.

Kerstetter, Earl E. "THE GLORIOUS CAMP MEETINGS OF THE NINETEENTH CENTURY," n.d., 13.

Kimball, Spencer W. "The Lamanite: Their Burden, Our Burden." BYU Speeches (blog). Accessed May 20, 2022. https://speeches.byu.edu/talks/spencer-w-kimball/lamanite-burden-burden/.

———. The Miracle of Forgiveness. Salt Lake City, Bookcraft, 1969. http://archive.org/details/miracleofforgivekimbookimb.

Kimball, Stanley B. "Heber C. Kimball: Mormon Patriarch and Pioneer." Urbana: University of Illinois Press, 1981, 93.

Kimball, Stanley B. "Kinderhook Plates Brought to Joseph Smith Appear to Be a Nineteenth-Century Hoax." Accessed June 26, 2022. https://www.churchofjesuschrist.org/study/eng/ensign/1981/08/kinderhook-plates-brought-to-joseph-smith-appear-to-be-a-nineteenth-century-hoax.

"Kinderhook Plates." Accessed June 26, 2022. https://www.churchofjesuschrist.org/study/eng/history/topics/kinderhook-plates.

"King Follett Discourse." Accessed October 5, 2023. https://www.churchofjesuschrist.org/study/eng/history/topics/king-follett-discourse.

Kraynak, Robert P. "The Idea of the Messiah in the Theology of Thomas Hobbes." Jewish Political Studies Review 4, no. 2 (1992): 115–37.

Kuznetsov, P. F. "The Emergence of Bronze Age Chariots in Eastern Europe." Antiquity 80, no. 309 (September 2006): 638–45. https://doi.org/10.1017/S0003598X00094096.

"Lamanite Identity." Accessed May 11, 2022. https://www.churchofjesuschrist.org/study/eng/history/topics/lamanite-identity.

Lambert, Patricia M. "The Archaeology of War: A North American Perspective." Journal of Archaeological Research, 2002.

Larson, Stan. "The Odyssey of Thomas Stuart Ferguson," n.d., 39.

Lashier, Jackson Jay. "The Trinitarian Theology of Irenaeus of Lyons," n.d.

LDS Discussions. "LDS Gospel Topics Essay: DNA and the Book of Mormon (Annotated)." Accessed May 20, 2022. https://www.ldsdiscussions.com/ldsessay-dna.

"Letter from Galileo to Grand Duchess Cristina (1615)." Accessed March 5, 2024. http://law2.umkc.edu/faculty/projects/ftrials/galileo/galileotograndduchess.html.

Ligonier Ministries. "Athanasius' Defense of the Incarnation |Reformed Bible Studies & Devotionals at Ligonier.Org |Reformed Bible Studies & Devotionals at Ligonier.Org." Accessed May 8, 2024. https://www.ligonier.org/learn/devotionals/athanasius-defense-of-incarnation.

Ligonier Ministries. "Good Works and the Christian Life." Accessed August 24, 2024. https://www.ligonier.org/learn/articles/good-works-christian-life.

"Lost Manuscript of the Book of Mormon." Accessed July 31, 2022. https://www.churchofjesuschrist.org/study/eng/history/topics/lost-manuscript-of-the-book-of-mormon.

Ludlow, Victor. "The Writings of Isaiah in the Book of Mormon." Search Isaiah (blog), January 4, 2018. https://searchisaiah.org/expert-insights/writings-isaiah-book-mormon/.

Luther, Martin, and Mark D. Tranvik. The Freedom of a Christian. Minneapolis: Fortress Press, 2008.

Lyman, Stanford M. "The Lost Tribes of Israel as a Problem in History and Sociology." International Journal of Politics, Culture, and Society 12, no. 1 (1998): 7–42.

Lyon, Keith Dwayne. "God's Brush Arbor: Camp Meeting Culture during the Second Great Awakening, 1800-1860," n.d., 408.

Machamer, Peter, and David Marshall Miller. "Galileo Galilei." In The Stanford Encyclopedia of Philosophy, edited by Edward N. Zalta, Summer 2021. Metaphysics Research Lab, Stanford University, 2021. https://plato.stanford.edu/archives/sum2021/entries/galileo/.

Magazines, Joshua J. Perkey Church. "Why Do I Need to Know Joseph Smith Is a Prophet?" Accessed August 24, 2024. https://www.churchofjesuschrist.org/study/eng/new-era/2015/12/why-do-i-need-to-know-joseph-smith-is-a-prophet.

"Marinda Nancy Johnson Hyde – Biography." Accessed August 27, 2022. https://www.josephsmithpapers.org/person/marinda-nancy-johnson-hyde.

"Martin Harris/Was He Unstable, Gullible and Superstitious - FAIR." Accessed August 28, 2022. https://www.fairlatterdaysaints.org/answers/Martin_Harris/Was_he_unstable,_gullible_and_superstitious.

"Martyrdom of Polycarp | Description, Importance, Date, & Facts |Britannica." Accessed March 18, 2024. https://www.britannica.com/topic/Martyrdom-of-Polycarp.

McBride, Matthew. "The Contributions of Martin Harris." Accessed May 28, 2022. https://www.churchofjesuschrist.org/study/eng/manual/revelations-in-context/the-contributions-of-martin-harris.

McDowell, Josh. Evidence That Demands a Verdict: Life-Changing Truth for a Skeptical World. Nashville, Tennessee: Thomas Nelson, 2017.

Meridian Magazine | Latter-day Saint News and Views. "The Longest Voyage: Lehi's Journey to the Promised Land | Meridian Magazine," April 7, 2016. https://latterdaysaintmag.com/the-longest-voyage-lehis-journey-to-the-promised-land/.

Michael D. Rhodes. Translation of The Hor Book of Breathings. Accessed August 20, 2024. http://archive.org/details/SnsnTranslation.

Michael Flournoy. Falling Into Grace, 2020.

Miller, Corey, Lynn K. Wilder, Vince Eccles, and Latayne Colvett Scott, eds. Leaving Mormonism: Why Four Scholars Changed Their Minds. Grand Rapids, Michigan: Kregel Publications, 2017.

Moreland, James Porter. Love Your God with All Your Mind: The Role of Reason in the Life of the Soul. 2nd ed. Colorado Springs, CO: NavPress, 2012.

"Mormons and Archaeology: An Outside View | The Dialogue Journal," April 27, 2018. https://www.dialoguejournal.com/articles/mormons-and-archaeology-an-outside-view/.

"Moroni, the Last of the Nephite Prophets | Religious Studies Center." Accessed May 24, 2022. https://rsc.byu.edu/book-mormon-fourth-nephi-through-moroni-zion-destruction/moroni-last-nephite-prophets.

Nash, Brittany Chapman. Let's Talk about Polygamy. Let's Talk About. Salt Lake City, Utah: Deseret Book, 2021.

"Native American Migrations." Accessed May 18, 2022. http://web-space.ship.edu/cgboer/nativeamericanmigrations.html.

Nelson, President Russell M. Nelson President of the Church ImagePresident Russell M. "The Correct Name of the Church." Accessed August 23, 2024. https://www.churchofjesuschrist.org/study/eng/general-conference/2018/10/the-correct-name-of-the-church.newsroom.churchofjesuschrist.org.

"What Latter-Day Saints Believe About Jesus Christ." Accessed March 14, 2024. http://newsroom.churchofjesuschrist.org/article/what-mormons-believe-about-jesus-christ.

Norwood, L Ara. "Vernal Holley, Book of Mormon Authorship: A Closer Look," n.d., 11.

"Oliver Cowdery/Related to Joseph Smith - FAIR." Accessed August 28, 2022. https://www.fairlatterdaysaints.org/answers/Oliver_Cowdery/Related_to_Joseph_Smith.

"Orson Hyde – Biography." Accessed August 27, 2022. https://www.josephsmithpapers.org/person/orson-hyde.

Packer, Boyd K. "Lehi's Dream and You." BYU Speeches (blog). Accessed August 26, 2022. https://speeches.byu.edu/talks/boyd-k-packer/lehis-dream/.

Palmer, Grant H. An Insider's View of Mormon Origins. Salt Lake City: Signature Books, 2002.

———. "Joseph Smith, Captain Kidd, Cumorah, and Moroni." The John Whitmer Historical Association Journal 34, no. 1 (2014): 50–57.

Pascal, Blaise, and A. J. Krailsheimer. Pensées. Rev. ed. Penguin Classics. London : New York: Penguin Books ; Penguin Books USA, 1995.

Peterson, Daniel C., and Stephen D. Ricks. "Comparing LDS Beliefs with First-Century Christianity." Accessed March 18, 2024. https://www.churchofjesuschrist.org/study/eng/ensign/1988/03/comparing-lds-beliefs-with-first-century-christianity.

"Plural Marriage in Kirtland and Nauvoo." Accessed August 27, 2022. https://www.churchofjesuschrist.org/study/eng/manual/gospel-topics-essays/plural-marriage-in-kirtland-and-nauvoo.

Porter, Larry. "The Joseph Knight Family." Accessed May 28, 2022. https://www.churchofjesuschrist.org/study/eng/ensign/1978/10/the-joseph-knight-family.

"Proboscidean | Evolution, Adaptations & Extinction | Britannica." Accessed May 19, 2024. https://www.britannica.com/animal/proboscidean.

"Question: Could Joseph Have Used a Bible during and Simply Dictated from It during Book of Mormon Translation? - FAIR." Accessed July 29, 2022. https://www.fairlatterdaysaints.org/answers/Question:_Could_Joseph_have_used_a_Bible_during_and_simply_dictated_from_it_during_Book_of_Mormon_translation%3F#cite_note-1.

"Question: Did Joseph Smith Begin His Prophetic Career with a 'Trinitarian' Idea of God? - FAIR." Accessed May 14, 2024. https://www.fairlatterdaysaints.org/answers/Question:_Did_Joseph_Smith_begin_his_prophetic_career_with_a_%22trinitarian%22_idea_of_God%3F.

"Question: Did Swords Exist in Pre-Columbian America during the Book of Mormon Time Period? - FAIR." Accessed May 19, 2024. https://www.fairlatterdaysaints.org/answers/Question:_Did_swords_exist_in_Pre-Columbian_America_during_the_Book_of_Mormon_time_period%3F.

"Question: Did the Witnesses Who Left the Church Continue to Maintain Their Witness of the Book of Mormon? - FAIR." Accessed August 28, 2022. https://www.fairlatterdaysaints.org/answers/Question:_Did_the_Witnesses_who_left_the_Church_continue_to_maintain_their_witness_of_the_Book_of_Mormon%3F.

Religious Education. "Dan Belnap." Accessed July 29, 2022. https://religion.byu.edu/directory/daniel-belnap.

"Repentance and Forgiveness." Accessed November 11, 2023. https://www.churchofjesuschrist.org/study/eng/new-era/2019/02/repentance-and-forgiveness.

Retief, F. P., and L. Cilliers. "The History and Pathology of Crucifixion." South African Medical Journal = Suid-Afrikaanse Tydskrif Vir Geneeskunde 93, no. 12 (December 2003): 938–41.

Richardson, James. "Quotes from the Early Church Fathers: On the Trinity." Apostles Creed, February 27, 2015. https://apostles-creed.org/confessional-reformed-christian-theology/theology/early-church-fathers-quotes-trinity/.

Richter, Kimberly. "The Book of Mormon: From Plates to Press." Accessed May 24, 2022. https://www.churchofjesuschrist.org/study/eng/new-era/2012/09/the-book-of-mormon-from-plates-to-press.

Ricks, Stephen D, and William J Hamblin. "Warfare in the Book of Mormon," n.d.

Ritner, Robert Kriech, Marc Coenen, and Robert Kriech Ritner. The Joseph Smith Egyptian Papyri: A Complete Edition ; P. JS 1 - 4 and the Hypocephalus of Sheshonq. Salt Lake City, Utah: Signature Books, 2013.

Roberts, B. H., and Brigham D. Madsen. Studies of the Book of Mormon. 2nd ed. Salt Lake City: Signature Books, 1992.

Runnells, Jeremy T. CES Letter: My Search for Answers to My Mormon Doubts. United States: CES Letter Foundation, 2017.

Ryan. "Heritage Goats." The Livestock Conservancy (blog). Accessed May 14, 2024. https://livestockconservancy.org/heritage-goats/.

"Saint Athanasius | Biography & Facts | Britannica." Accessed May 8, 2024. https://www.britannica.com/biography/Saint-Athanasius.

"Saint Augustine | Biography, Philosophy, Major Works, & Facts |Britannica," January 5, 2024. https://www.britannica.com/biography/Saint-Augustine.

"Saint Clement of Alexandria | Biography, Apologist, Works, & Facts| Britannica." Accessed May 8, 2024. https://www.britannica.com/biography/Clement-of-Alexandria.

"Saint Ignatius of Antioch | Biography, Writings, & Martyrdom |Britannica," March 14, 2024. https://www.britannica.com/biography/Saint-Ignatius-of-Antioch.

Saints, The Church of Jesus Christ of Latter-day. "The Living Christ." Accessed March 14, 2024. https://www.churchofjesuschrist.org/study/eng/scriptures/the-living-christ-the-testimony-of-the-apostles/the-living-christ-the-testimony-of-the-apostles.

Schreiner, Thomas R. Faith Alone— the Doctrine of Justification: What the Reformers Taught ... and Why It Matters. Grand Rapids, Michigan: Zondervan, 2015.

ScienceDaily. "Gone But Not Forgotten: Bring Back North American Elephants." Accessed May 19, 2024. https://www.sciencedaily.com/releases/1999/06/990607154315.htm.

ScienceDaily. "Study Confirms Widespread Literacy in Biblical-Period Kingdom of Judah." Accessed May 19, 2024. https://www.sciencedaily.com/releases/2020/09/200910110828.htm.

Skousen, Royal. "Textual Variants in the Isaiah Quotations in the Book of Mormon," n.d., 23.

Smith, Ethan. View of the Hebrews: Or The Tribes of Israel in America. [Repr. of the] 2. ed., Improved and Enlarged, 1825. Colfax, Wis: Ancient American Archaeology Foundation, 2002.

Smith Joseph. History of the Church: 1839-1842. Place of publication not identified: Deseret Book, 1991.

"Source:The True Latter Day Saints' Herald:15 November 1879:A 'Seer Stone,' Which Was Placed in the Crown of a Hat, into Which Joseph Put His Face, so as to Exclude the External Light - FAIR." Accessed June 1, 2022. https://www.fairlatterdaysaints.org/evidences/Source:The_True_Latter_Day_Saints%E2%80%99_Herald:15_November_1879:a_%27Seer_Stone,%27_which_was_placed_in_the_crown_of_a_hat,_into_which_Joseph_put_his_face,_so_as_to_exclude_the_external_light.

Specht, Walter F. "THE USE OF ITALICS I N ENGLISH VERSIONS OF THE NEW TESTAMENT," n.d., 22.

"Steel | Britannica." Accessed May 19, 2024. https://www.britannica.com/technology/steel/additional-info.

Stuff You Missed in Sunday School. "Tree of Life," April 7, 2018. https://missedinsunday.com/memes/other/tree-of-life/.

Swinburne, Richard. Is There a God? New York: Oxford University Press, 1996

"Testimony of Eight Witnesses." Accessed August 28, 2022. https://www.churchofjesuschrist.org/study/eng/scriptures/bofm/eight.

"The Book of Mormon and The Late War." Accessed August 16, 2022. http://wordtree.org/thelatewar/.

The Center for Biblical Studies. "April 3, AD 33: Why We Believe We Can Know the Exact Date Jesus Died," April 8, 2020. https://cbs.mbts.edu/2020/04/08/april-3-ad-33-why-we-believe-we-can-know-the-exact-date-jesus-died/.

"The Dead Sea Scrolls | The Israel Museum, Jerusalem." Accessed May 19, 2024. https://www.imj.org.il/en/wings/shrine-book/dead-sea-scrolls.

The Doctrines and Discipline of the Methodist Episcopal Church in America. With Explanatory Notes by Thomas Coke and Francis Asbury. The Tenth Edition, n.d.

"The Eleven Witnesses | Religious Studies Center." Accessed August 28, 2022. https://rsc.byu.edu/coming-forth-book-mormon/eleven-witnesses.

The Good Book Blog - Biola University Blogs. "Old Testament Prophecies of Jesus' Resurrection," September 20, 2019. https://www.biola.edu/blogs/good-book-blog/2019/old-testament-prophecies-of-jesus-resurrection.

"The Great Awakening and George Whitefield – Mapping the Great Awakening." Accessed August 20, 2022. https://people.smu.edu/mappingthega/stories/s1/.

"The Great Isaiah Scroll MS A (1QIsa) | The Israel Museum, Jerusalem." Accessed September 4, 2022. https://www.imj.org.il/en/collections/198208.

The Holy Word Church of God. "How Many Words in Each Book of the Bible." Accessed July 29, 2022. https://holyword.church/miscellaneous-resources/how-many-words-in-each-book-of-the-bible/.

"The Introduction to the Book of Mormon." Accessed May 20, 2022. https://www.churchofjesuschrist.org/manual/book-of-mormon-teacher-resource-manual/the-introduction-to-the-book-of-mormon?lang=eng.

"The Joy and Gift of Repentance—Recent Messages from Prophets and Apostles." Accessed November 11, 2023. https://www.churchofjesuschrist.org/study/eng/liahona/2022/10/digital-only/the-joy-and-gift-of-repentance-recent-messages-from-prophets-and-apostles.

"The King James Bible and the Book of Mormon | Religious Studies Center." Accessed July 23, 2022. https://rsc.byu.edu/king-james-bible-restoration/king-james-bible-book-mormon#_ednref9.

"The Lost 116 Pages Story: What We Do Know, What We Don't Know, and What We Might Know | Religious Studies Center." Accessed July 31, 2022. https://rsc.byu.edu/coming-forth-book-mormon/lost-116-pages-story-what-we-do-know-what-we-dont-know-what-we-might-know.

The Saints Herald Volume 26 1879. Accessed May 25, 2022. http://archive.org/details/TheSaintsHerald_Volume_26_1879.

"The Surprising History of America's Wild Horses | Live Science." Accessed May 19, 2024. https://www.livescience.com/9589-surprising-history-america-wild-horses.html.

The Westminster Shorter Catechism: With Scripture Proofs. Edinburgh: Banner of Truth Trust, 2008.

Times & Seasons. "Jonathan Green," March 23, 2024. http://timesandseasons.org.

"Times and Seasons Vol 4." Accessed June 26, 2022. https://contentdm.lib.byu.edu/digital/collection/NCMP1820-1846/id/8618/.

Tornau, Christian. "Saint Augustine." In The Stanford Encyclopedia of Philosophy, edited by Edward N. Zalta, Summer 2020. Metaphysics Research Lab, Stanford University, 2020. https://plato.stanford.edu/archives/sum2020/entries/augustine/.

"Tracing the Thread of Trinitarian Thought from Ignatius to Origen | Maranatha Baptist Seminary." Accessed March 18, 2024. https://www.mbu.edu/seminary/tracing-the-thread-of-trinitarian-thought-from-ignatius-to-origen/.

"Trajan." Accessed March 18, 2024. https://education.nationalgeographic.org/resource/trajan.

"Translation and Historicity of the Book of Abraham." Accessed April 18, 2022. https://www.churchofjesuschrist.org/study/eng/manual/gospel-topics-essays/translation-and-historicity-of-the-book-of-abraham.

Turner, O. (Orasmus). History of the Pioneer Settlement of Phelps and Gorham's Purchase, and Morris' Reserve; Embracing the Counties of Monroe, Ontario, Livingston, Yates, Steuben, Most of Wayne and Allegany, and Parts of Orleans, Genesee and Wyoming. To Which Is Added, a Supplement, or Extension of the Pioneer History of Monroe County ... Rochester: W. Alling, 1851.

Twain, Mark, and Elizabeth Frank. Roughing It. New York: Signet Classics, 2008.

Vogel, Dan. Early Mormon Documents. Salt Lake City: Signature Books, 2000.

Vogt, Katja. "Ancient Skepticism." In The Stanford Encyclopedia of Philosophy, edited by Edward N. Zalta, Summer 2021. Metaphysics Research Lab, Stanford University, 2021. https://plato.stanford.edu/archives/sum2021/entries/skepticism-ancient/.

"Was Haman Hanged, Impaled or Crucified? - TheTorah.Com." Accessed May 19, 2024. https://www.thetorah.com/article/was-haman-hanged-impaled-or-crucified.

"Was Martin Harris Ever Excommunicated from the Church?" Accessed August 28, 2022. https://www.churchofjesuschrist.org/study/eng/ensign/1979/06/i-have-a-question/was-martin-harris-ever-excommunicated-from-the-church.

Welch, John, Greg Welch, Greg Welch, and Greg Welch. "Testimony of the Three Witnesses." Provo, UT: Foundation for Ancient Research and Mormon Studies, 1999.

Wesley, John. An address to the clergy. By John Wesley, ... 1756, 1756. http://archive.org/details/bim_eighteenth-century_an-address-to-the-clergy_wesley-john_1756.

"What Do We Know of the Life of John the Apostle after the Day of Pentecost?" Accessed March 18, 2024. https://www.churchofjesuschrist.org/study/eng/ensign/1984/01/i-have-a-question/what-do-we-know-of-the-life-of-john-the-apostle-after-the-day-of-pentecost.

Wheeler, Brannon M. "Deciphering the Signs of God: A Phenomenological Approach to Islam. Annemarie Schimmel." History of Religions 36, no. 3 (February 1997): 283–85. https://doi.org/10.1086/463472.

"Whitney, Helen Mar, 1828-1896." Accessed August 27, 2022. https://contentdm.lib.byu.edu/digital/collection/rsc/id/42564.

"Who Was Isaiah?" Accessed July 29, 2022. https://www.churchofjesuschrist.org/study/eng/ensign/2020/02/weekly-book-of-mormon-insights/who-was-isaiah.

"Why Are Some Words Italicized in the Bible?" Accessed July 29, 2022. https://www.churchofjesuschrist.org/study/eng/ensign/1978/02/i-have-a-question/why-are-some-words-italicized-in-the-bible.

"Why Is the Phrase 'and It Came to Pass' so Prevalent in the Book of Mormon?" Accessed August 8, 2022. https://www.churchofjesuschrist.org/study/eng/ensign/1992/12/i-have-a-question/why-is-the-phrase-and-it-came-to-pass-so-prevalent-in-the-book-of-mormon.

"Why It Took So Long to Invent the Wheel | Scientific American." Accessed May 19, 2024. https://www.scientificamerican.com/article/why-it-took-so-long-to-inv/.

Wilder, Micah. Passport to Heaven. Eugene, Oregon: Harvest House Publishers, 2021.

Witchger, Andy. "Arianism, Athanasius, and the Effect on Trinitarian Thought," n.d.

YaleNews. "Michael Coe: Influential Archaeologist Helped Un-lock Secrets of Mesoamerica," October 8, 2019. https://news.yale.edu/2019/10/08/michael-coe-influential-archaeologist-helped-unlock-secrets-mesoamerica.

"Zina D. H. Jacobs Young." Accessed August 27, 2022. https://www.churchofjesuschrist.org/st

www.ingramcontent.com/pod-product-compliance
Lightning Source LLC
Chambersburg PA
CBHW071232230426
43668CB00011B/1401